ASSASSIN'S CREED

TRIAL BY FIRE

WRITERS
ANTHONY DEL COL &
CONOR MCCREERY

ARTIST
NEIL EDWARDS

COLORIST
IVAN NUNES

LETTERER
RICHARD STARKINGS AND COMICRAFT'S
JIMMY BETANCOURT

TITAN
COMICS

Assassin's Creed: Trial by Fire
9781782763055

Published by Titan Comics
A division of Titan Publishing Group Ltd.
144 Southwark St.
London
SE1 0UP

A CIP catalogue record for this title is available from the British Library

First edition: May 2016

10 9 8 7 6 5 4 3 2

Printed in China.
Titan Comics. 0123

TITAN COMICS

EDITOR: LIZZIE KAYE
DESIGNER: ROB FARMER

Senior Comics Editor: Andrew James
Titan Comics Editorial: Steve White, Tom Williams, Jessica Burton, Gabriela Houston
Production Supervisions: Jackie Flook, Maria Pearson
Production Assistant: Peter James
Production Manager: Obi Onuora
Art Director: Oz Browne
Studio Manager: Emma Smith
Senior Sales Manager: Steve Tothill
Press Officer: Cara Fielder
Senior Marketing & Press Executive: Owen Johnson
Direct Sales & Marketing Manager: Ricky Claydon
Publishing Manager: Darryl Tothill
Publishing Director: Chris Teather
Operations Director: Leigh Baulch
Executive Director: Vivian Cheung
Publisher: Nick Landau

WWW.TITAN-COMICS.COM

Follow us on Twitter @ComicsTitan

Visit us at facebook.com/comicstitan

ACKNOWLEDGEMENTS:
Many thanks to Aymar Azaizia, Anouk Bachman, Richard Farrese,
Raphaël Lacoste, Caroline Lamache and Clémence Deleuze.

CHAPTER
ONE

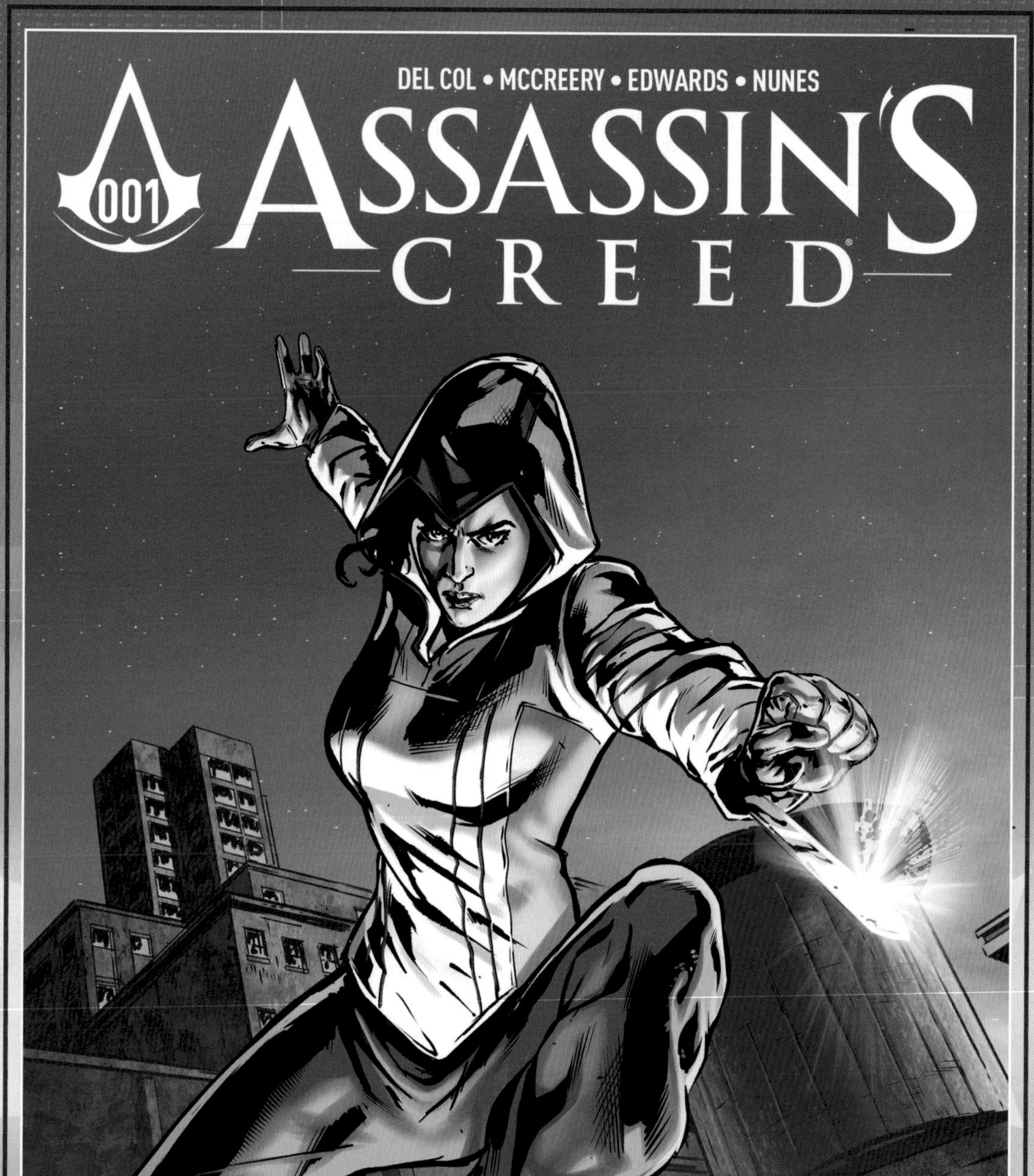
DEL COL • MCCREERY • EDWARDS • NUNES
001
ASSASSIN'S CREED
UBISOFT
TITAN COMICS

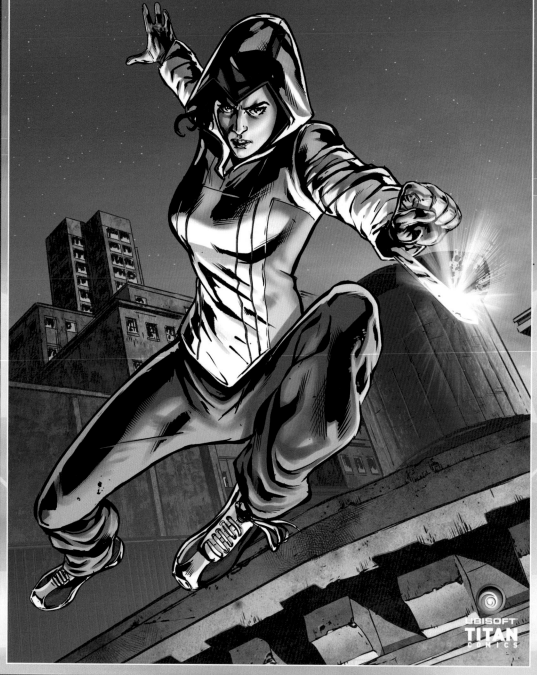

COVER A - ISSUE 1
NEIL EDWARDS & IVAN NUNES

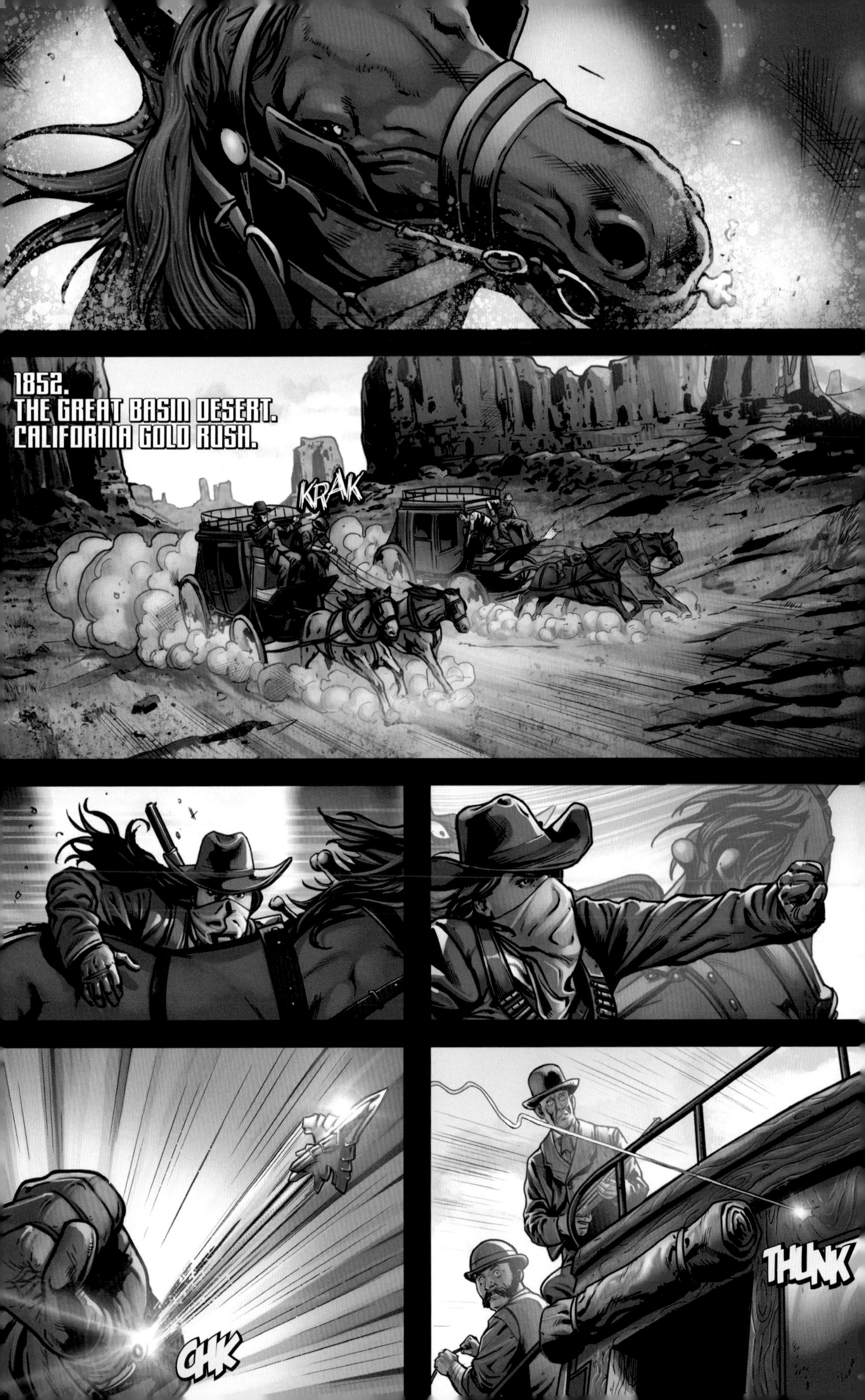
1852.
THE GREAT BASIN DESERT.
CALIFORNIA GOLD RUSH.
KRAK
CHK
THUNK

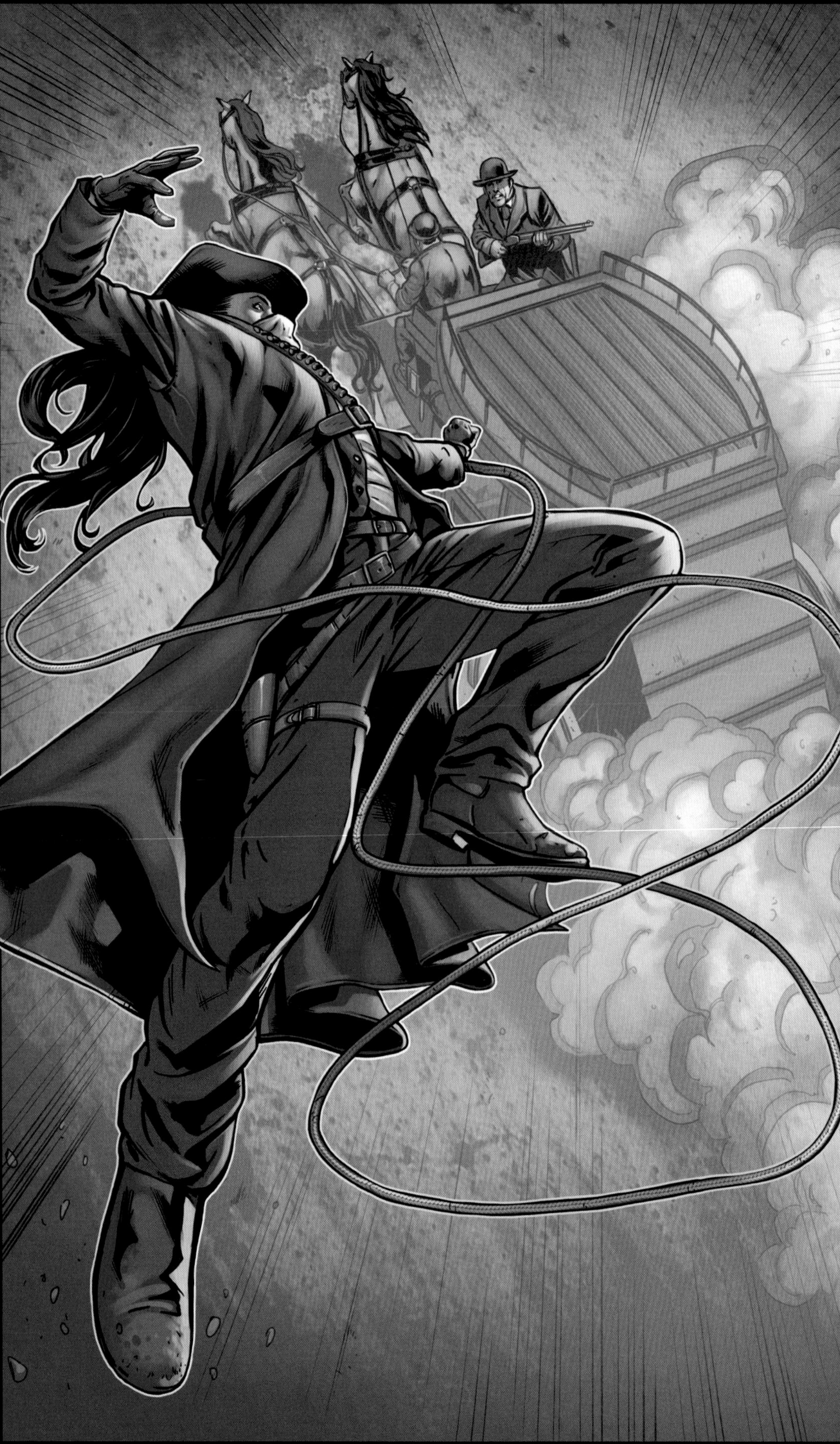

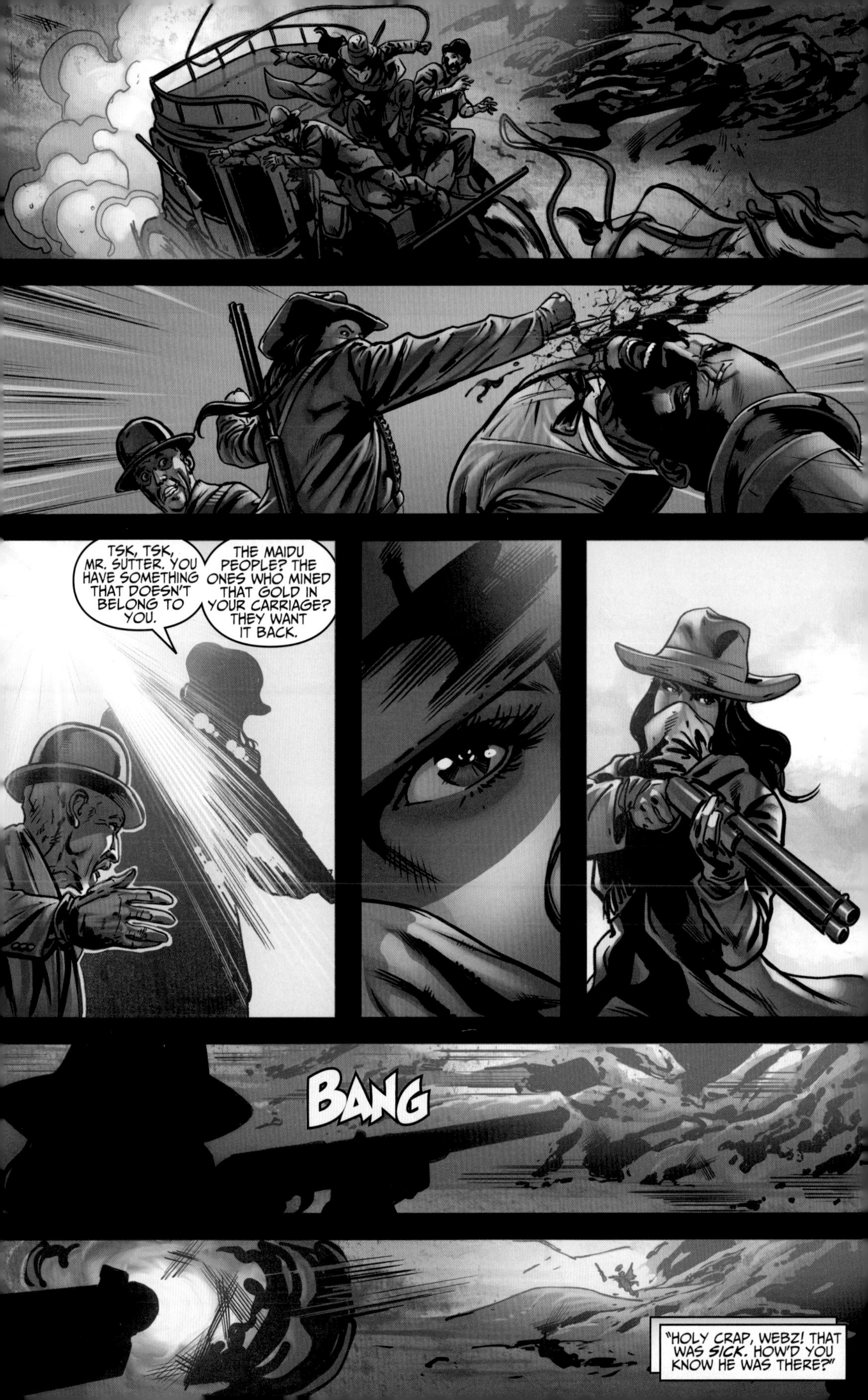
TSK, TSK, MR. SUTTER. YOU HAVE SOMETHING THAT DOESN'T BELONG TO YOU.
THE MAIDU PEOPLE? THE ONES WHO MINED THAT GOLD IN YOUR CARRIAGE? THEY WANT IT BACK.
BANG
"HOLY CRAP, WEBZ! THAT WAS SICK. HOW'D YOU KNOW HE WAS THERE?"

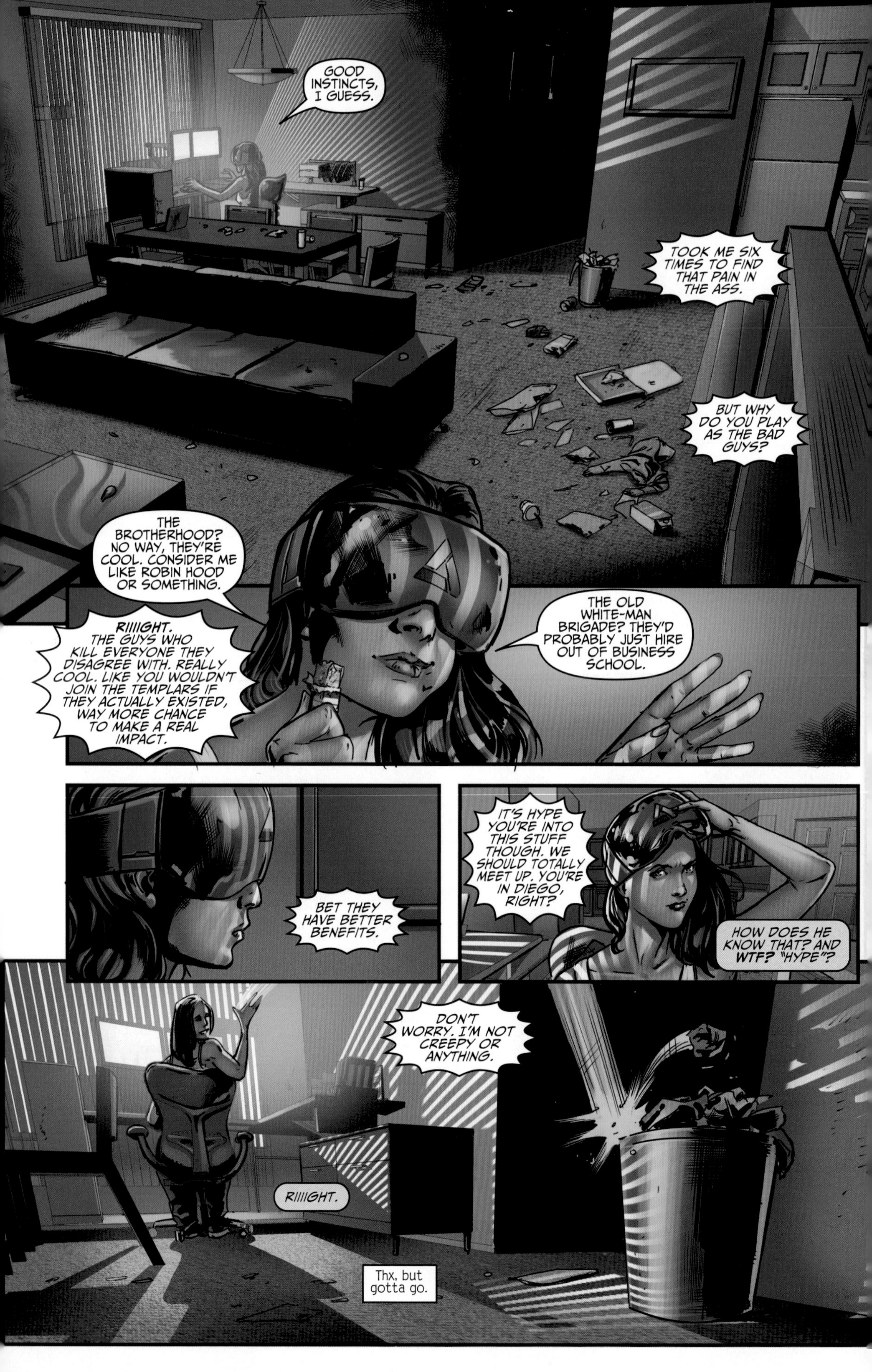
GOOD INSTINCTS, I GUESS.
TOOK ME SIX TIMES TO FIND THAT PAIN IN THE ASS.
BUT WHY DO YOU PLAY AS THE BAD GUYS?
THE BROTHERHOOD? NO WAY, THEY'RE COOL. CONSIDER ME LIKE ROBIN HOOD OR SOMETHING.
RIIIGHT. THE GUYS WHO KILL EVERYONE THEY DISAGREE WITH. REALLY COOL. LIKE YOU WOULDN'T JOIN THE TEMPLARS IF THEY ACTUALLY EXISTED, WAY MORE CHANCE TO MAKE A REAL IMPACT.
THE OLD WHITE-MAN BRIGADE? THEY'D PROBABLY JUST HIRE OUT OF BUSINESS SCHOOL.
BET THEY HAVE BETTER BENEFITS.
IT'S HYPE YOU'RE INTO THIS STUFF THOUGH. WE SHOULD TOTALLY MEET UP. YOU'RE IN DIEGO, RIGHT?
HOW DOES HE KNOW THAT? AND WTF? "HYPE"?
DON'T WORRY. I'M NOT CREEPY OR ANYTHING.
RIIIGHT.
Thx, but gotta go.

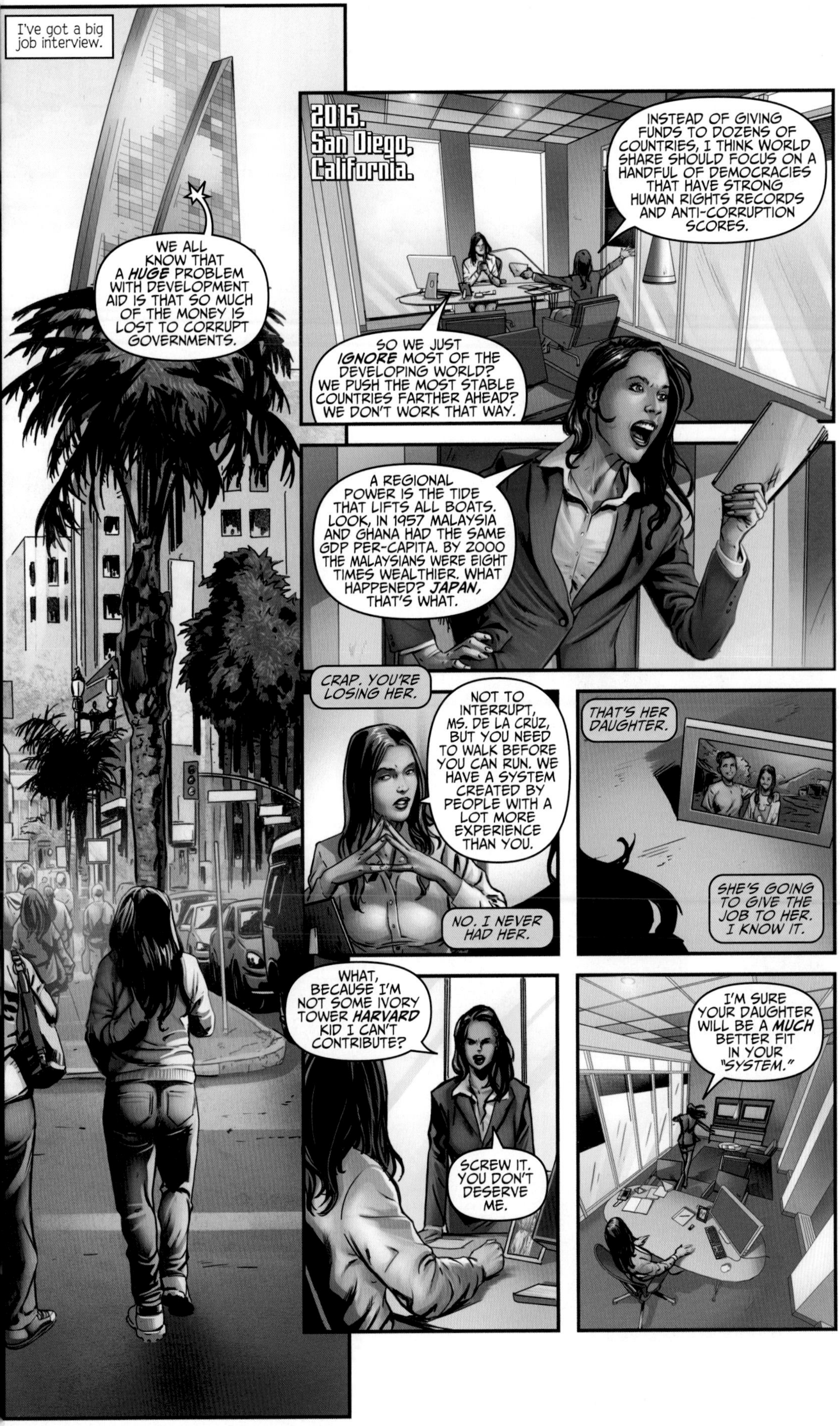
I've got a big job interview.
WE ALL KNOW THAT A HUGE PROBLEM WITH DEVELOPMENT AID IS THAT SO MUCH OF THE MONEY IS LOST TO CORRUPT GOVERNMENTS.
2015. San Diego, California.
INSTEAD OF GIVING FUNDS TO DOZENS OF COUNTRIES, I THINK WORLD SHARE SHOULD FOCUS ON A HANDFUL OF DEMOCRACIES THAT HAVE STRONG HUMAN RIGHTS RECORDS AND ANTI-CORRUPTION SCORES.
SO WE JUST IGNORE MOST OF THE DEVELOPING WORLD? WE PUSH THE MOST STABLE COUNTRIES FARTHER AHEAD? WE DON'T WORK THAT WAY.
A REGIONAL POWER IS THE TIDE THAT LIFTS ALL BOATS. LOOK, IN 1957 MALAYSIA AND GHANA HAD THE SAME GDP PER-CAPITA. BY 2000 THE MALAYSIANS WERE EIGHT TIMES WEALTHIER. WHAT HAPPENED? JAPAN, THAT'S WHAT.
CRAP. YOU'RE LOSING HER.
NOT TO INTERRUPT, MS. DE LA CRUZ, BUT YOU NEED TO WALK BEFORE YOU CAN RUN. WE HAVE A SYSTEM CREATED BY PEOPLE WITH A LOT MORE EXPERIENCE THAN YOU.
NO. I NEVER HAD HER.
THAT'S HER DAUGHTER.
SHE'S GOING TO GIVE THE JOB TO HER. I KNOW IT.
WHAT, BECAUSE I'M NOT SOME IVORY TOWER HARVARD KID I CAN'T CONTRIBUTE?
SCREW IT. YOU DON'T DESERVE ME.
I'M SURE YOUR DAUGHTER WILL BE A MUCH BETTER FIT IN YOUR "SYSTEM."

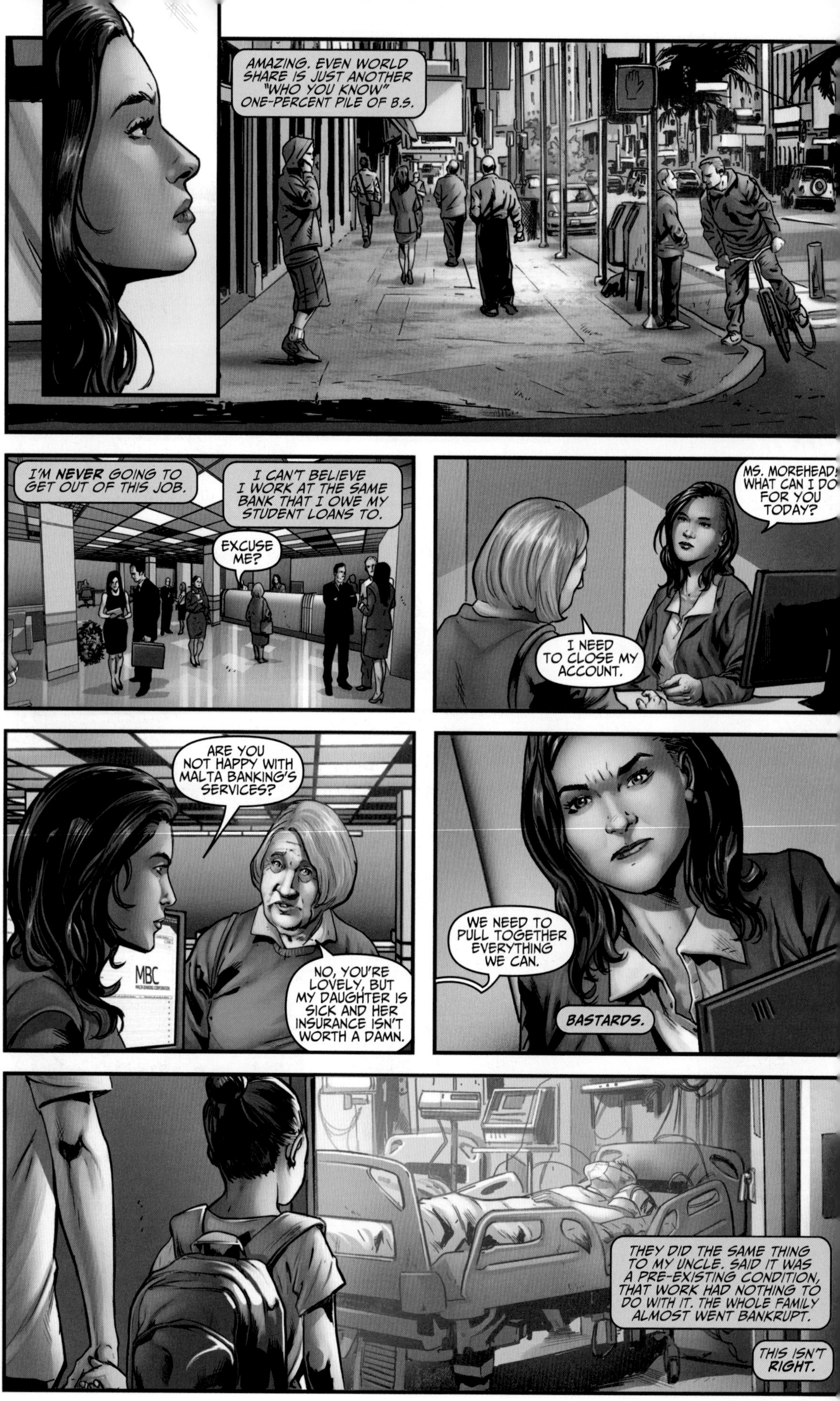
AMAZING. EVEN WORLD SHARE IS JUST ANOTHER "WHO YOU KNOW" ONE-PERCENT PILE OF B.S.
I'M **NEVER** GOING TO GET OUT OF THIS JOB.
I CAN'T BELIEVE I WORK AT THE SAME BANK THAT I OWE MY STUDENT LOANS TO.
EXCUSE ME?
MS. MOREHEAD! WHAT CAN I DO FOR YOU TODAY?
I NEED TO CLOSE MY ACCOUNT.
ARE YOU NOT HAPPY WITH MALTA BANKING'S SERVICES?
MBC
NO, YOU'RE LOVELY, BUT MY DAUGHTER IS SICK AND HER INSURANCE ISN'T WORTH A DAMN.
WE NEED TO PULL TOGETHER EVERYTHING WE CAN.
BASTARDS.
THEY DID THE SAME THING TO MY UNCLE. SAID IT WAS A PRE-EXISTING CONDITION, THAT WORK HAD NOTHING TO DO WITH IT. THE WHOLE FAMILY ALMOST WENT BANKRUPT.
THIS ISN'T **RIGHT**.

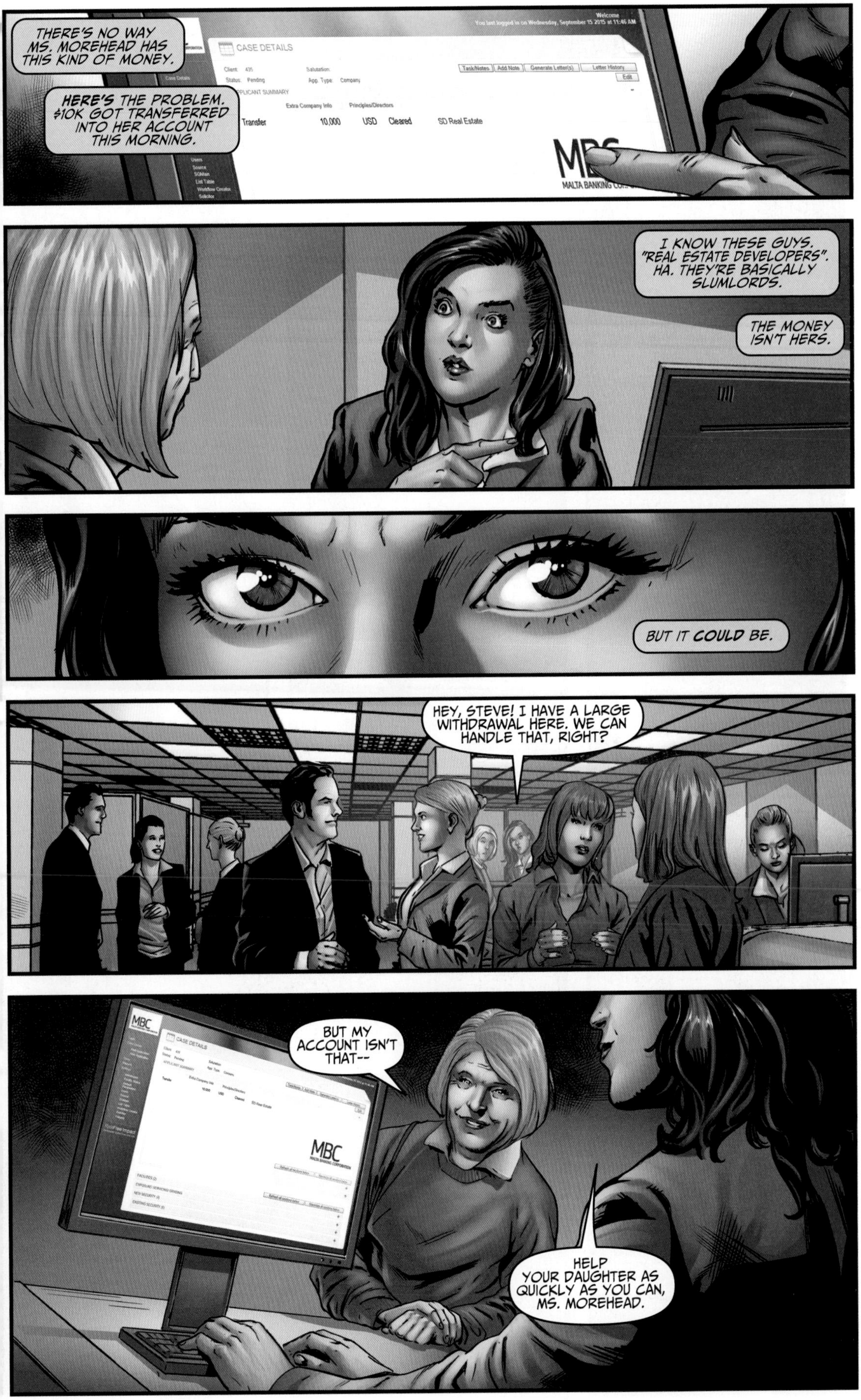
THERE'S NO WAY MS. MOREHEAD HAS THIS KIND OF MONEY.
Welcome
You last logged in on Wednesday, September 15 2015 at 11:46 AM
CASE DETAILS
Task/Notes
Add Note
Generate Letter(s)
Letter History
Edit
Transfer 10,000 USD Cleared SD Real Estate
HERE'S THE PROBLEM. $10K GOT TRANSFERRED INTO HER ACCOUNT THIS MORNING.
I KNOW THESE GUYS. "REAL ESTATE DEVELOPERS". HA. THEY'RE BASICALLY SLUMLORDS.
THE MONEY ISN'T HERS.
BUT IT COULD BE.
HEY, STEVE! I HAVE A LARGE WITHDRAWAL HERE. WE CAN HANDLE THAT, RIGHT?
MBC
CASE DETAILS
MBC
MALTA BANKING CORPORATION
BUT MY ACCOUNT ISN'T THAT--
HELP YOUR DAUGHTER AS QUICKLY AS YOU CAN, MS. MOREHEAD.

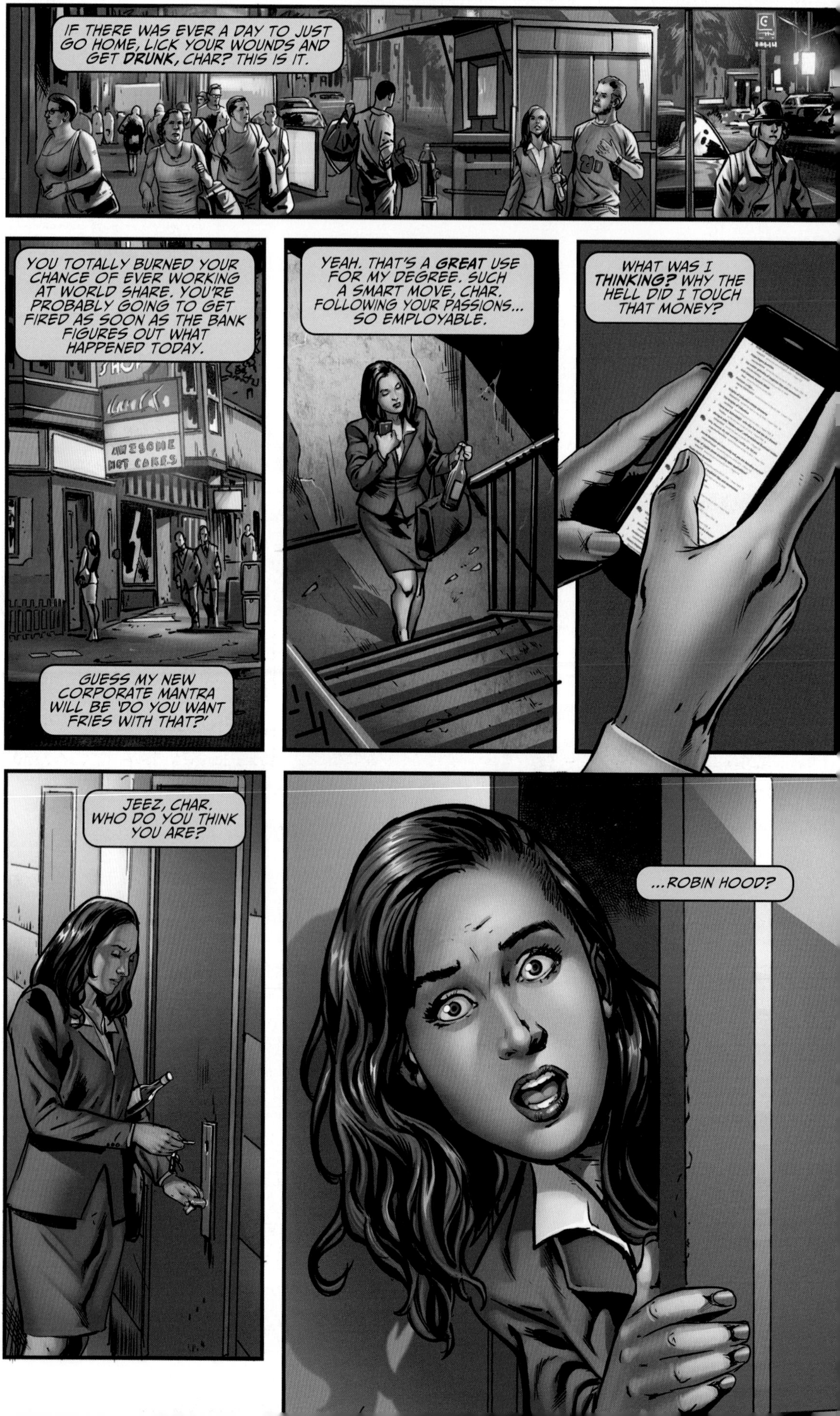

IF THERE WAS EVER A DAY TO JUST GO HOME, LICK YOUR WOUNDS AND GET **DRUNK**, CHAR? THIS IS IT.
YOU TOTALLY BURNED YOUR CHANCE OF EVER WORKING AT WORLD SHARE. YOU'RE PROBABLY GOING TO GET FIRED AS SOON AS THE BANK FIGURES OUT WHAT HAPPENED TODAY.
AWESOME HOT CAKES
GUESS MY NEW CORPORATE MANTRA WILL BE 'DO YOU WANT FRIES WITH THAT?'
YEAH. THAT'S A **GREAT** USE FOR MY DEGREE. SUCH A SMART MOVE, CHAR. FOLLOWING YOUR PASSIONS... SO EMPLOYABLE.
WHAT WAS I **THINKING?** WHY THE HELL DID I TOUCH THAT MONEY?
JEEZ, CHAR. WHO DO YOU THINK YOU ARE?
...ROBIN HOOD?

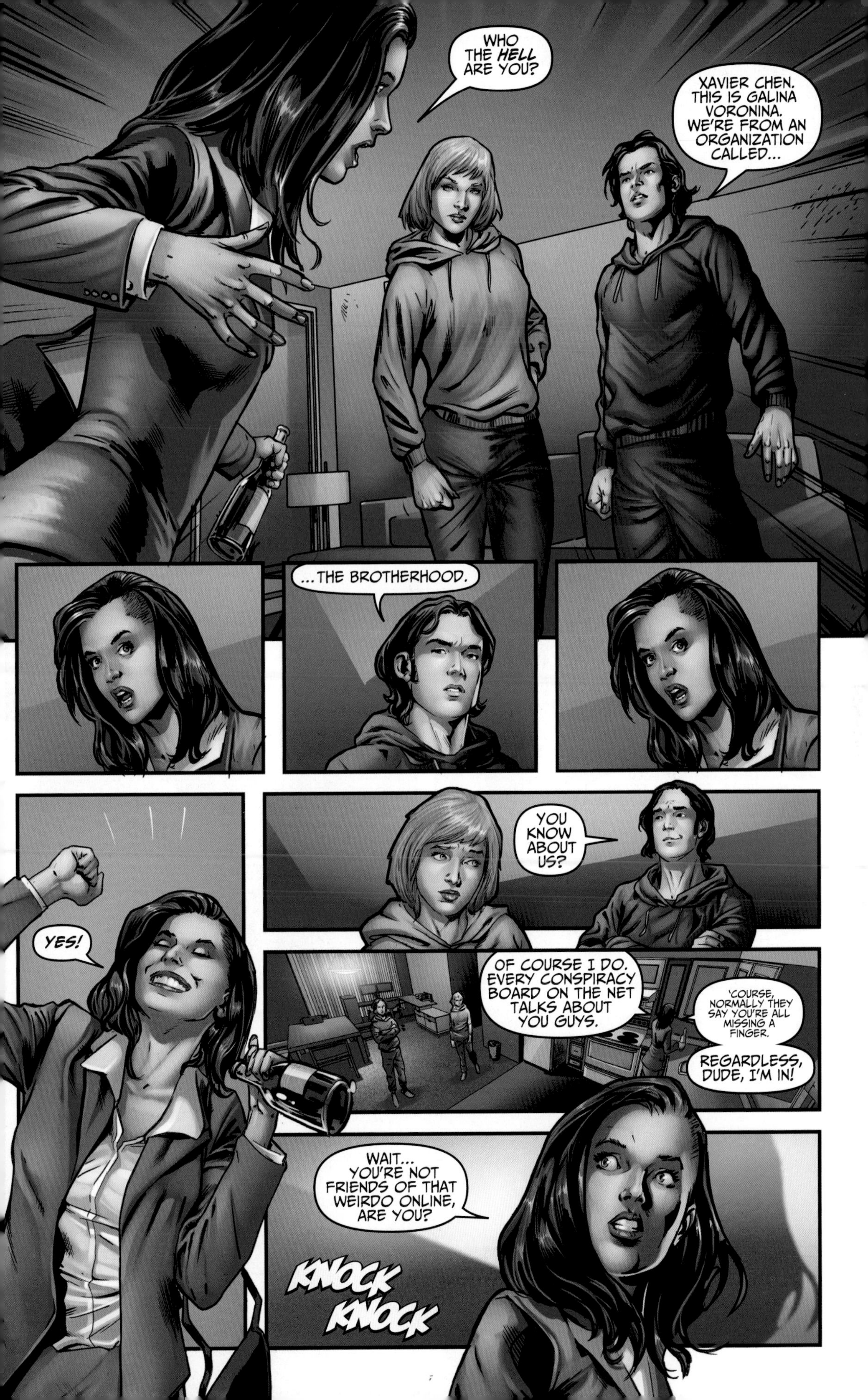
WHO THE *HELL* ARE YOU?
XAVIER CHEN. THIS IS GALINA VORONINA. WE'RE FROM AN ORGANIZATION CALLED...
...THE BROTHERHOOD.
YES!
YOU KNOW ABOUT US?
OF COURSE I DO. EVERY CONSPIRACY BOARD ON THE NET TALKS ABOUT YOU GUYS.
'COURSE, NORMALLY THEY SAY YOU'RE ALL MISSING A FINGER.
REGARDLESS, DUDE, I'M IN!
WAIT... YOU'RE NOT FRIENDS OF THAT WEIRDO ONLINE, ARE YOU?
KNOCK KNOCK

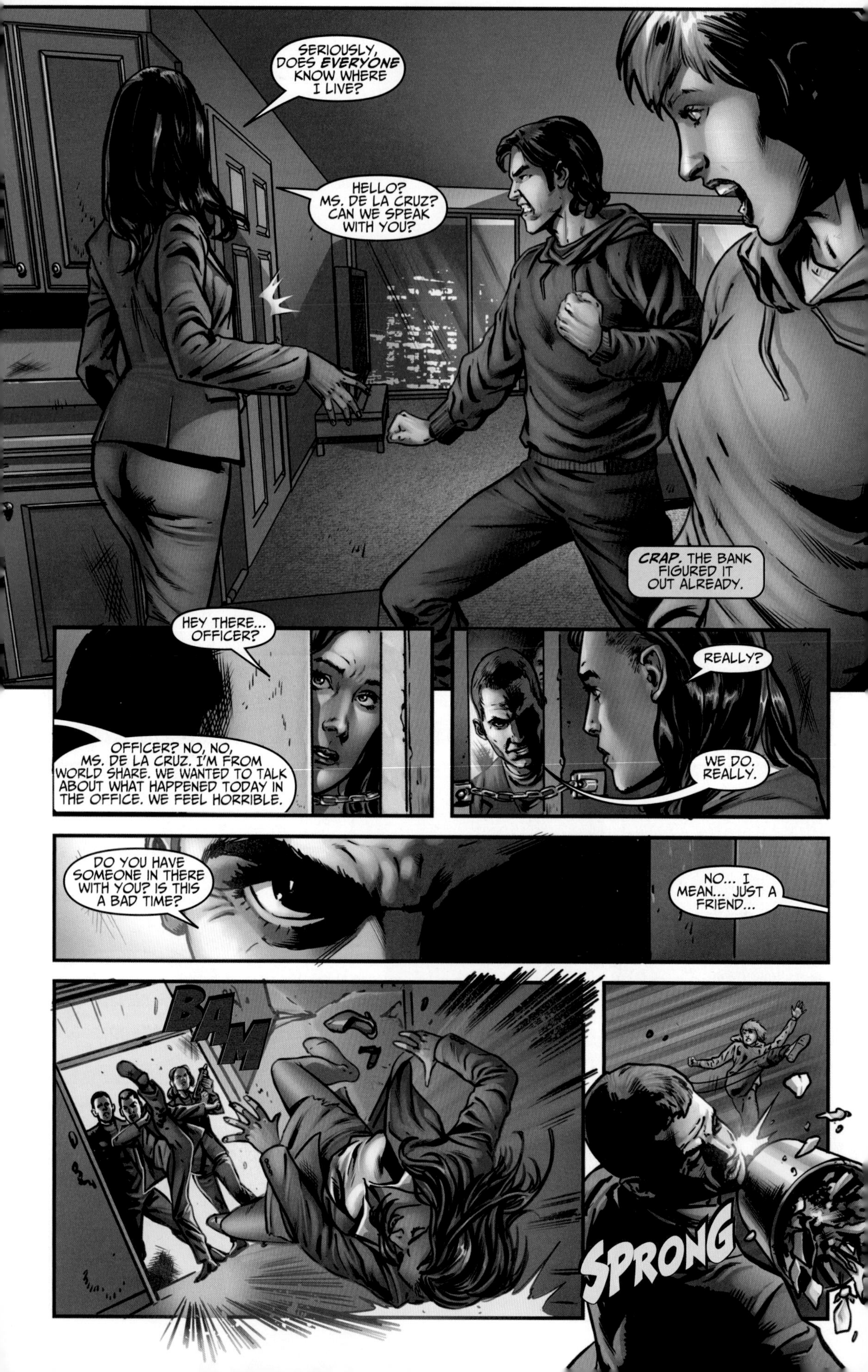
SERIOUSLY, DOES EVERYONE KNOW WHERE I LIVE?
HELLO? MS. DE LA CRUZ? CAN WE SPEAK WITH YOU?
CRAP. THE BANK FIGURED IT OUT ALREADY.
HEY THERE... OFFICER?
OFFICER? NO, NO, MS. DE LA CRUZ. I'M FROM WORLD SHARE. WE WANTED TO TALK ABOUT WHAT HAPPENED TODAY IN THE OFFICE. WE FEEL HORRIBLE.
REALLY?
WE DO. REALLY.
DO YOU HAVE SOMEONE IN THERE WITH YOU? IS THIS A BAD TIME?
NO... I MEAN... JUST A FRIEND...
BAM
SPRONG

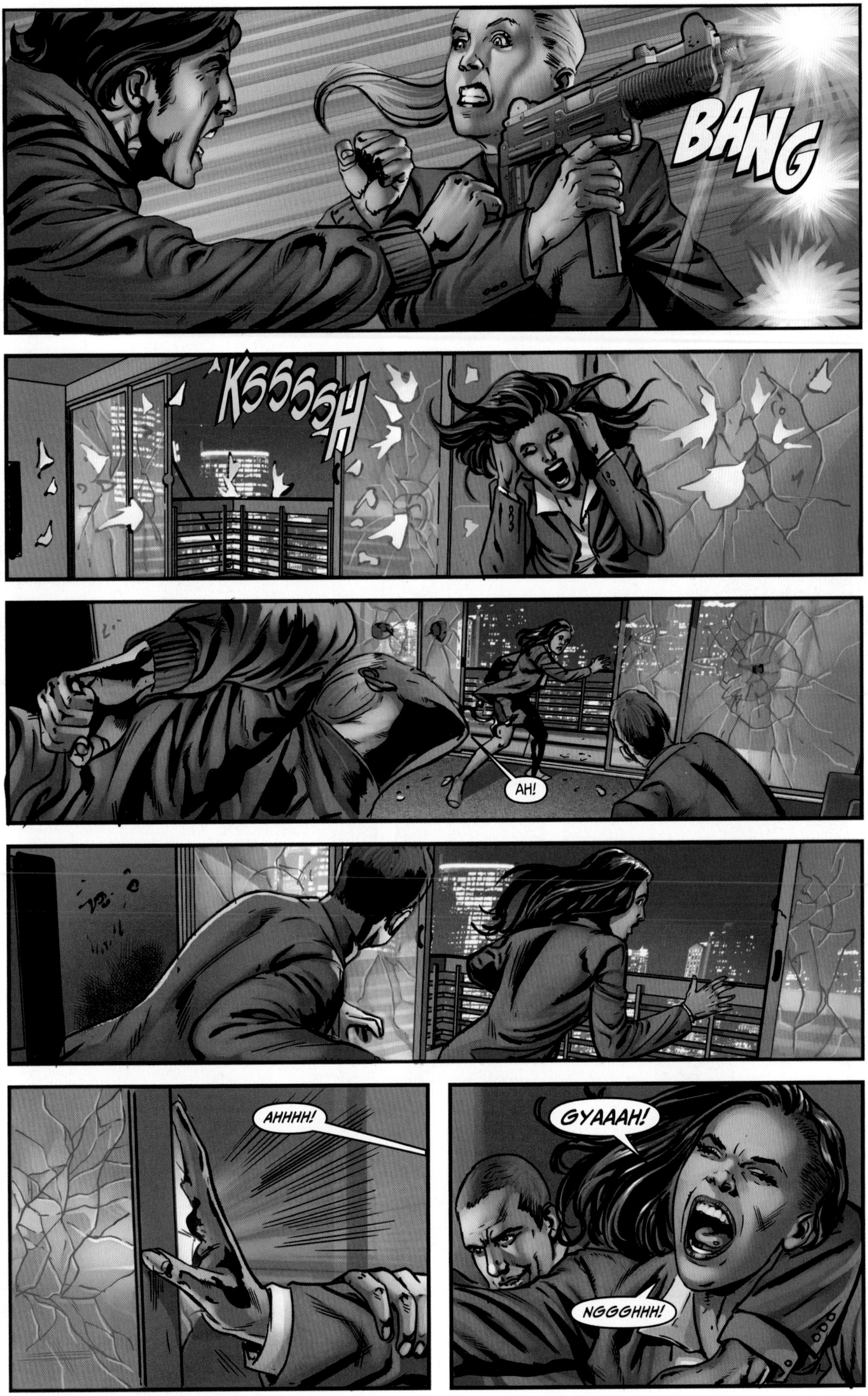
BANG
KSSSSH
AH!
AHHHH!
GYAAAH!
NGGGHHH!

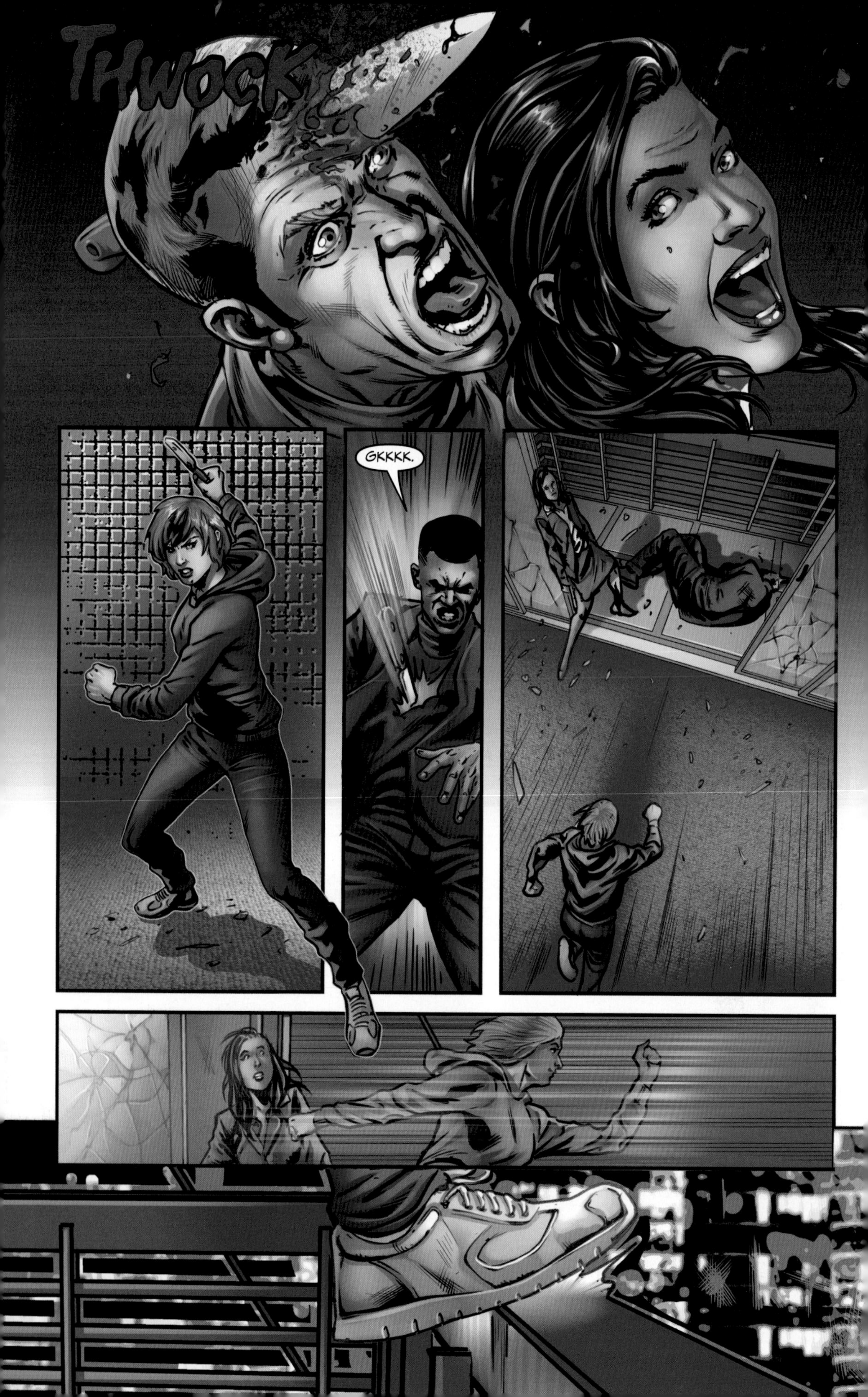
THWOCK
GKKKK.

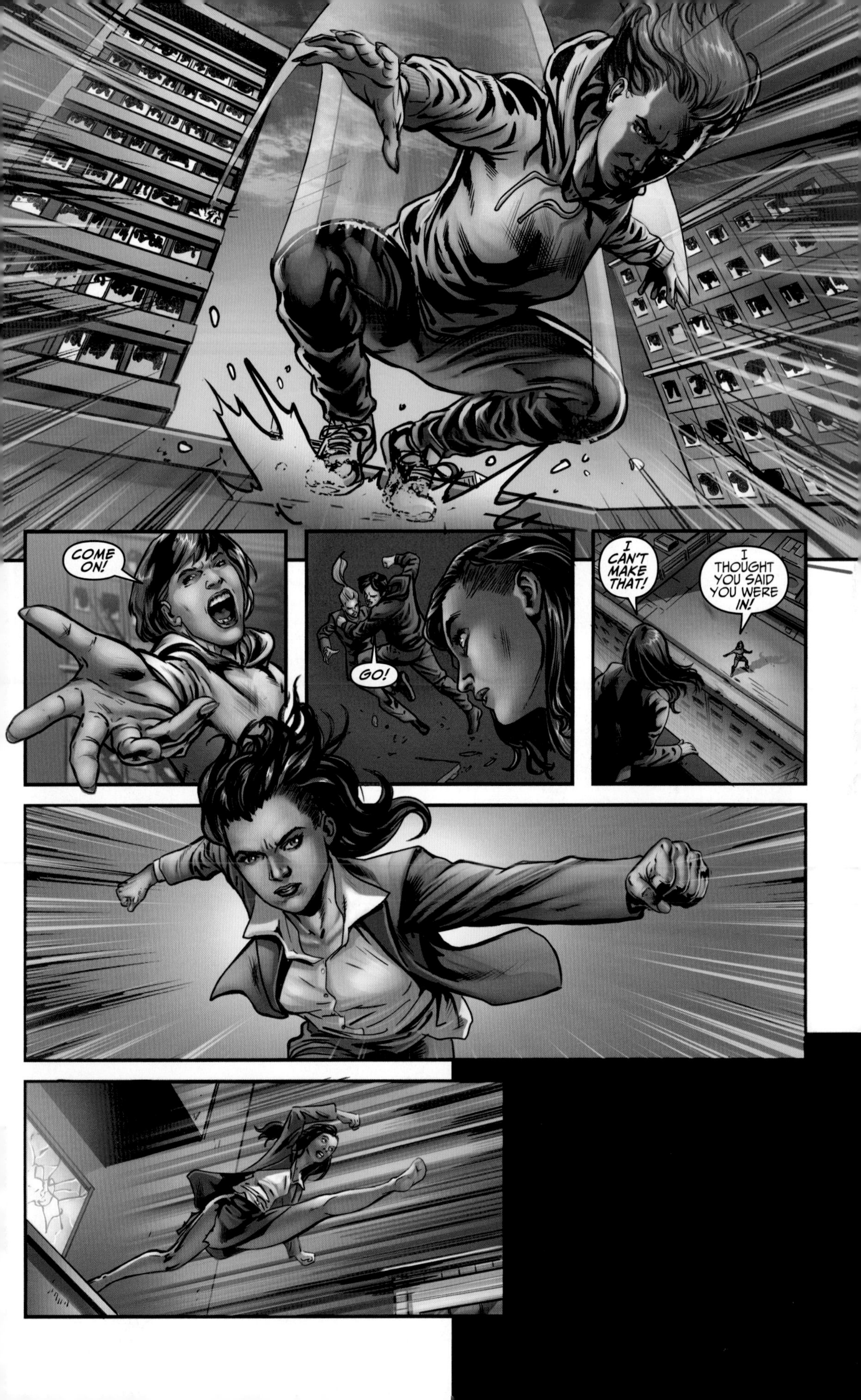
COME ON!
GO!
I CAN'T MAKE THAT!
I THOUGHT YOU SAID YOU WERE IN!

UNNNH.

AH!

HEY.

WHAT HAPPENED?

YOU MOSTLY MADE IT.

WHAT IS THIS PLACE?

THE SALTON SEA. USED TO BE A PARADISE BEFORE THEY DRAINED HALF OF IT.

XAVIER LIKES THE IRONY OF NURTURING OUR PLANS FOR REBELLION IN A DESERT.

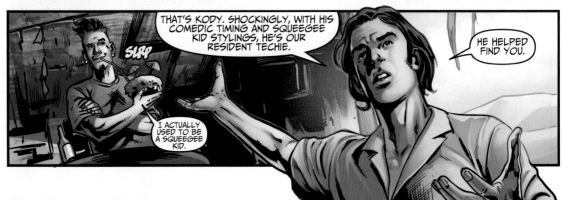

THAT'S KODY. SHOCKINGLY, WITH HIS COMEDIC TIMING AND SQUEEGEE KID STYLINGS, HE'S OUR RESIDENT TECHIE.

HE HELPED FIND YOU.

SLRP

I ACTUALLY USED TO BE A SQUEEGEE KID.

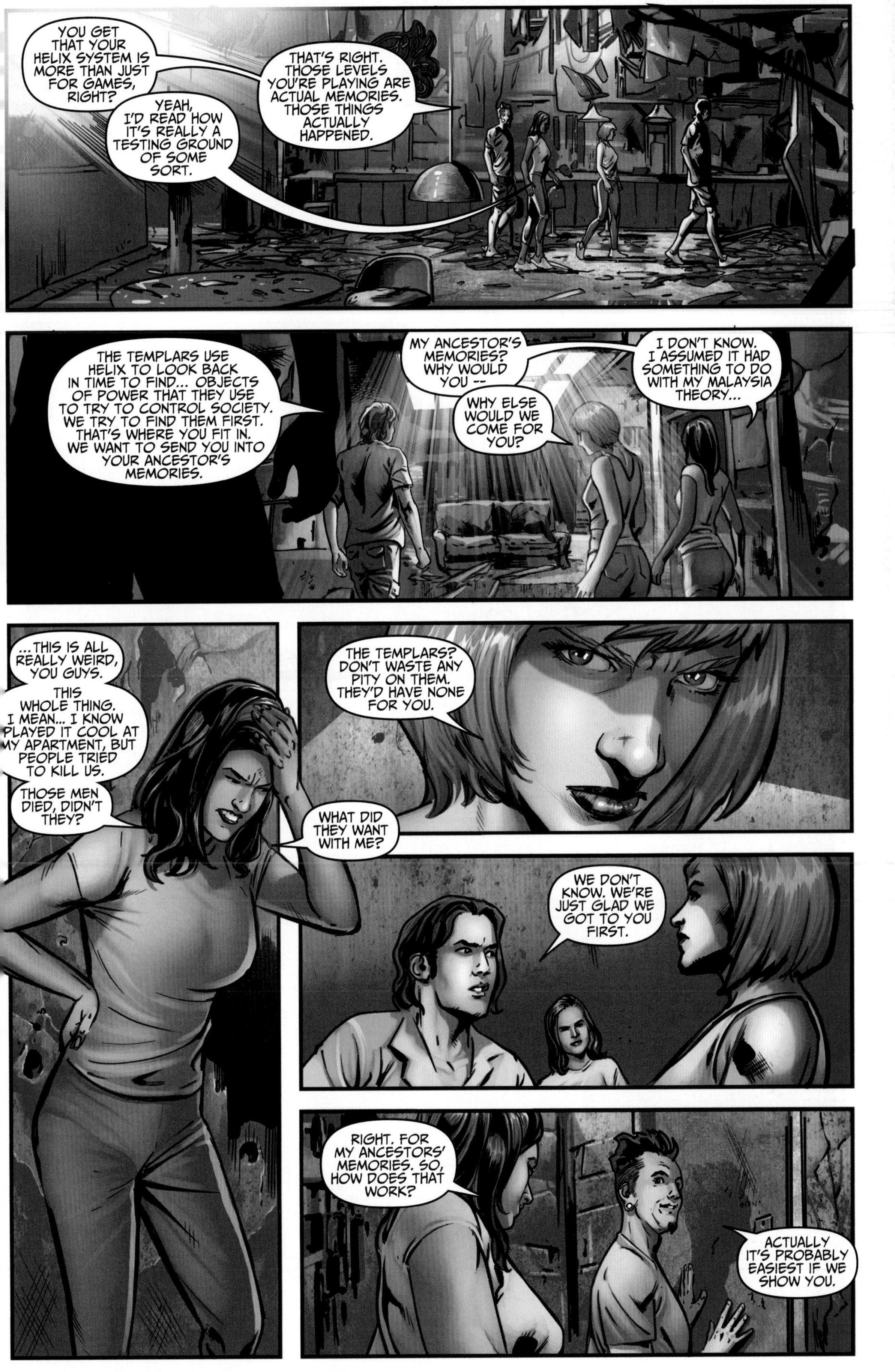
YOU GET THAT YOUR HELIX SYSTEM IS MORE THAN JUST FOR GAMES, RIGHT?
YEAH, I'D READ HOW IT'S REALLY A TESTING GROUND OF SOME SORT.
THAT'S RIGHT. THOSE LEVELS YOU'RE PLAYING ARE ACTUAL MEMORIES. THOSE THINGS ACTUALLY HAPPENED.
THE TEMPLARS USE HELIX TO LOOK BACK IN TIME TO FIND... OBJECTS OF POWER THAT THEY USE TO TRY TO CONTROL SOCIETY. WE TRY TO FIND THEM FIRST. THAT'S WHERE YOU FIT IN. WE WANT TO SEND YOU INTO YOUR ANCESTOR'S MEMORIES.
MY ANCESTOR'S MEMORIES? WHY WOULD YOU --
WHY ELSE WOULD WE COME FOR YOU?
I DON'T KNOW. I ASSUMED IT HAD SOMETHING TO DO WITH MY MALAYSIA THEORY...
...THIS IS ALL REALLY WEIRD, YOU GUYS.
THIS WHOLE THING. I MEAN... I KNOW PLAYED IT COOL AT MY APARTMENT, BUT PEOPLE TRIED TO KILL US.
THOSE MEN DIED, DIDN'T THEY?
THE TEMPLARS? DON'T WASTE ANY PITY ON THEM. THEY'D HAVE NONE FOR YOU.
WHAT DID THEY WANT WITH ME?
WE DON'T KNOW. WE'RE JUST GLAD WE GOT TO YOU FIRST.
RIGHT. FOR MY ANCESTORS' MEMORIES. SO, HOW DOES THAT WORK?
ACTUALLY IT'S PROBABLY EASIEST IF WE SHOW YOU.

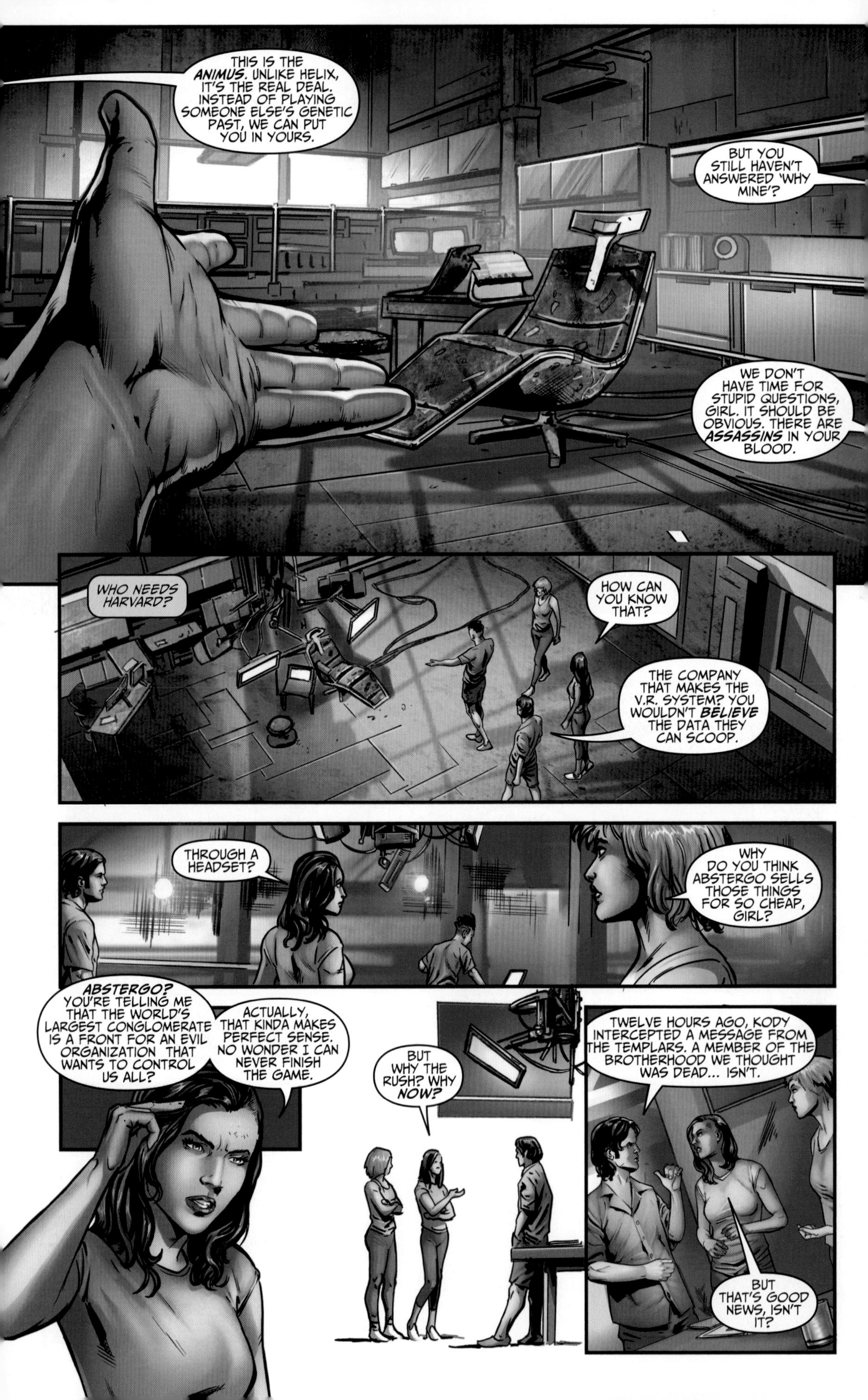
THIS IS THE ANIMUS. UNLIKE HELIX, IT'S THE REAL DEAL. INSTEAD OF PLAYING SOMEONE ELSE'S GENETIC PAST, WE CAN PUT YOU IN YOURS.
BUT YOU STILL HAVEN'T ANSWERED 'WHY MINE'?
WE DON'T HAVE TIME FOR STUPID QUESTIONS, GIRL. IT SHOULD BE OBVIOUS. THERE ARE ASSASSINS IN YOUR BLOOD.
WHO NEEDS HARVARD?
HOW CAN YOU KNOW THAT?
THE COMPANY THAT MAKES THE V.R. SYSTEM? YOU WOULDN'T BELIEVE THE DATA THEY CAN SCOOP.
THROUGH A HEADSET?
WHY DO YOU THINK ABSTERGO SELLS THOSE THINGS FOR SO CHEAP, GIRL?
ABSTERGO? YOU'RE TELLING ME THAT THE WORLD'S LARGEST CONGLOMERATE IS A FRONT FOR AN EVIL ORGANIZATION THAT WANTS TO CONTROL US ALL?
ACTUALLY, THAT KINDA MAKES PERFECT SENSE. NO WONDER I CAN NEVER FINISH THE GAME.
BUT WHY THE RUSH? WHY NOW?
TWELVE HOURS AGO, KODY INTERCEPTED A MESSAGE FROM THE TEMPLARS. A MEMBER OF THE BROTHERHOOD WE THOUGHT WAS DEAD... ISN'T.
BUT THAT'S GOOD NEWS, ISN'T IT?

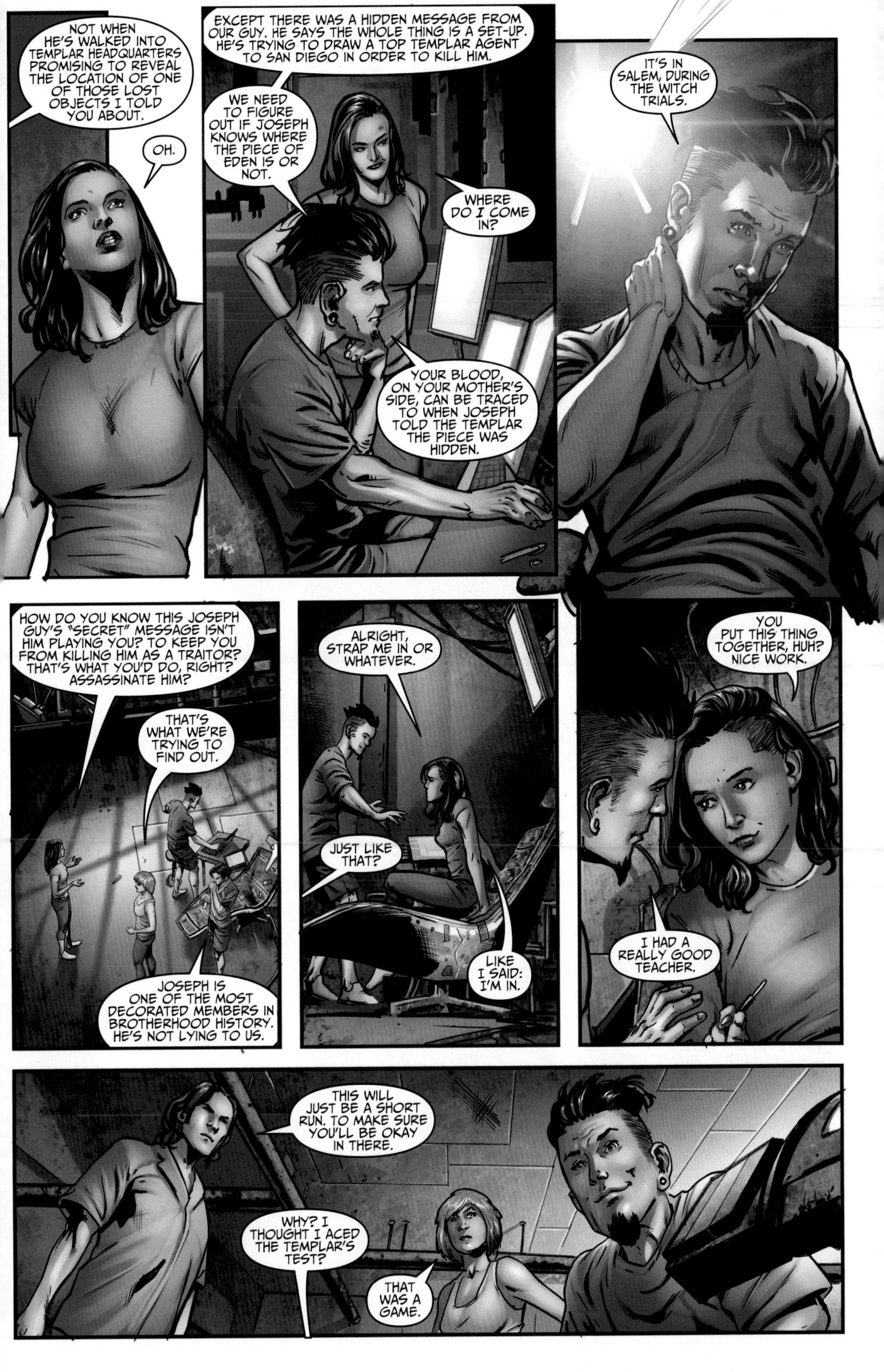
NOT WHEN HE'S WALKED INTO TEMPLAR HEADQUARTERS PROMISING TO REVEAL THE LOCATION OF ONE OF THOSE LOST OBJECTS I TOLD YOU ABOUT.
OH.
EXCEPT THERE WAS A HIDDEN MESSAGE FROM OUR GUY. HE SAYS THE WHOLE THING IS A SET-UP. HE'S TRYING TO DRAW A TOP TEMPLAR AGENT TO SAN DIEGO IN ORDER TO KILL HIM.
WE NEED TO FIGURE OUT IF JOSEPH KNOWS WHERE THE PIECE OF EDEN IS OR NOT.
WHERE DO I COME IN?
YOUR BLOOD, ON YOUR MOTHER'S SIDE, CAN BE TRACED TO WHEN JOSEPH TOLD THE TEMPLAR THE PIECE WAS HIDDEN.
IT'S IN SALEM, DURING THE WITCH TRIALS.
HOW DO YOU KNOW THIS JOSEPH GUY'S "SECRET" MESSAGE ISN'T HIM PLAYING YOU? TO KEEP YOU FROM KILLING HIM AS A TRAITOR? THAT'S WHAT YOU'D DO, RIGHT? ASSASSINATE HIM?
THAT'S WHAT WE'RE TRYING TO FIND OUT.
JOSEPH IS ONE OF THE MOST DECORATED MEMBERS IN BROTHERHOOD HISTORY. HE'S NOT LYING TO US.
ALRIGHT, STRAP ME IN OR WHATEVER.
JUST LIKE THAT?
LIKE I SAID: I'M IN.
YOU PUT THIS THING TOGETHER, HUH? NICE WORK.
I HAD A REALLY GOOD TEACHER.
THIS WILL JUST BE A SHORT RUN. TO MAKE SURE YOU'LL BE OKAY IN THERE.
WHY? I THOUGHT I ACED THE TEMPLAR'S TEST?
THAT WAS A GAME.

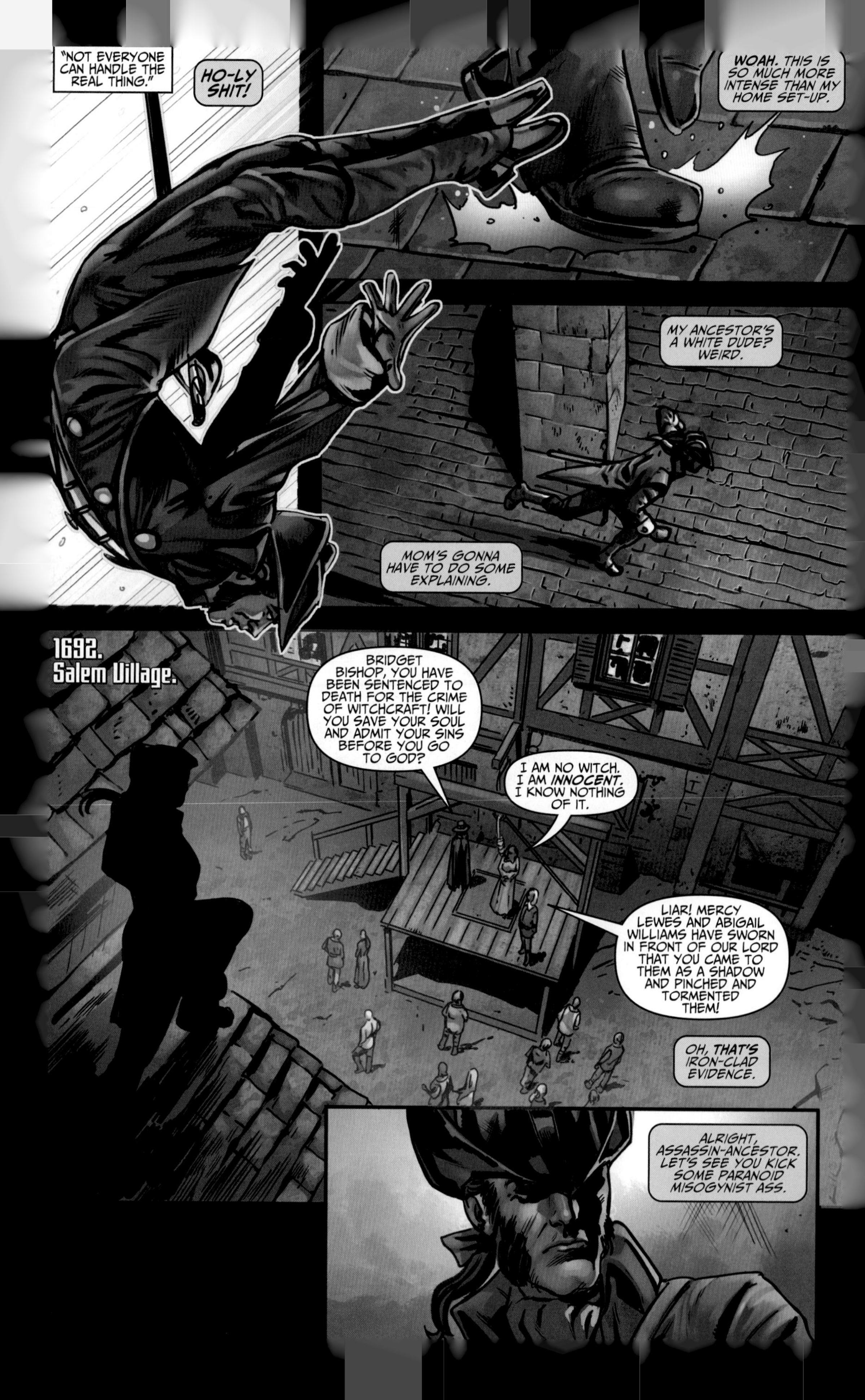
"NOT EVERYONE CAN HANDLE THE REAL THING."
HO-LY SHIT!
WOAH. THIS IS SO MUCH MORE INTENSE THAN MY HOME SET-UP.
MY ANCESTOR'S A WHITE DUDE? WEIRD.
MOM'S GONNA HAVE TO DO SOME EXPLAINING.
1692. Salem Village.
BRIDGET BISHOP, YOU HAVE BEEN SENTENCED TO DEATH FOR THE CRIME OF WITCHCRAFT! WILL YOU SAVE YOUR SOUL AND ADMIT YOUR SINS BEFORE YOU GO TO GOD?
I AM NO WITCH. I AM INNOCENT. I KNOW NOTHING OF IT.
LIAR! MERCY LEWES AND ABIGAIL WILLIAMS HAVE SWORN IN FRONT OF OUR LORD THAT YOU CAME TO THEM AS A SHADOW AND PINCHED AND TORMENTED THEM!
OH, THAT'S IRON-CLAD EVIDENCE.
ALRIGHT, ASSASSIN-ANCESTOR. LET'S SEE YOU KICK SOME PARANOID MISOGYNIST ASS.

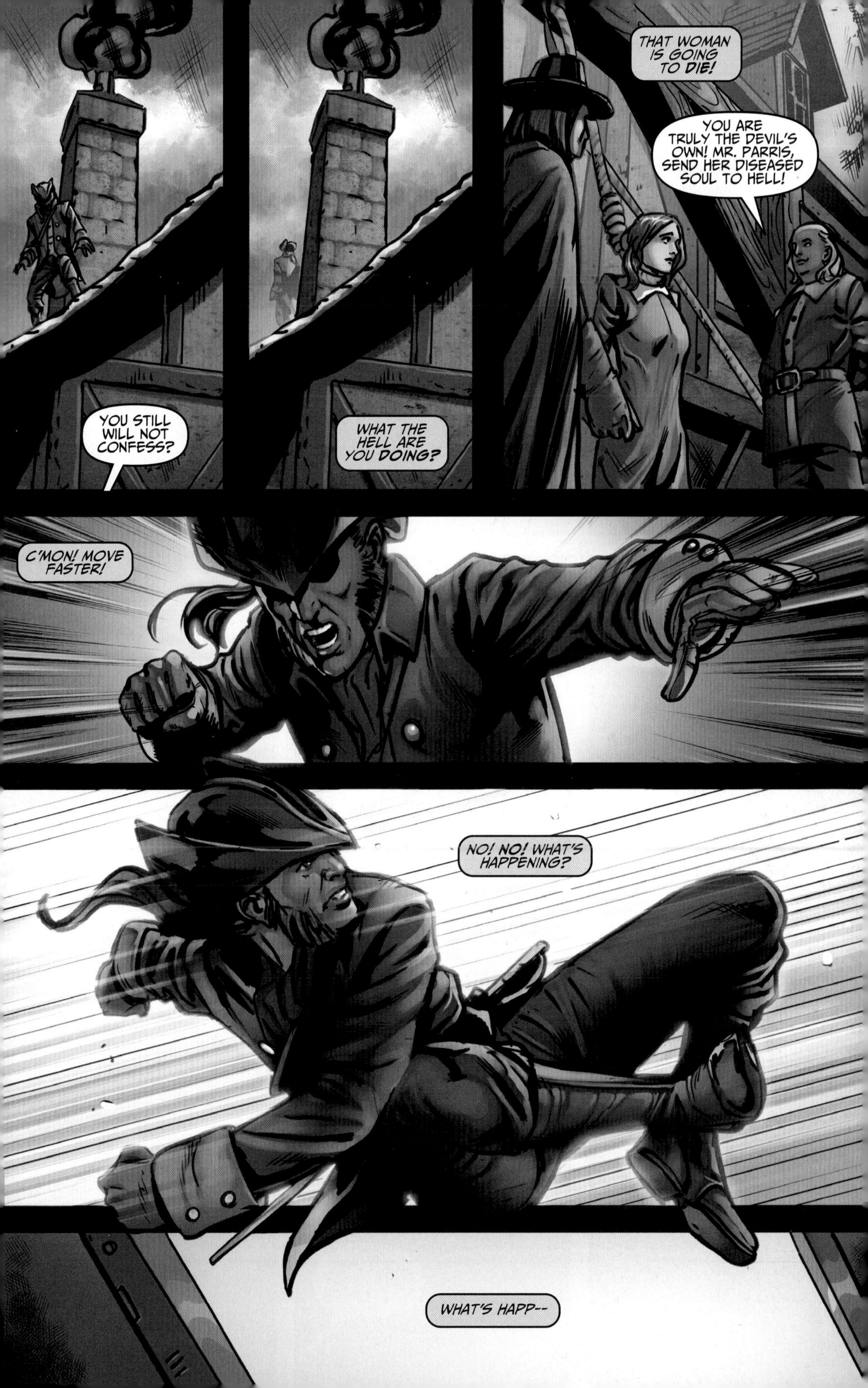
YOU STILL WILL NOT CONFESS?
WHAT THE HELL ARE YOU DOING?
THAT WOMAN IS GOING TO DIE!
YOU ARE TRULY THE DEVIL'S OWN! MR. PARRIS, SEND HER DISEASED SOUL TO HELL!
C'MON! MOVE FASTER!
NO! NO! WHAT'S HAPPENING?
WHAT'S HAPP--

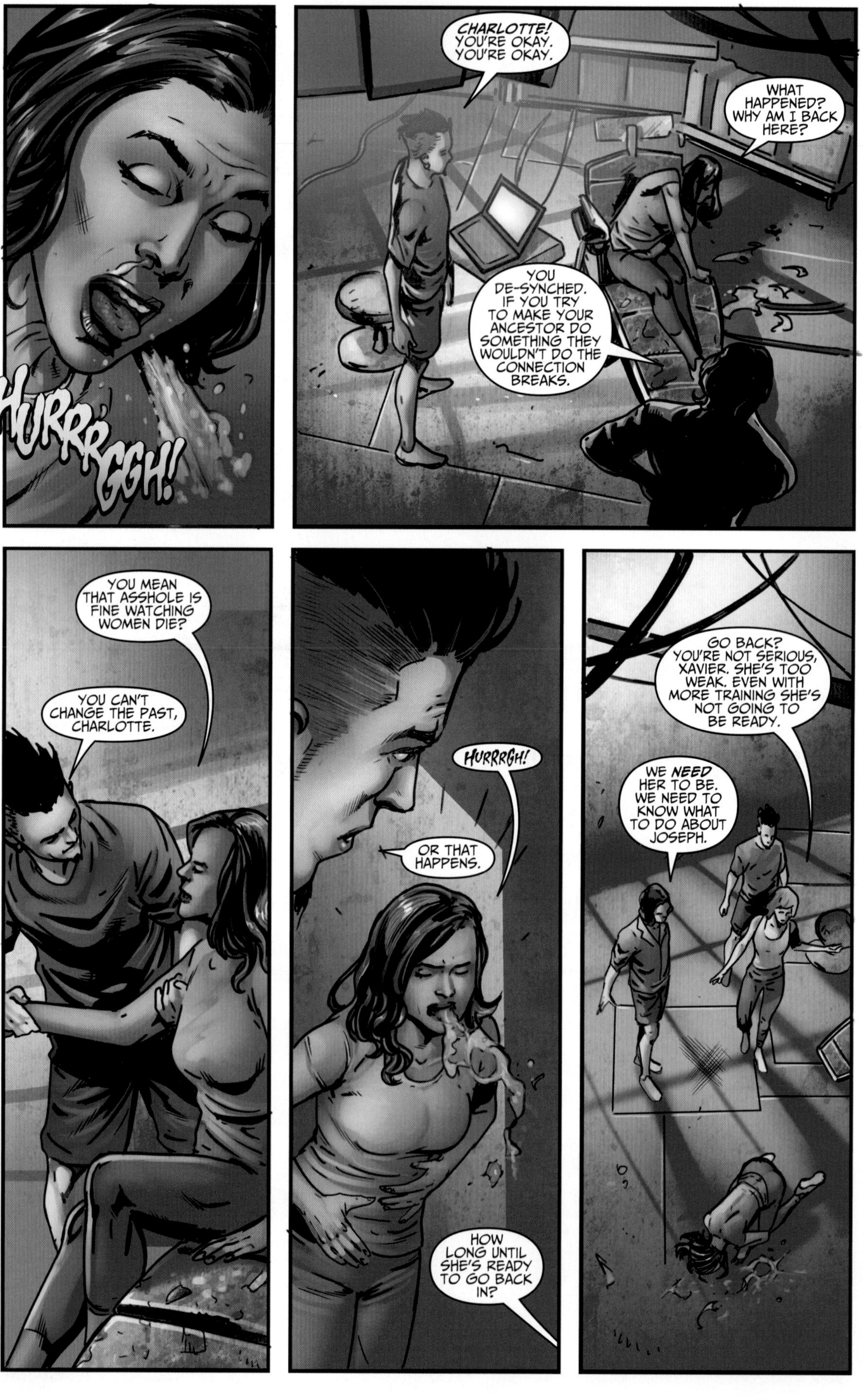
HURRRGGH!
CHARLOTTE! YOU'RE OKAY. YOU'RE OKAY.
WHAT HAPPENED? WHY AM I BACK HERE?
YOU DE-SYNCHED. IF YOU TRY TO MAKE YOUR ANCESTOR DO SOMETHING THEY WOULDN'T DO THE CONNECTION BREAKS.
YOU MEAN THAT ASSHOLE IS FINE WATCHING WOMEN DIE?
YOU CAN'T CHANGE THE PAST, CHARLOTTE.
HURRRGH!
OR THAT HAPPENS.
HOW LONG UNTIL SHE'S READY TO GO BACK IN?
GO BACK? YOU'RE NOT SERIOUS, XAVIER. SHE'S TOO WEAK. EVEN WITH MORE TRAINING SHE'S NOT GOING TO BE READY.
WE NEED HER TO BE. WE NEED TO KNOW WHAT TO DO ABOUT JOSEPH.

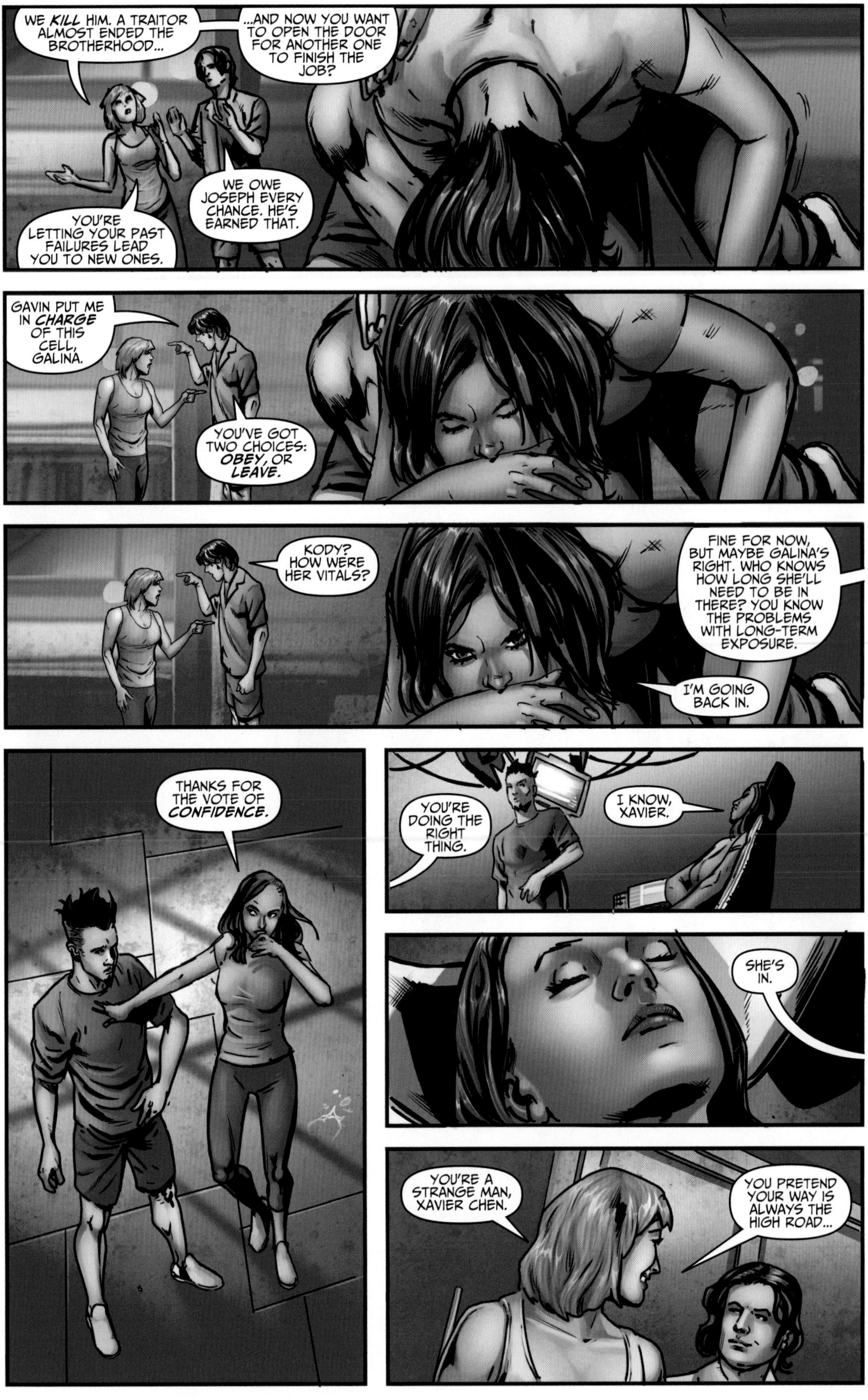
WE KILL HIM. A TRAITOR ALMOST ENDED THE BROTHERHOOD...
...AND NOW YOU WANT TO OPEN THE DOOR FOR ANOTHER ONE TO FINISH THE JOB?
YOU'RE LETTING YOUR PAST FAILURES LEAD YOU TO NEW ONES.
WE OWE JOSEPH EVERY CHANCE. HE'S EARNED THAT.
GAVIN PUT ME IN CHARGE OF THIS CELL, GALINA.
YOU'VE GOT TWO CHOICES: OBEY, OR LEAVE.
KODY? HOW WERE HER VITALS?
FINE FOR NOW, BUT MAYBE GALINA'S RIGHT. WHO KNOWS HOW LONG SHE'LL NEED TO BE IN THERE? YOU KNOW THE PROBLEMS WITH LONG-TERM EXPOSURE.
I'M GOING BACK IN.
THANKS FOR THE VOTE OF CONFIDENCE.
YOU'RE DOING THE RIGHT THING.
I KNOW, XAVIER.
SHE'S IN.
YOU'RE A STRANGE MAN, XAVIER CHEN.
YOU PRETEND YOUR WAY IS ALWAYS THE HIGH ROAD...

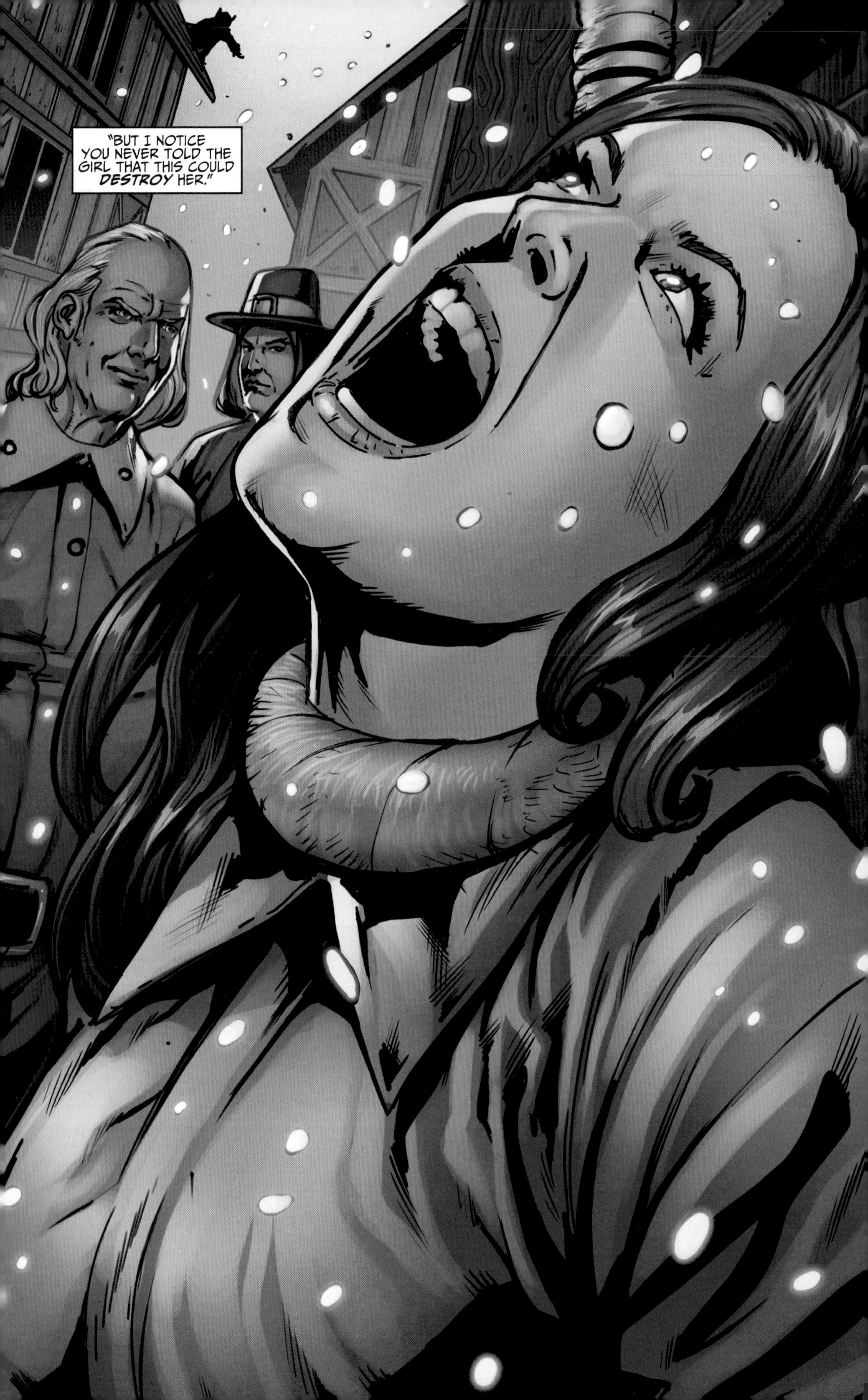
"BUT I NOTICE YOU NEVER TOLD THE GIRL THAT THIS COULD *DESTROY* HER."

CHAPTER
TWO

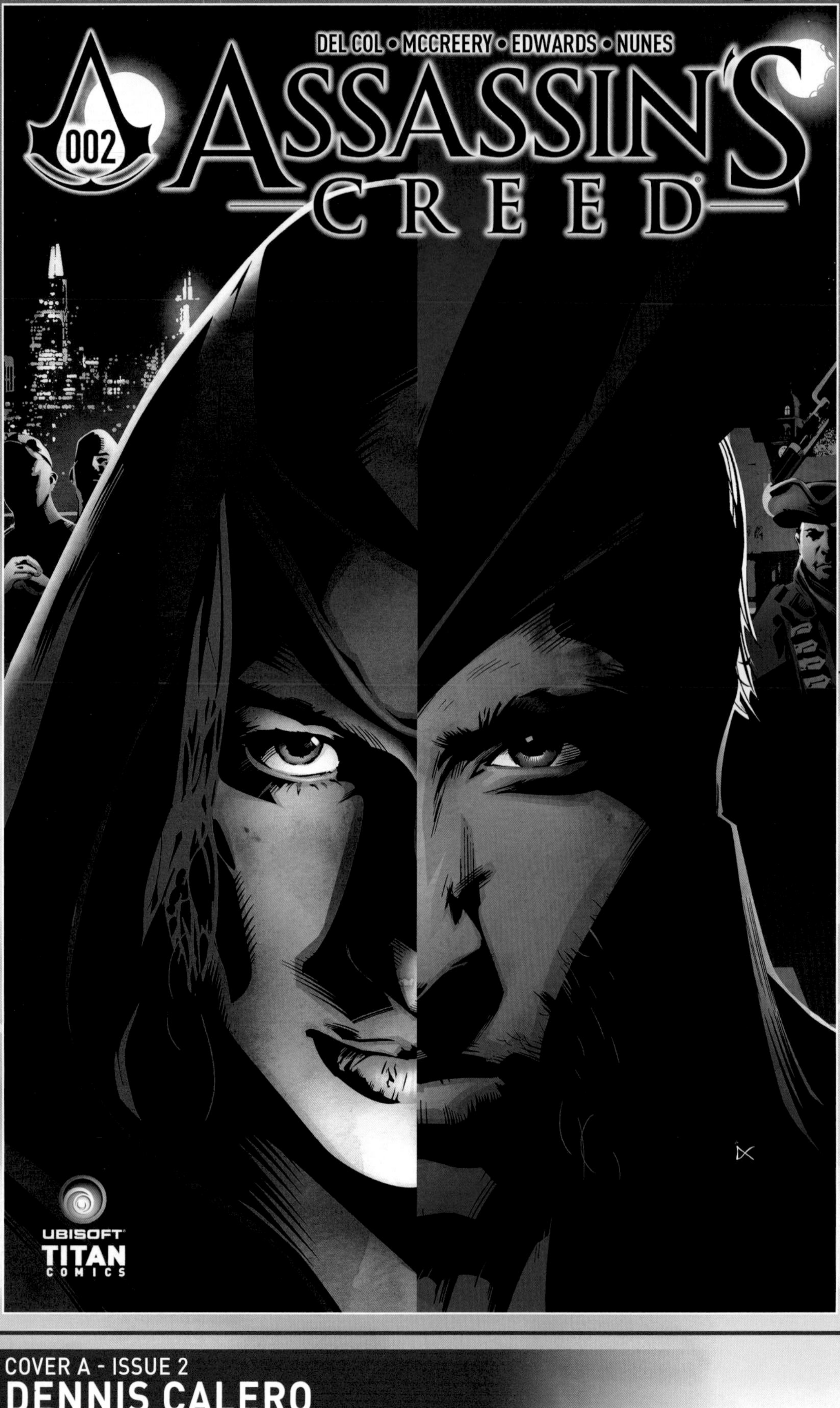
DEL COL • MCCREERY • EDWARDS • NUNES
002
ASSASSIN'S CREED
UBISOFT
TITAN COMICS

COVER A - ISSUE 2
DENNIS CALERO

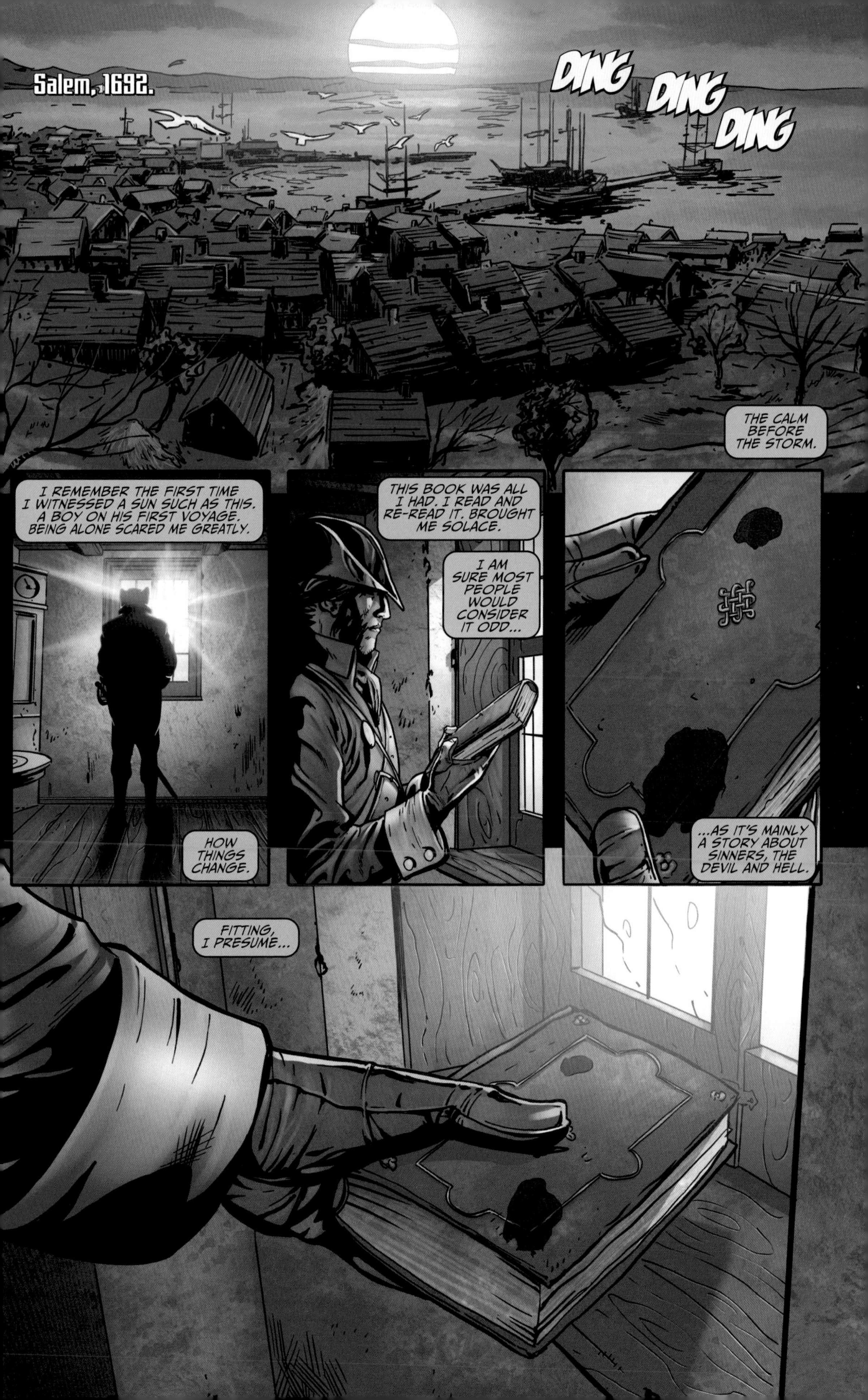
Salem, 1692.
DING DING DING
THE CALM BEFORE THE STORM.
I REMEMBER THE FIRST TIME I WITNESSED A SUN SUCH AS THIS. A BOY ON HIS FIRST VOYAGE. BEING ALONE SCARED ME GREATLY.
HOW THINGS CHANGE.
THIS BOOK WAS ALL I HAD. I READ AND RE-READ IT. BROUGHT ME SOLACE.
I AM SURE MOST PEOPLE WOULD CONSIDER IT ODD...
...AS IT'S MAINLY A STORY ABOUT SINNERS, THE DEVIL AND HELL.
FITTING, I PRESUME...

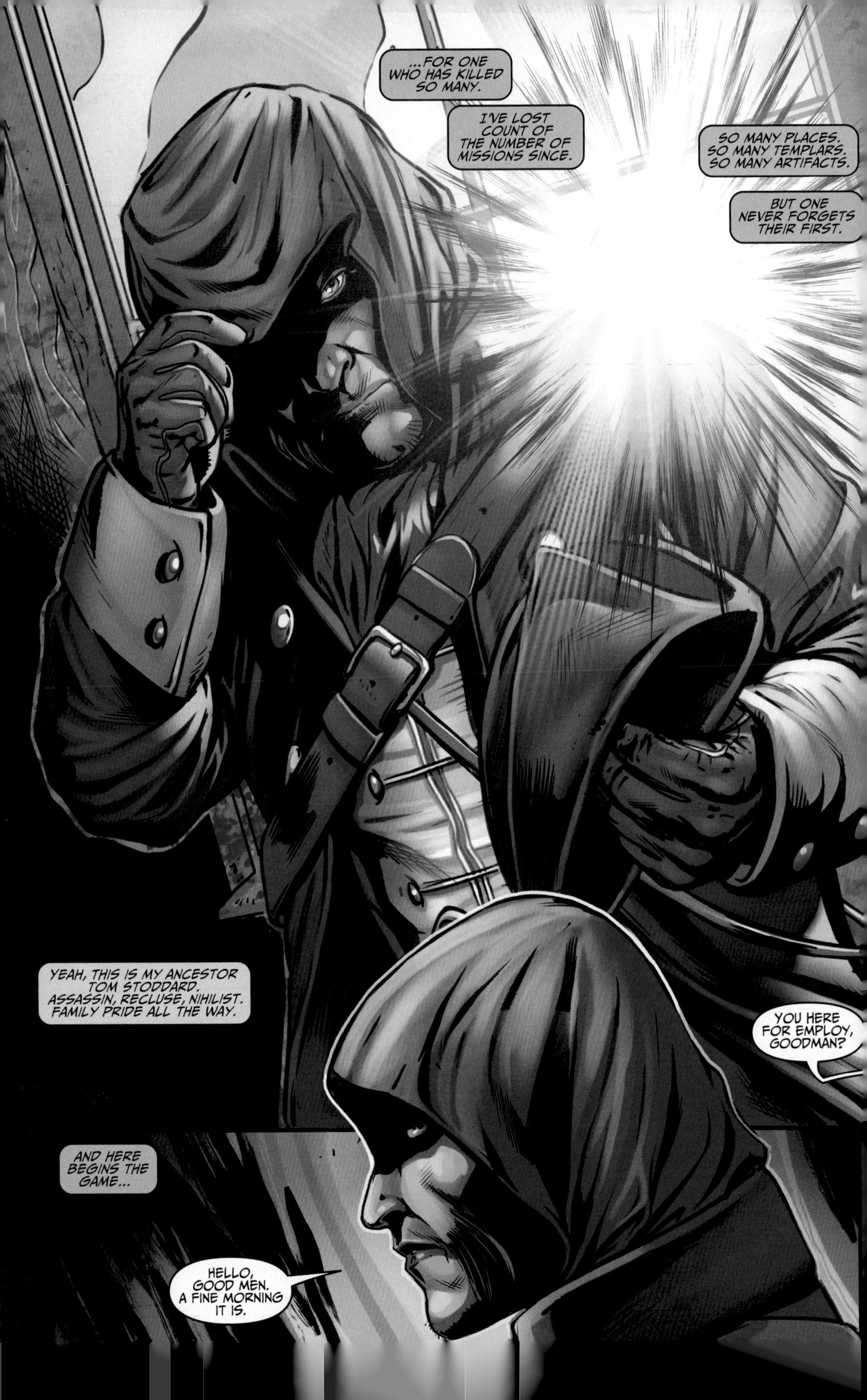
...FOR ONE WHO HAS KILLED SO MANY.
I'VE LOST COUNT OF THE NUMBER OF MISSIONS SINCE.
SO MANY PLACES. SO MANY TEMPLARS. SO MANY ARTIFACTS.
BUT ONE NEVER FORGETS THEIR FIRST.
YEAH, THIS IS MY ANCESTOR TOM STODDARD. ASSASSIN, RECLUSE, NIHILIST. FAMILY PRIDE ALL THE WAY.
YOU HERE FOR EMPLOY, GOODMAN?
AND HERE BEGINS THE GAME...
HELLO, GOOD MEN. A FINE MORNING IT IS.

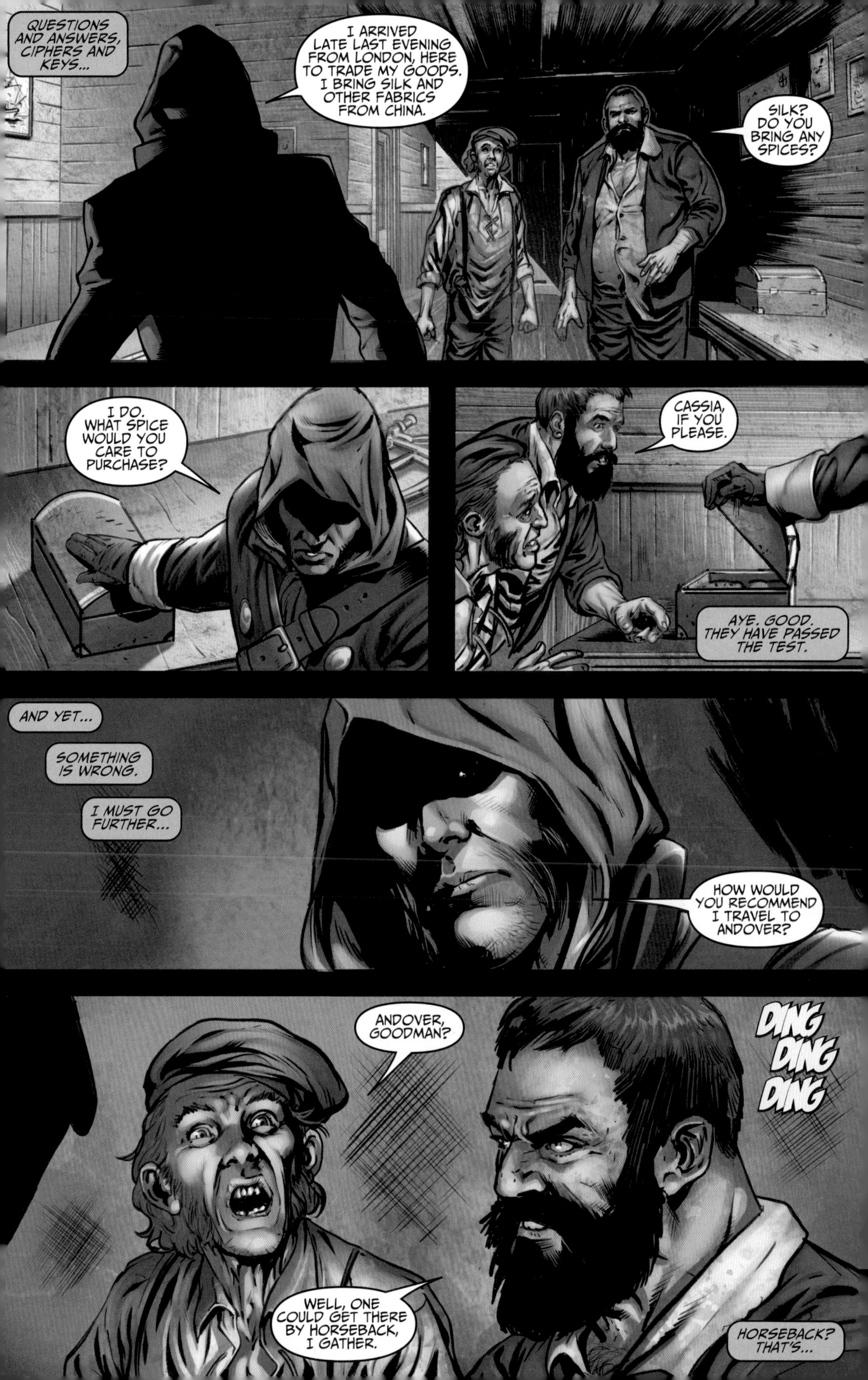

QUESTIONS AND ANSWERS, CIPHERS AND KEYS...
I ARRIVED LATE LAST EVENING FROM LONDON, HERE TO TRADE MY GOODS. I BRING SILK AND OTHER FABRICS FROM CHINA.
SILK? DO YOU BRING ANY SPICES?
I DO. WHAT SPICE WOULD YOU CARE TO PURCHASE?
CASSIA, IF YOU PLEASE.
AYE. GOOD. THEY HAVE PASSED THE TEST.
AND YET...
SOMETHING IS WRONG.
I MUST GO FURTHER...
HOW WOULD YOU RECOMMEND I TRAVEL TO ANDOVER?
ANDOVER, GOODMAN?
DING DING DING
WELL, ONE COULD GET THERE BY HORSEBACK, I GATHER.
HORSEBACK? THAT'S...

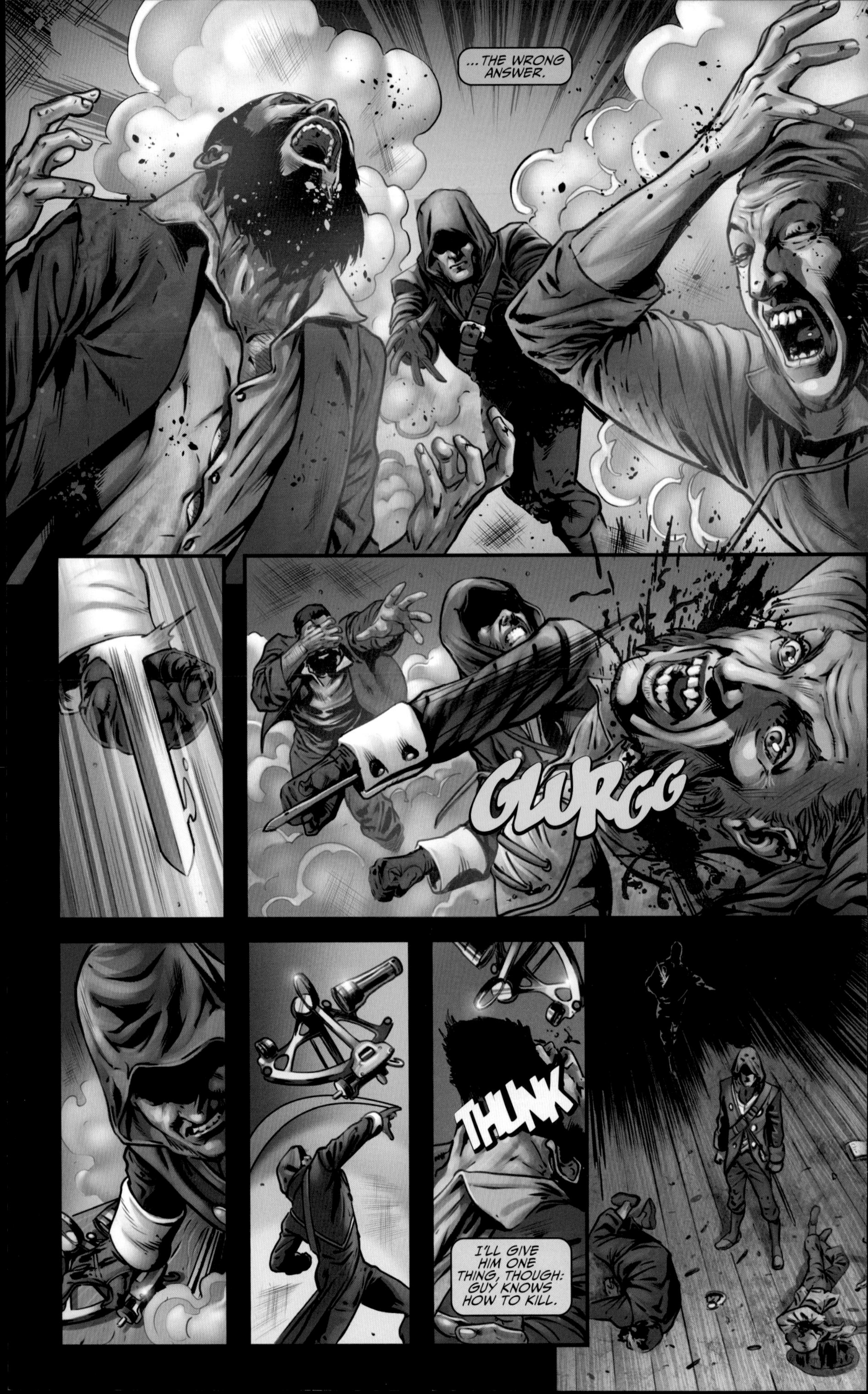
...THE WRONG ANSWER.
GLURGG
THUNK
I'LL GIVE HIM ONE THING, THOUGH: GUY KNOWS HOW TO KILL.

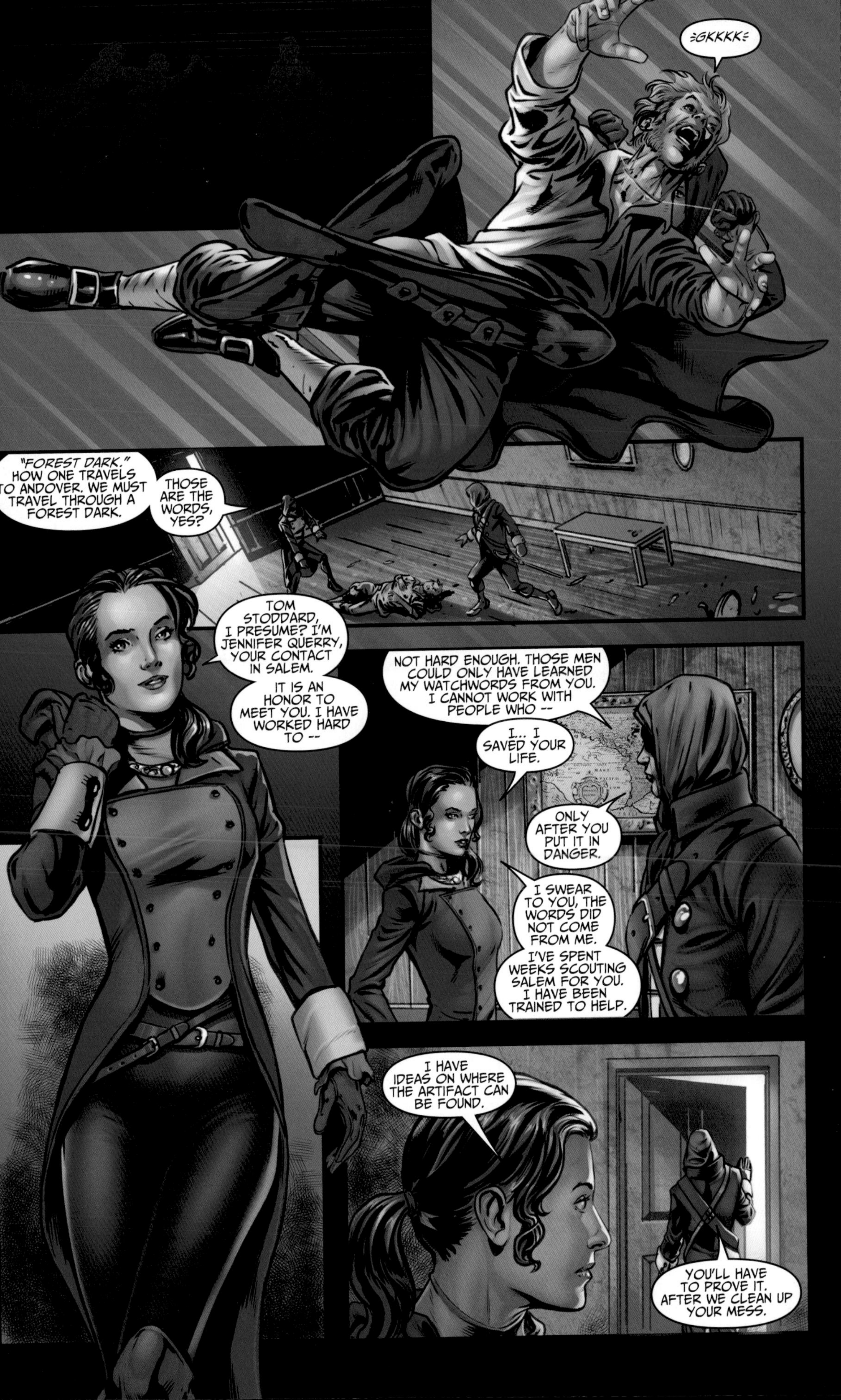

=GKKKK=
"FOREST DARK." HOW ONE TRAVELS TO ANDOVER. WE MUST TRAVEL THROUGH A FOREST DARK.
THOSE ARE THE WORDS, YES?
TOM STODDARD, I PRESUME? I'M JENNIFER QUERRY, YOUR CONTACT IN SALEM.
IT IS AN HONOR TO MEET YOU. I HAVE WORKED HARD TO --
NOT HARD ENOUGH. THOSE MEN COULD ONLY HAVE LEARNED MY WATCHWORDS FROM YOU. I CANNOT WORK WITH PEOPLE WHO --
I... I SAVED YOUR LIFE.
ONLY AFTER YOU PUT IT IN DANGER.
I SWEAR TO YOU, THE WORDS DID NOT COME FROM ME.
I'VE SPENT WEEKS SCOUTING SALEM FOR YOU. I HAVE BEEN TRAINED TO HELP.
I HAVE IDEAS ON WHERE THE ARTIFACT CAN BE FOUND.
YOU'LL HAVE TO PROVE IT. AFTER WE CLEAN UP YOUR MESS.

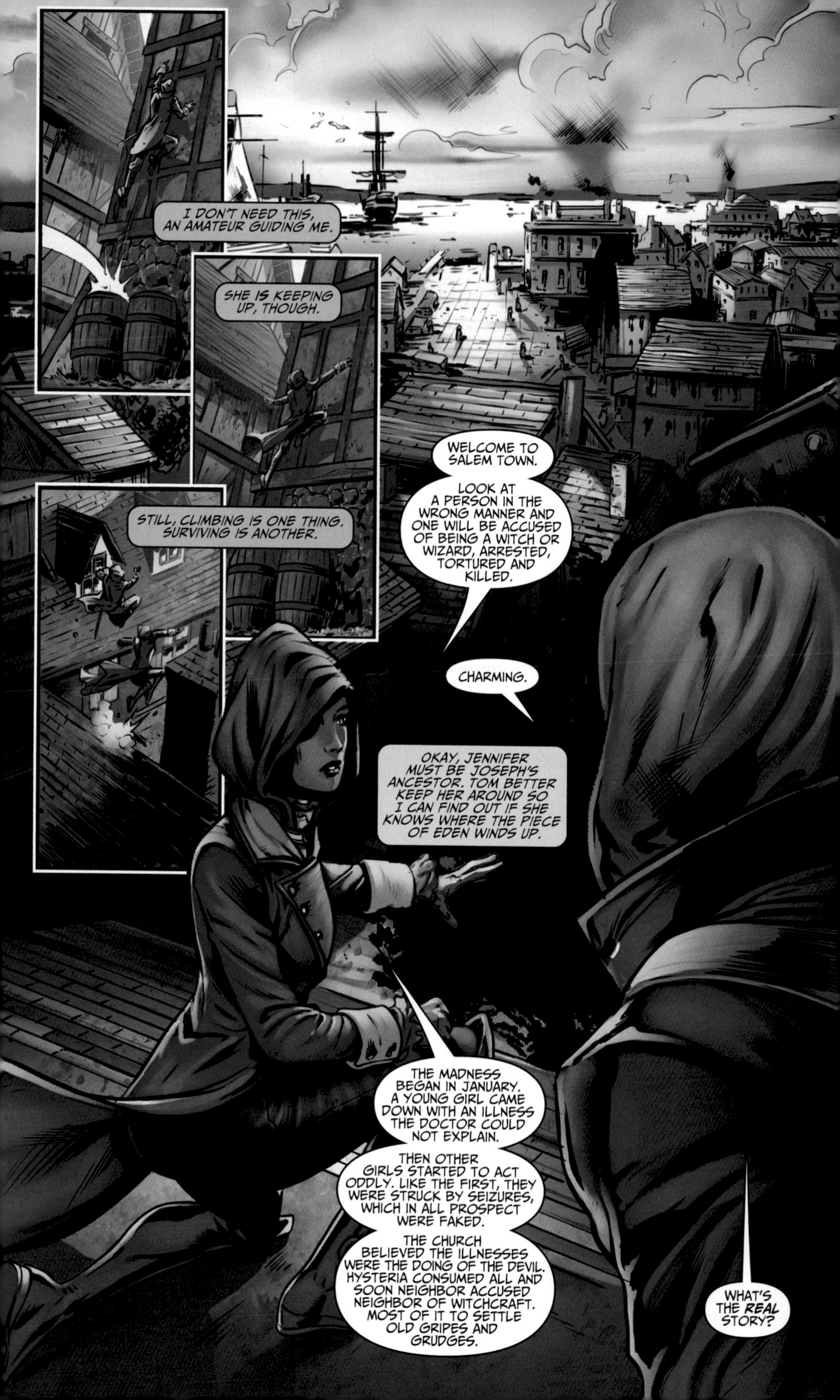

I DON'T NEED THIS, AN AMATEUR GUIDING ME.
SHE IS KEEPING UP, THOUGH.
STILL, CLIMBING IS ONE THING. SURVIVING IS ANOTHER.
WELCOME TO SALEM TOWN.
LOOK AT A PERSON IN THE WRONG MANNER AND ONE WILL BE ACCUSED OF BEING A WITCH OR WIZARD, ARRESTED, TORTURED AND KILLED.
CHARMING.
OKAY, JENNIFER MUST BE JOSEPH'S ANCESTOR. TOM BETTER KEEP HER AROUND SO I CAN FIND OUT IF SHE KNOWS WHERE THE PIECE OF EDEN WINDS UP.
THE MADNESS BEGAN IN JANUARY. A YOUNG GIRL CAME DOWN WITH AN ILLNESS THE DOCTOR COULD NOT EXPLAIN.
THEN OTHER GIRLS STARTED TO ACT ODDLY. LIKE THE FIRST, THEY WERE STRUCK BY SEIZURES, WHICH IN ALL PROSPECT WERE FAKED.
THE CHURCH BELIEVED THE ILLNESSES WERE THE DOING OF THE DEVIL. HYSTERIA CONSUMED ALL AND SOON NEIGHBOR ACCUSED NEIGHBOR OF WITCHCRAFT. MOST OF IT TO SETTLE OLD GRIPES AND GRUDGES.
WHAT'S THE REAL STORY?

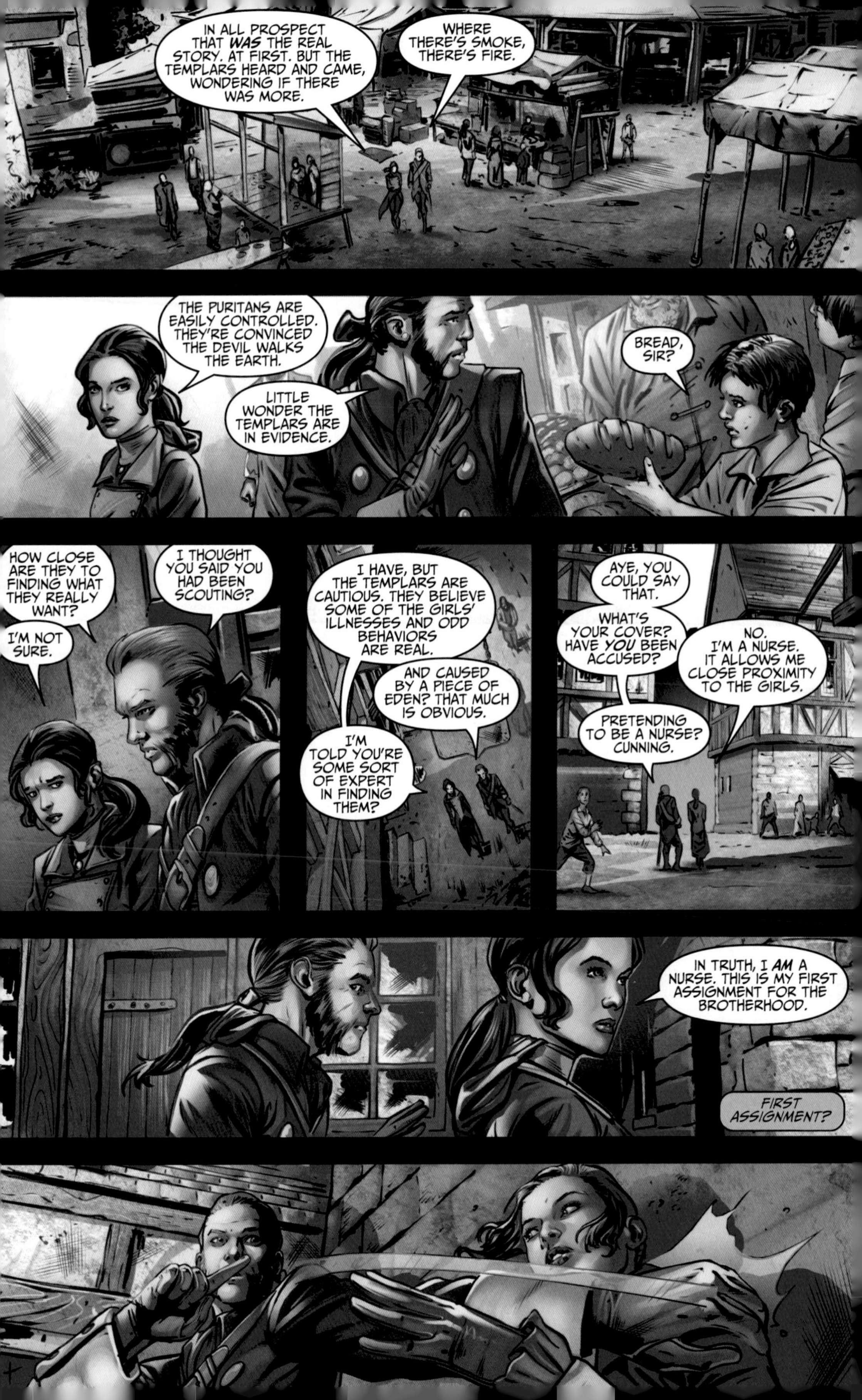
IN ALL PROSPECT THAT WAS THE REAL STORY. AT FIRST. BUT THE TEMPLARS HEARD AND CAME, WONDERING IF THERE WAS MORE.
WHERE THERE'S SMOKE, THERE'S FIRE.
THE PURITANS ARE EASILY CONTROLLED. THEY'RE CONVINCED THE DEVIL WALKS THE EARTH.
LITTLE WONDER THE TEMPLARS ARE IN EVIDENCE.
BREAD, SIR?
HOW CLOSE ARE THEY TO FINDING WHAT THEY REALLY WANT?
I'M NOT SURE.
I THOUGHT YOU SAID YOU HAD BEEN SCOUTING?
I HAVE, BUT THE TEMPLARS ARE CAUTIOUS. THEY BELIEVE SOME OF THE GIRLS' ILLNESSES AND ODD BEHAVIORS ARE REAL.
AND CAUSED BY A PIECE OF EDEN? THAT MUCH IS OBVIOUS.
I'M TOLD YOU'RE SOME SORT OF EXPERT IN FINDING THEM?
AYE, YOU COULD SAY THAT.
WHAT'S YOUR COVER? HAVE YOU BEEN ACCUSED?
NO. I'M A NURSE. IT ALLOWS ME CLOSE PROXIMITY TO THE GIRLS.
PRETENDING TO BE A NURSE? CUNNING.
IN TRUTH, I AM A NURSE. THIS IS MY FIRST ASSIGNMENT FOR THE BROTHERHOOD.
FIRST ASSIGNMENT?

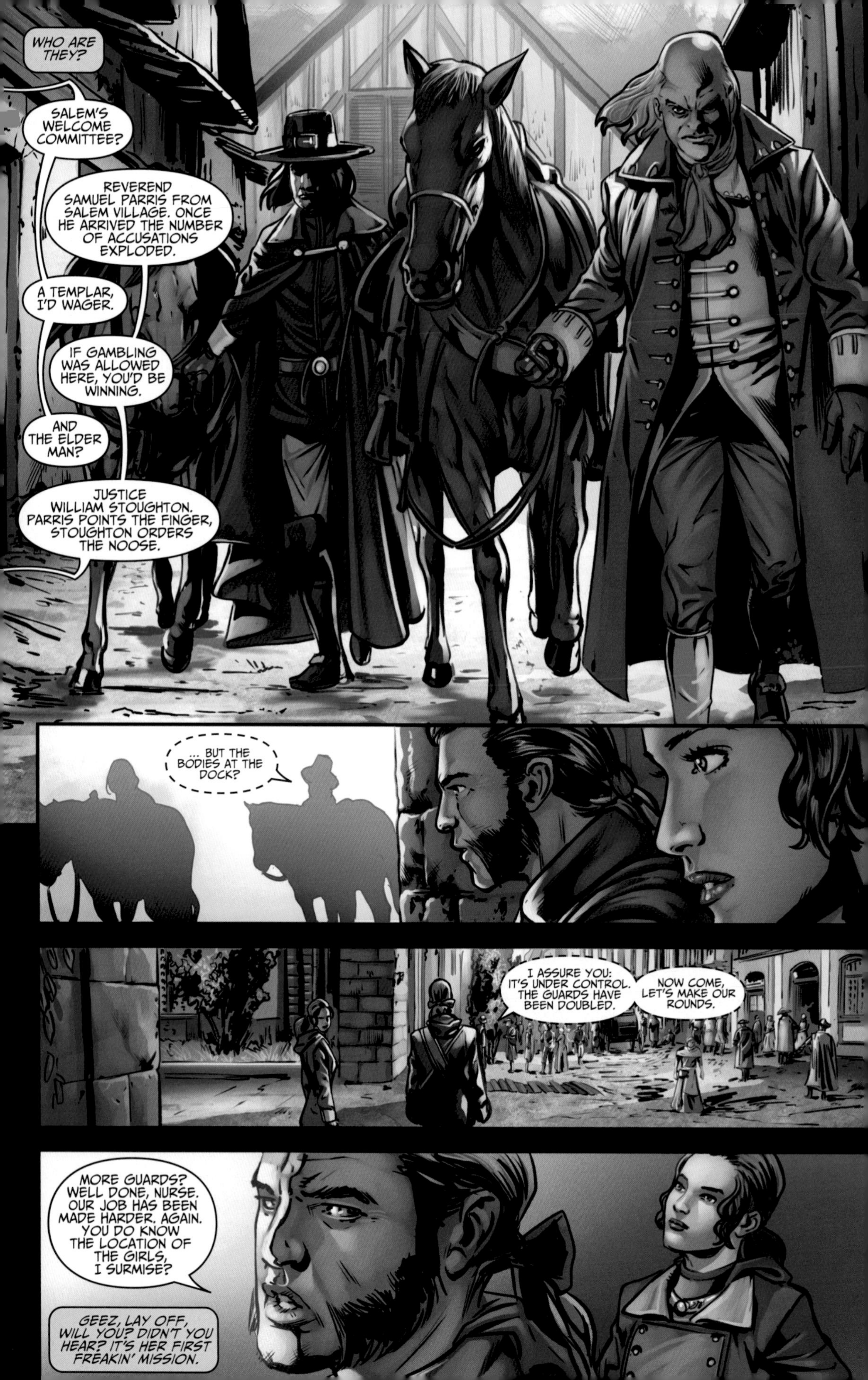
WHO ARE THEY?
SALEM'S WELCOME COMMITTEE?
REVEREND SAMUEL PARRIS FROM SALEM VILLAGE. ONCE HE ARRIVED THE NUMBER OF ACCUSATIONS EXPLODED.
A TEMPLAR, I'D WAGER.
IF GAMBLING WAS ALLOWED HERE, YOU'D BE WINNING.
AND THE ELDER MAN?
JUSTICE WILLIAM STOUGHTON. PARRIS POINTS THE FINGER, STOUGHTON ORDERS THE NOOSE.
... BUT THE BODIES AT THE DOCK?
I ASSURE YOU: IT'S UNDER CONTROL. THE GUARDS HAVE BEEN DOUBLED.
NOW COME, LET'S MAKE OUR ROUNDS.
MORE GUARDS? WELL DONE, NURSE. OUR JOB HAS BEEN MADE HARDER. AGAIN. YOU DO KNOW THE LOCATION OF THE GIRLS, I SURMISE?
GEEZ, LAY OFF, WILL YOU? DIDN'T YOU HEAR? IT'S HER FIRST FREAKIN' MISSION.

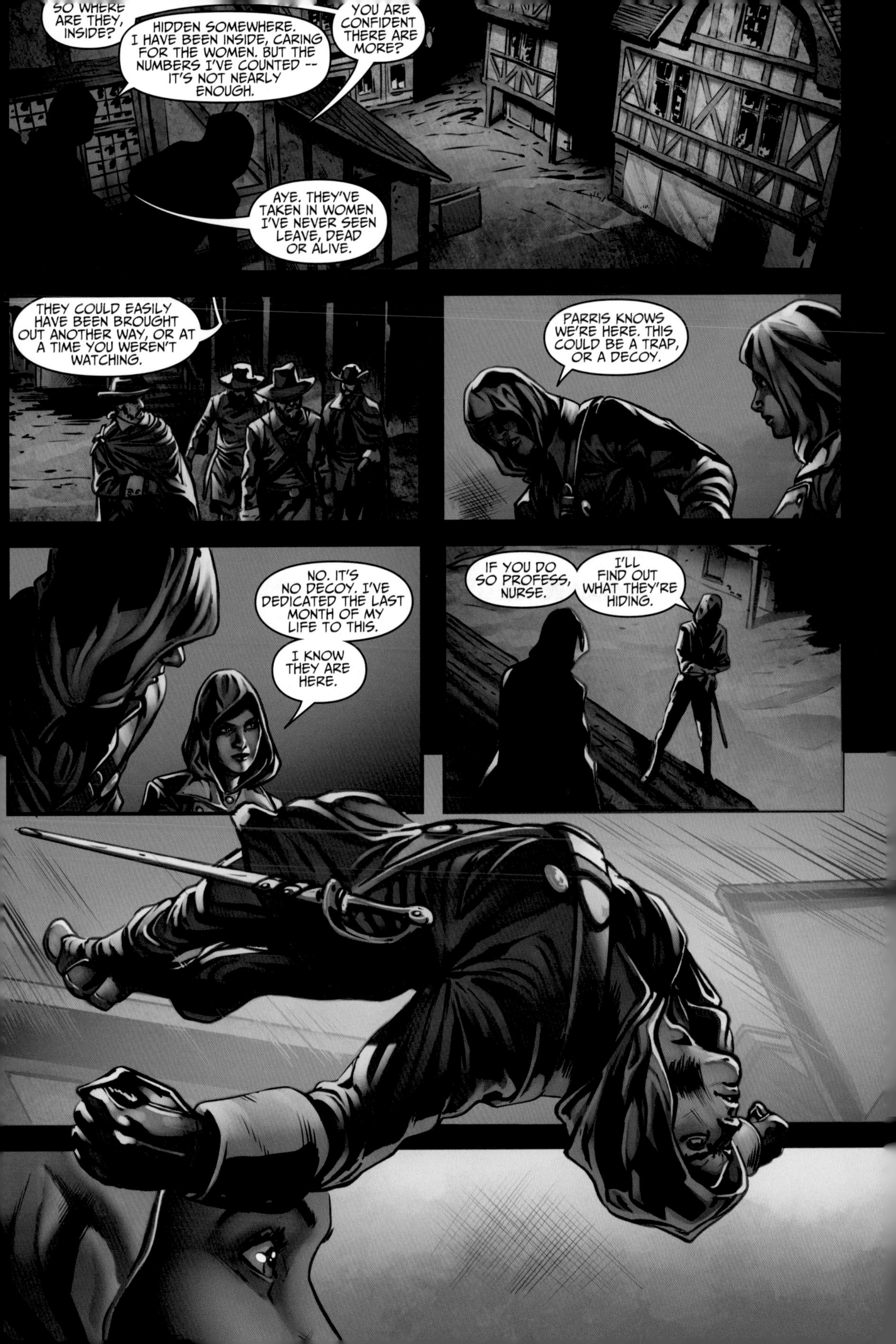
SO WHERE ARE THEY, INSIDE?
HIDDEN SOMEWHERE. I HAVE BEEN INSIDE, CARING FOR THE WOMEN. BUT THE NUMBERS I'VE COUNTED -- IT'S NOT NEARLY ENOUGH.
YOU ARE CONFIDENT THERE ARE MORE?
AYE. THEY'VE TAKEN IN WOMEN I'VE NEVER SEEN LEAVE, DEAD OR ALIVE.
THEY COULD EASILY HAVE BEEN BROUGHT OUT ANOTHER WAY, OR AT A TIME YOU WEREN'T WATCHING.
PARRIS KNOWS WE'RE HERE. THIS COULD BE A TRAP, OR A DECOY.
NO. IT'S NO DECOY. I'VE DEDICATED THE LAST MONTH OF MY LIFE TO THIS.
I KNOW THEY ARE HERE.
IF YOU DO SO PROFESS, NURSE.
I'LL FIND OUT WHAT THEY'RE HIDING.

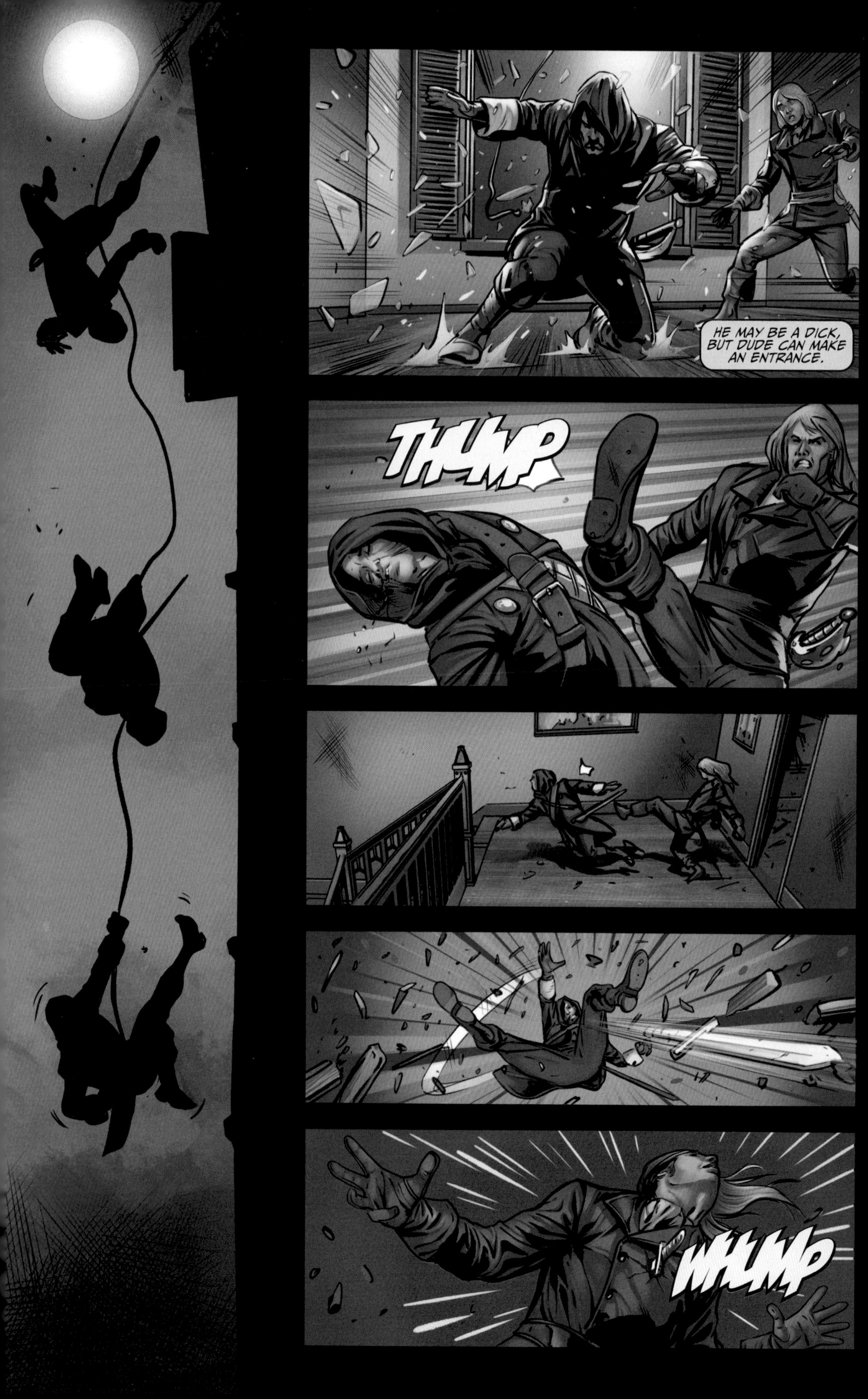
HE MAY BE A DICK, BUT DUDE CAN MAKE AN ENTRANCE.
THUMP
WHUMP

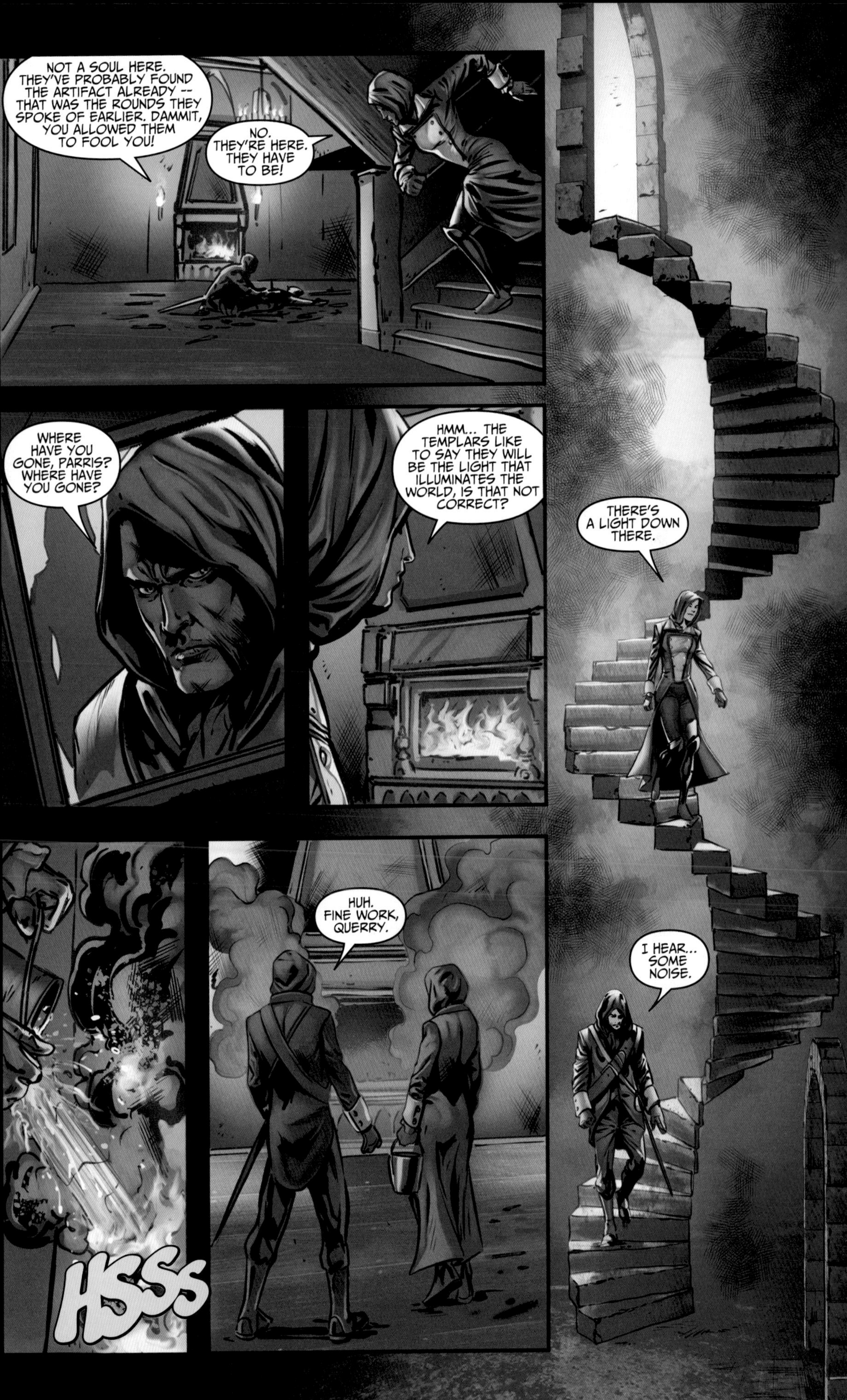
NOT A SOUL HERE. THEY'VE PROBABLY FOUND THE ARTIFACT ALREADY -- THAT WAS THE ROUNDS THEY SPOKE OF EARLIER. DAMMIT, YOU ALLOWED THEM TO FOOL YOU!
NO. THEY'RE HERE. THEY HAVE TO BE!
WHERE HAVE YOU GONE, PARRIS? WHERE HAVE YOU GONE?
HMM... THE TEMPLARS LIKE TO SAY THEY WILL BE THE LIGHT THAT ILLUMINATES THE WORLD, IS THAT NOT CORRECT?
HSSS
HUH. FINE WORK, QUERRY.
THERE'S A LIGHT DOWN THERE.
I HEAR... SOME NOISE.

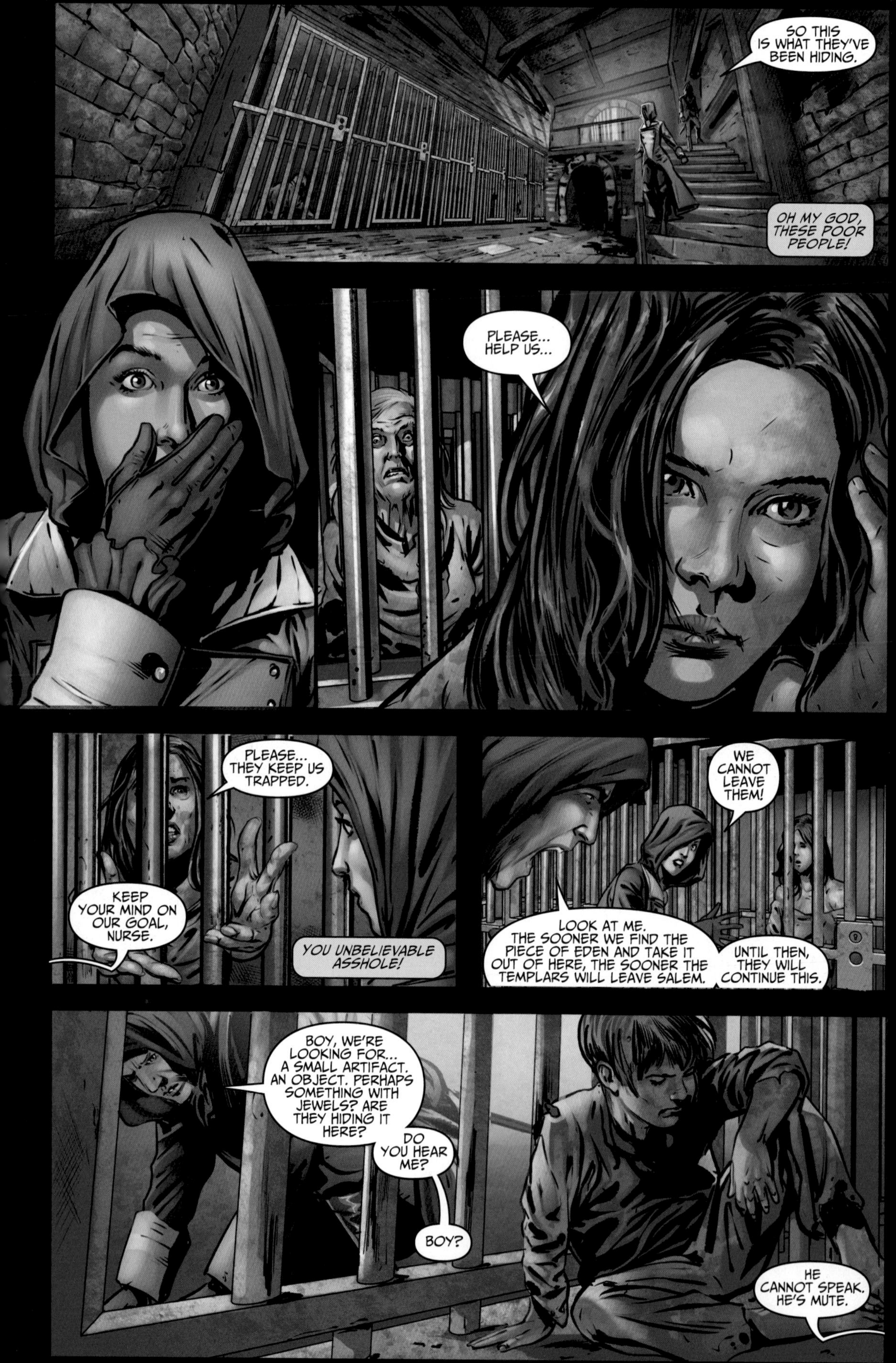
SO THIS IS WHAT THEY'VE BEEN HIDING.
OH MY GOD, THESE POOR PEOPLE!
PLEASE... HELP US...
PLEASE... THEY KEEP US TRAPPED.
KEEP YOUR MIND ON OUR GOAL, NURSE.
YOU UNBELIEVABLE ASSHOLE!
WE CANNOT LEAVE THEM!
LOOK AT ME. THE SOONER WE FIND THE PIECE OF EDEN AND TAKE IT OUT OF HERE, THE SOONER THE TEMPLARS WILL LEAVE SALEM.
UNTIL THEN, THEY WILL CONTINUE THIS.
BOY, WE'RE LOOKING FOR... A SMALL ARTIFACT. AN OBJECT. PERHAPS SOMETHING WITH JEWELS? ARE THEY HIDING IT HERE?
DO YOU HEAR ME?
BOY?
HE CANNOT SPEAK. HE'S MUTE.

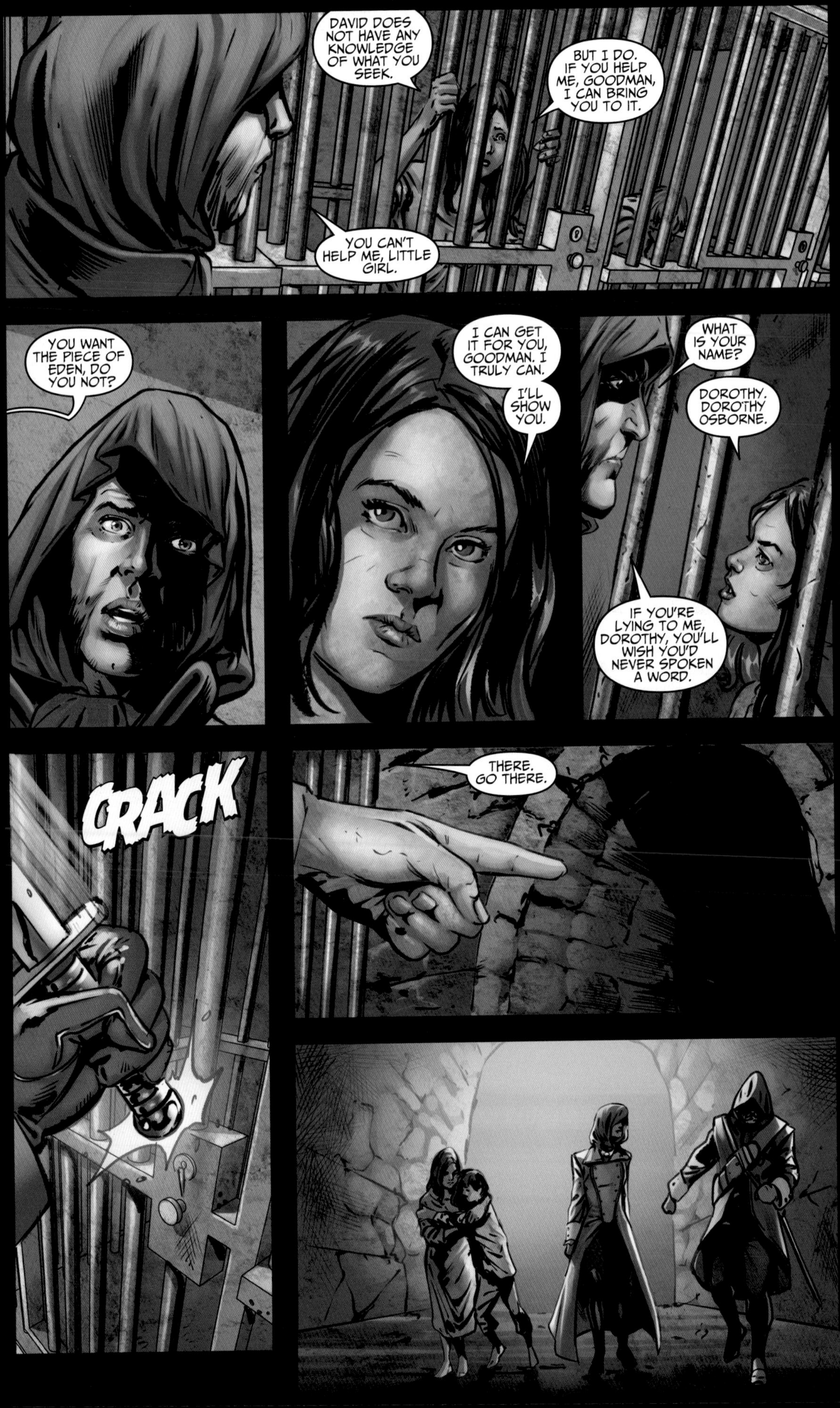
DAVID DOES NOT HAVE ANY KNOWLEDGE OF WHAT YOU SEEK.
BUT I DO. IF YOU HELP ME, GOODMAN, I CAN BRING YOU TO IT.
YOU CAN'T HELP ME, LITTLE GIRL.
YOU WANT THE PIECE OF EDEN, DO YOU NOT?
I CAN GET IT FOR YOU, GOODMAN. I TRULY CAN.
I'LL SHOW YOU.
WHAT IS YOUR NAME?
DOROTHY. DOROTHY OSBORNE.
IF YOU'RE LYING TO ME, DOROTHY, YOU'LL WISH YOU'D NEVER SPOKEN A WORD.
CRACK
THERE. GO THERE.

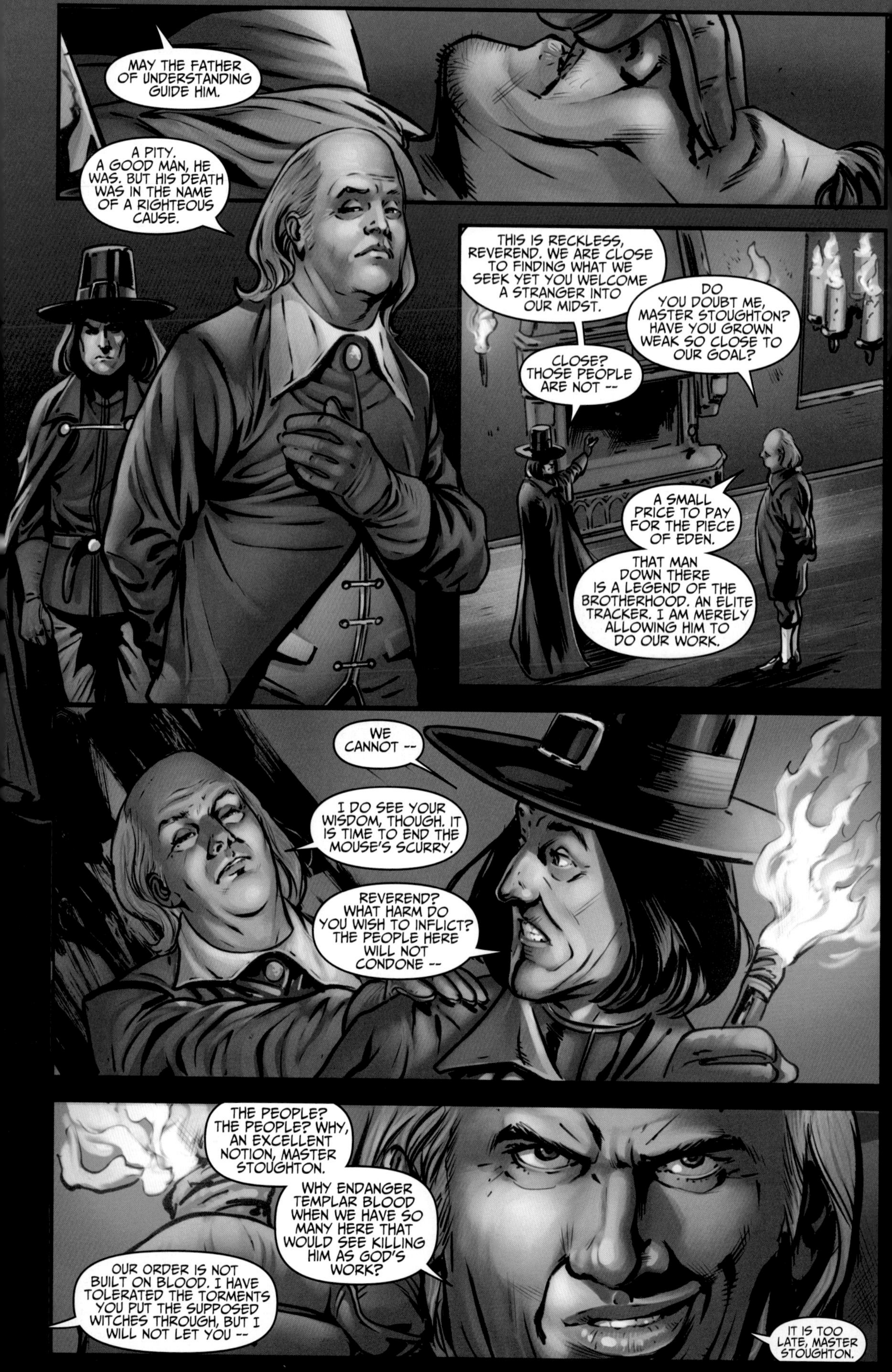
MAY THE FATHER OF UNDERSTANDING GUIDE HIM.
A PITY. A GOOD MAN, HE WAS. BUT HIS DEATH WAS IN THE NAME OF A RIGHTEOUS CAUSE.
THIS IS RECKLESS, REVEREND. WE ARE CLOSE TO FINDING WHAT WE SEEK YET YOU WELCOME A STRANGER INTO OUR MIDST.
DO YOU DOUBT ME, MASTER STOUGHTON? HAVE YOU GROWN WEAK SO CLOSE TO OUR GOAL?
CLOSE? THOSE PEOPLE ARE NOT --
A SMALL PRICE TO PAY FOR THE PIECE OF EDEN.
THAT MAN DOWN THERE IS A LEGEND OF THE BROTHERHOOD. AN ELITE TRACKER. I AM MERELY ALLOWING HIM TO DO OUR WORK.
WE CANNOT --
I DO SEE YOUR WISDOM, THOUGH. IT IS TIME TO END THE MOUSE'S SCURRY.
REVEREND? WHAT HARM DO YOU WISH TO INFLICT? THE PEOPLE HERE WILL NOT CONDONE --
THE PEOPLE? THE PEOPLE? WHY, AN EXCELLENT NOTION, MASTER STOUGHTON.
WHY ENDANGER TEMPLAR BLOOD WHEN WE HAVE SO MANY HERE THAT WOULD SEE KILLING HIM AS GOD'S WORK?
OUR ORDER IS NOT BUILT ON BLOOD. I HAVE TOLERATED THE TORMENTS YOU PUT THE SUPPOSED WITCHES THROUGH, BUT I WILL NOT LET YOU --
IT IS TOO LATE, MASTER STOUGHTON.

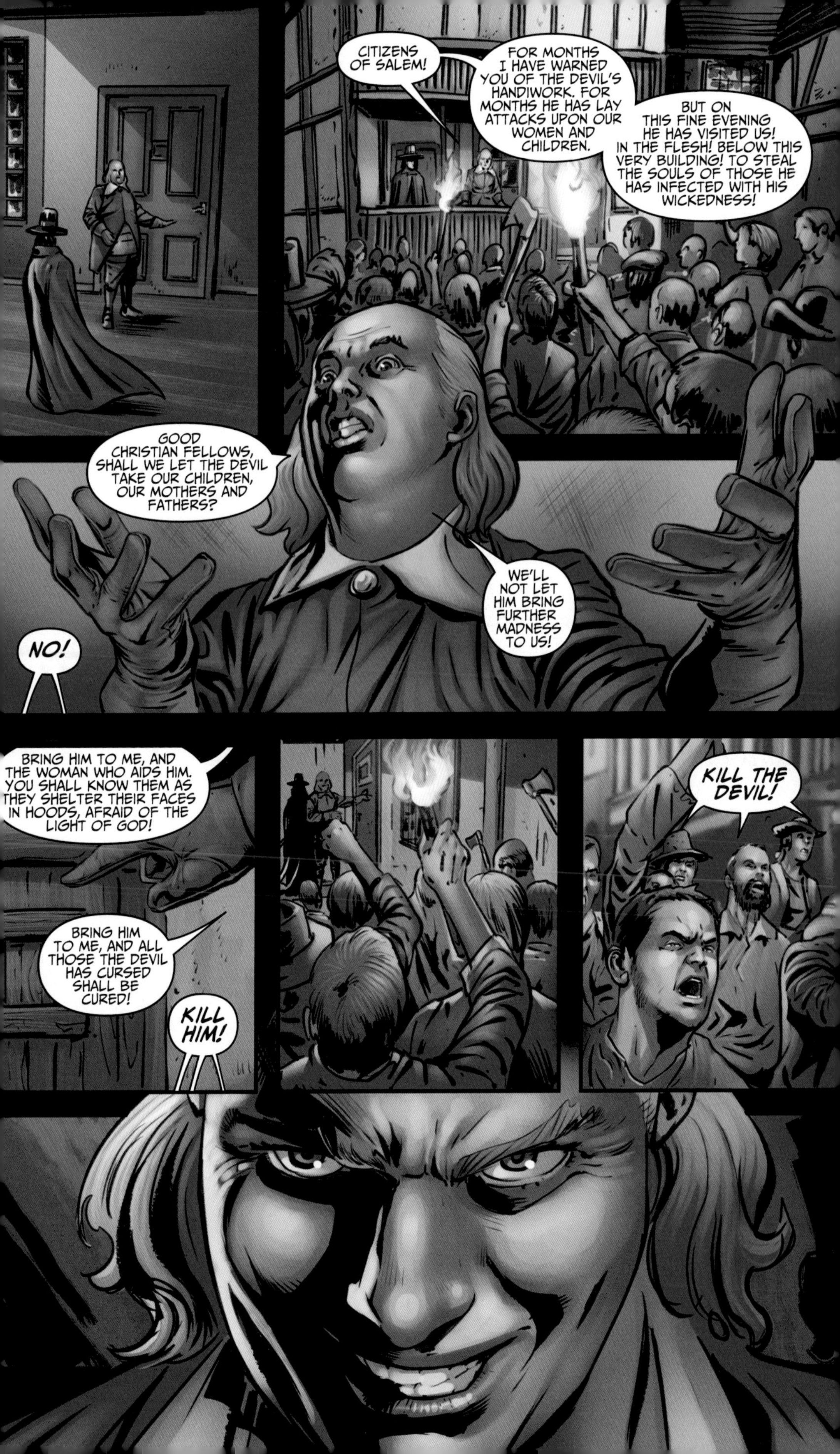
CITIZENS OF SALEM!
FOR MONTHS I HAVE WARNED YOU OF THE DEVIL'S HANDIWORK. FOR MONTHS HE HAS LAY ATTACKS UPON OUR WOMEN AND CHILDREN.
BUT ON THIS FINE EVENING HE HAS VISITED US! IN THE FLESH! BELOW THIS VERY BUILDING! TO STEAL THE SOULS OF THOSE HE HAS INFECTED WITH HIS WICKEDNESS!
GOOD CHRISTIAN FELLOWS, SHALL WE LET THE DEVIL TAKE OUR CHILDREN, OUR MOTHERS AND FATHERS?
WE'LL NOT LET HIM BRING FURTHER MADNESS TO US!
NO!
BRING HIM TO ME, AND THE WOMAN WHO AIDS HIM. YOU SHALL KNOW THEM AS THEY SHELTER THEIR FACES IN HOODS, AFRAID OF THE LIGHT OF GOD!
BRING HIM TO ME, AND ALL THOSE THE DEVIL HAS CURSED SHALL BE CURED!
KILL HIM!
KILL THE DEVIL!

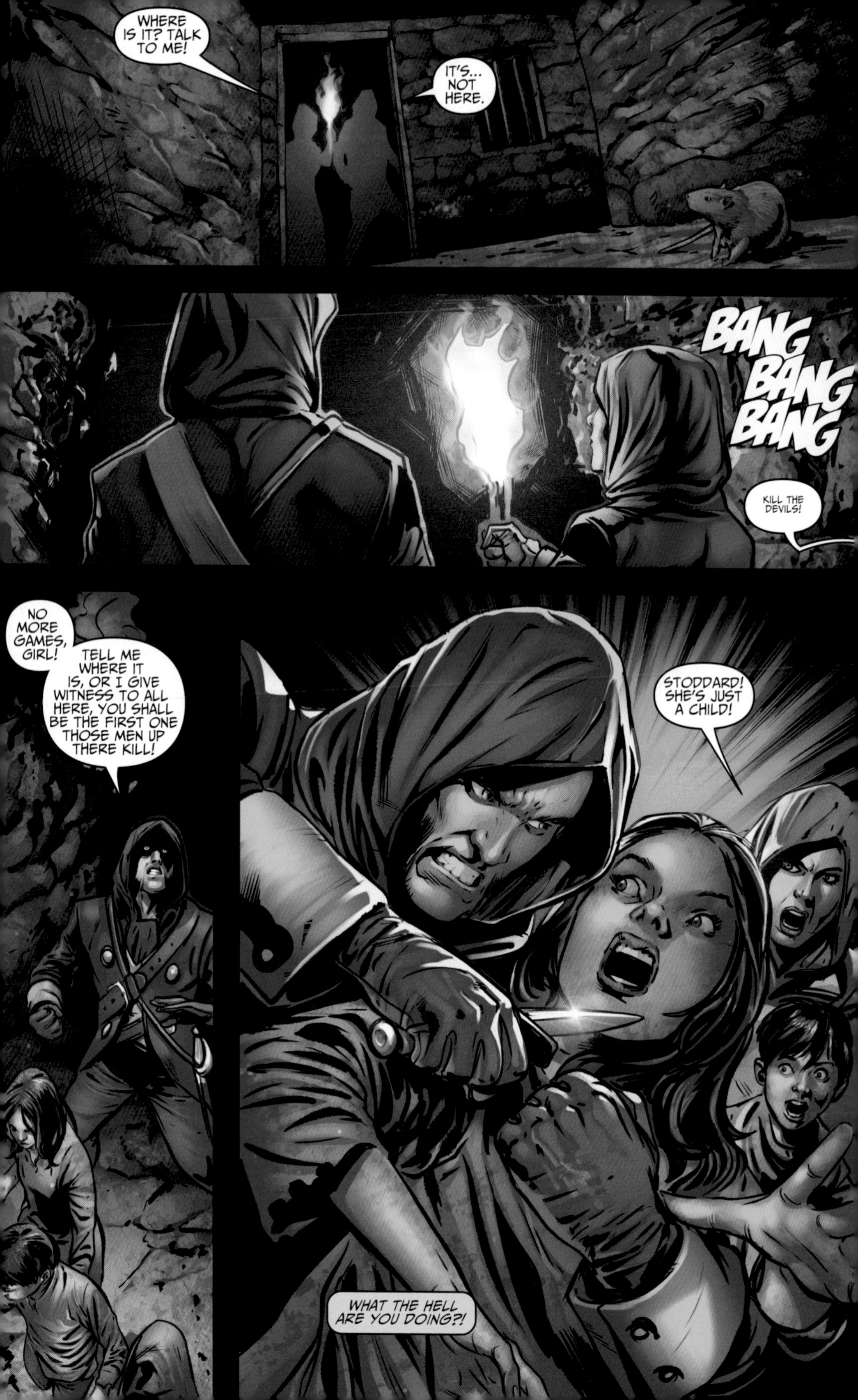
WHERE IS IT? TALK TO ME!
IT'S... NOT HERE.
BANG BANG BANG
KILL THE DEVILS!
NO MORE GAMES, GIRL!
TELL ME WHERE IT IS, OR I GIVE WITNESS TO ALL HERE, YOU SHALL BE THE FIRST ONE THOSE MEN UP THERE KILL!
STODDARD! SHE'S JUST A CHILD!
WHAT THE HELL ARE YOU DOING?!

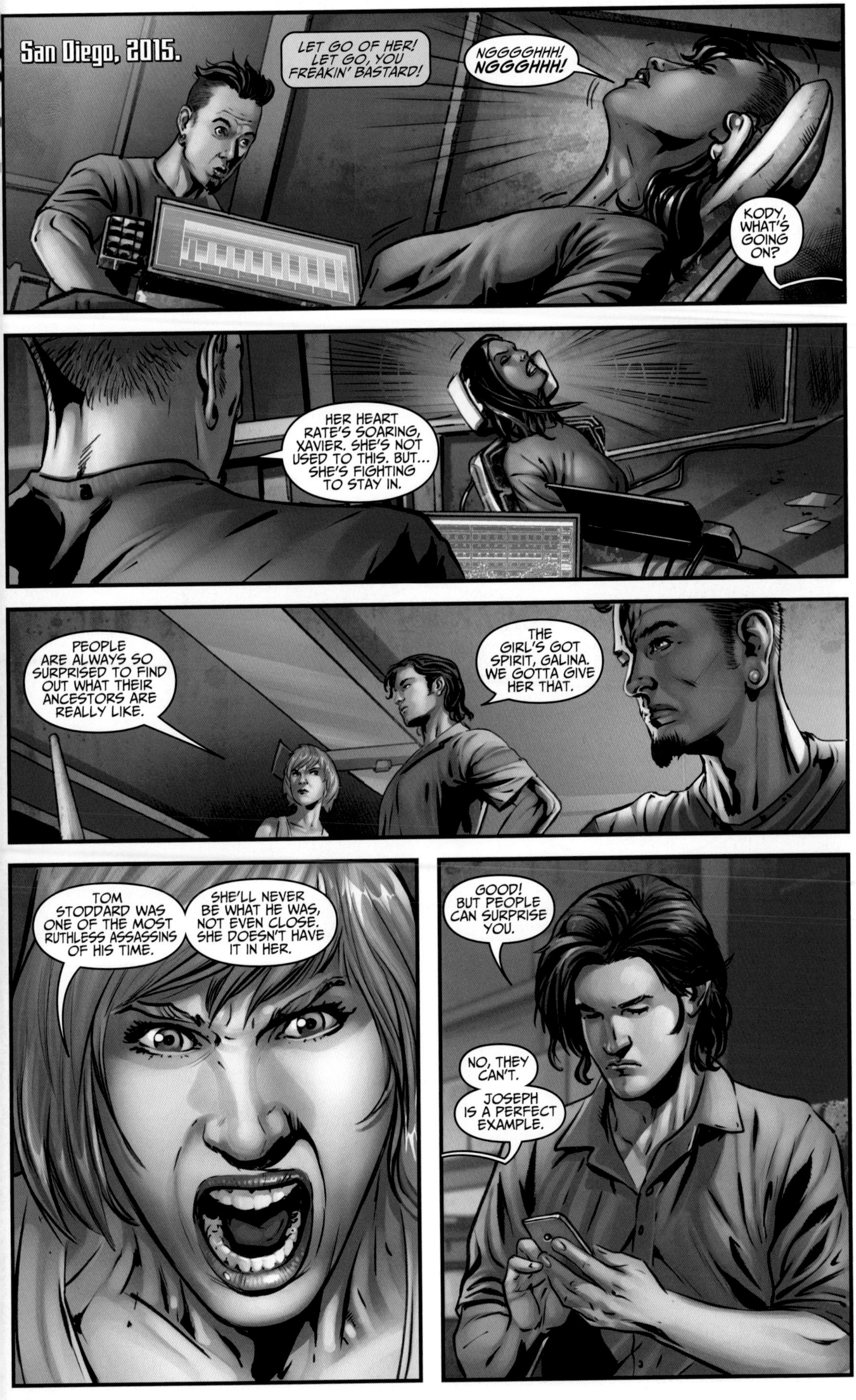
San Diego, 2015.
LET GO OF HER! LET GO, YOU FREAKIN' BASTARD!
NGGGGHHH! NGGGHHH!
KODY, WHAT'S GOING ON?
HER HEART RATE'S SOARING, XAVIER. SHE'S NOT USED TO THIS. BUT... SHE'S FIGHTING TO STAY IN.
PEOPLE ARE ALWAYS SO SURPRISED TO FIND OUT WHAT THEIR ANCESTORS ARE REALLY LIKE.
THE GIRL'S GOT SPIRIT, GALINA. WE GOTTA GIVE HER THAT.
TOM STODDARD WAS ONE OF THE MOST RUTHLESS ASSASSINS OF HIS TIME.
SHE'LL NEVER BE WHAT HE WAS, NOT EVEN CLOSE. SHE DOESN'T HAVE IT IN HER.
GOOD! BUT PEOPLE CAN SURPRISE YOU.
NO, THEY CAN'T.
JOSEPH IS A PERFECT EXAMPLE.

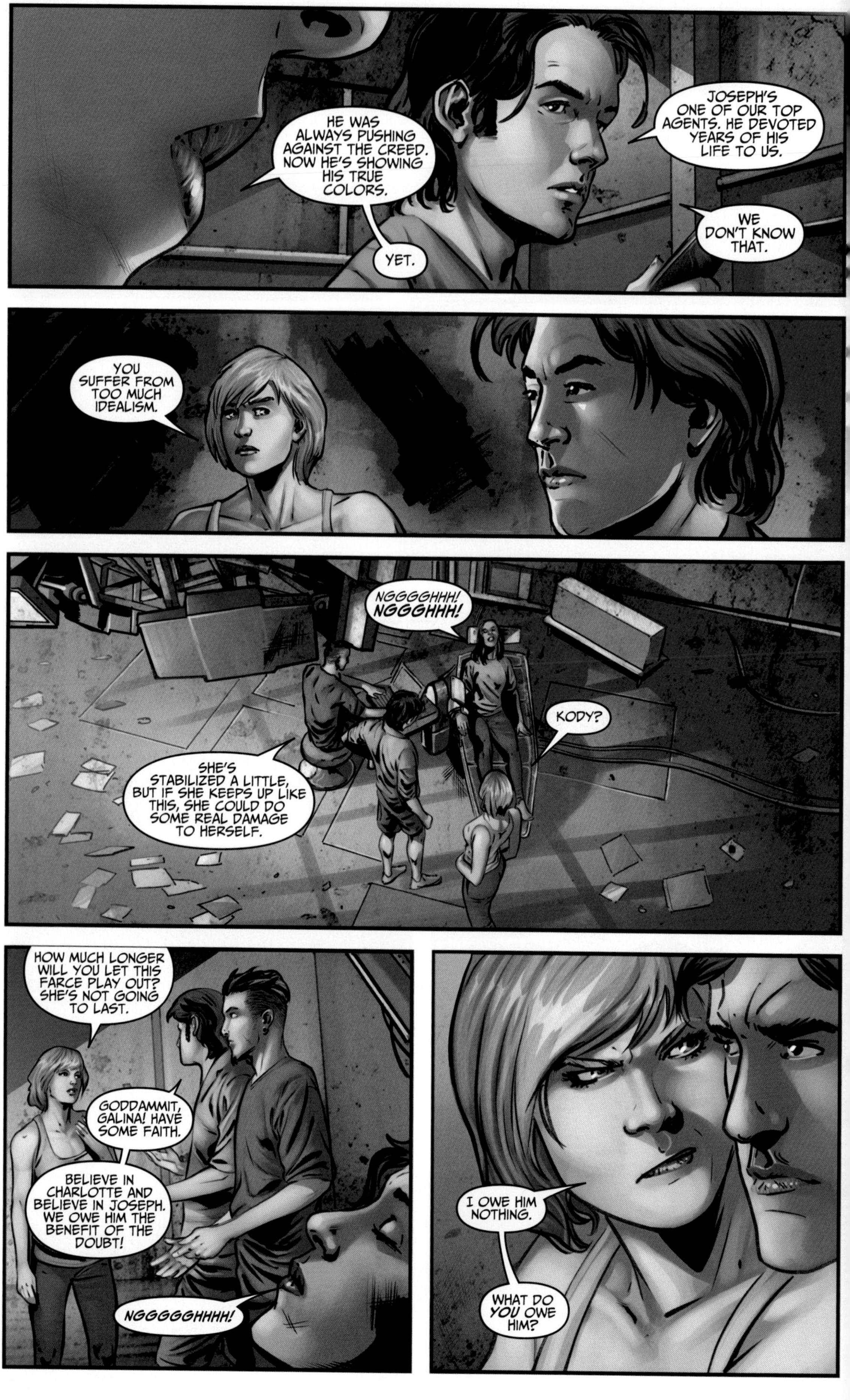

HE WAS ALWAYS PUSHING AGAINST THE CREED. NOW HE'S SHOWING HIS TRUE COLORS.
YET.
JOSEPH'S ONE OF OUR TOP AGENTS. HE DEVOTED YEARS OF HIS LIFE TO US.
WE DON'T KNOW THAT.
YOU SUFFER FROM TOO MUCH IDEALISM.
NGGGGHHH! NGGGHHH!
KODY?
SHE'S STABILIZED A LITTLE, BUT IF SHE KEEPS UP LIKE THIS, SHE COULD DO SOME REAL DAMAGE TO HERSELF.
HOW MUCH LONGER WILL YOU LET THIS FARCE PLAY OUT? SHE'S NOT GOING TO LAST.
GODDAMMIT, GALINA! HAVE SOME FAITH.
BELIEVE IN CHARLOTTE AND BELIEVE IN JOSEPH. WE OWE HIM THE BENEFIT OF THE DOUBT!
NGGGGGHHHH!
I OWE HIM NOTHING.
WHAT DO YOU OWE HIM?

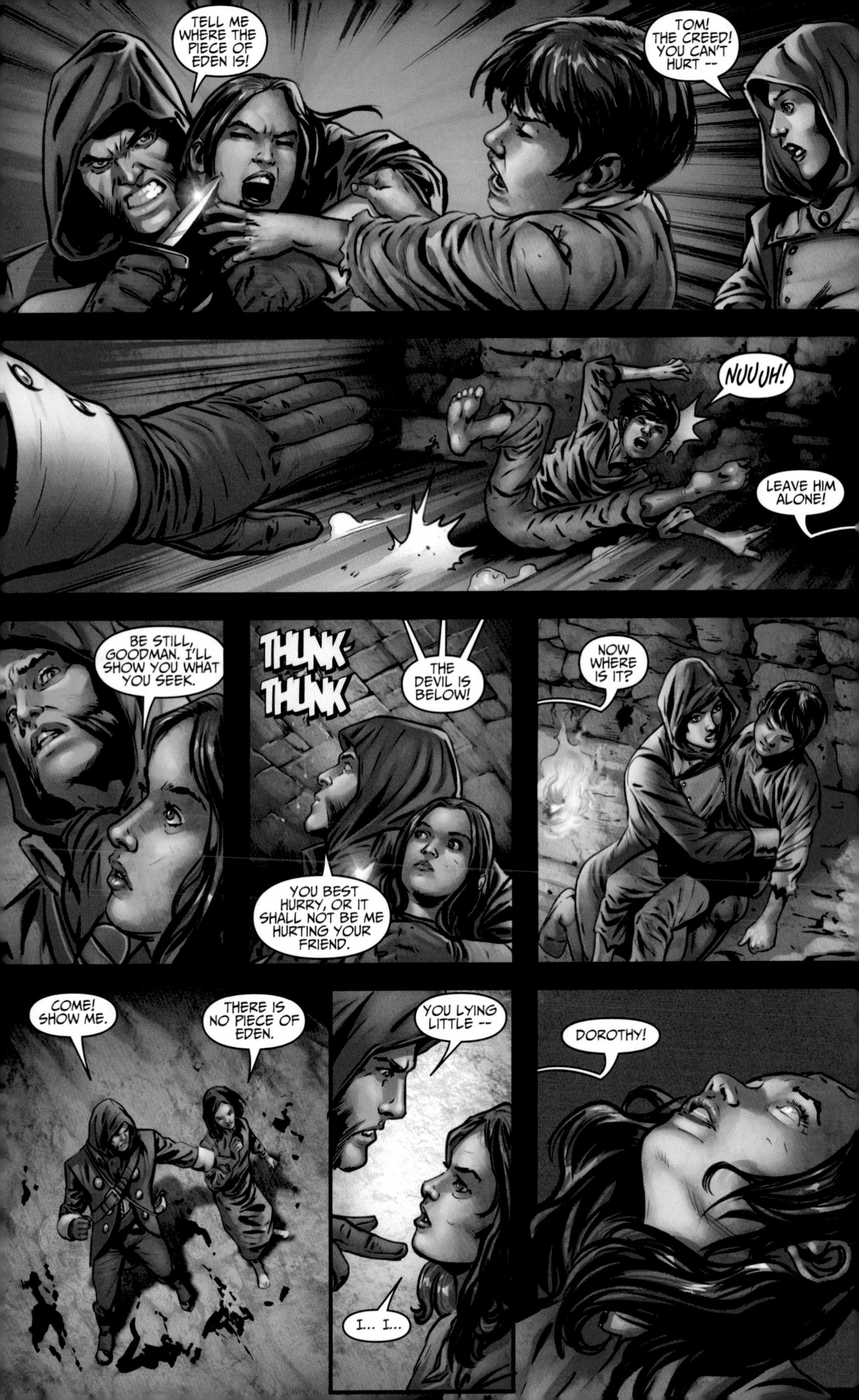
TELL ME WHERE THE PIECE OF EDEN IS!
TOM! THE CREED! YOU CAN'T HURT --
NUUUH!
LEAVE HIM ALONE!
BE STILL, GOODMAN. I'LL SHOW YOU WHAT YOU SEEK.
THUNK-THUNK
THE DEVIL IS BELOW!
YOU BEST HURRY, OR IT SHALL NOT BE ME HURTING YOUR FRIEND.
NOW WHERE IS IT?
COME! SHOW ME.
THERE IS NO PIECE OF EDEN.
YOU LYING LITTLE --
I... I...
DOROTHY!

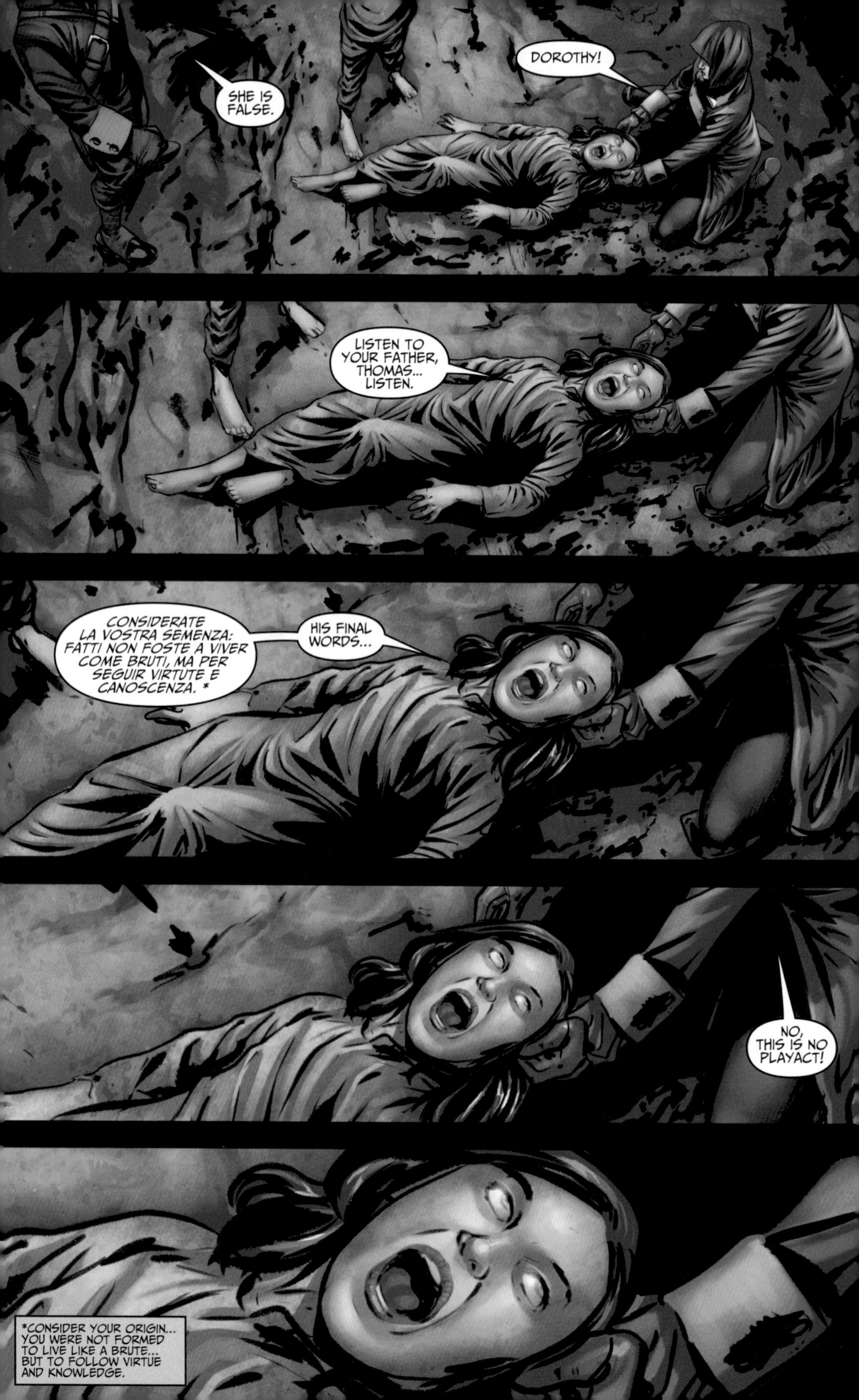
SHE IS FALSE.
DOROTHY!
LISTEN TO YOUR FATHER, THOMAS... LISTEN.
CONSIDERATE LA VOSTRA SEMENZA: FATTI NON FOSTE A VIVER COME BRUTI, MA PER SEGUIR VIRTUTE E CANOSCENZA. *
HIS FINAL WORDS...
NO, THIS IS NO PLAYACT!
*CONSIDER YOUR ORIGIN... YOU WERE NOT FORMED TO LIVE LIKE A BRUTE... BUT TO FOLLOW VIRTUE AND KNOWLEDGE.

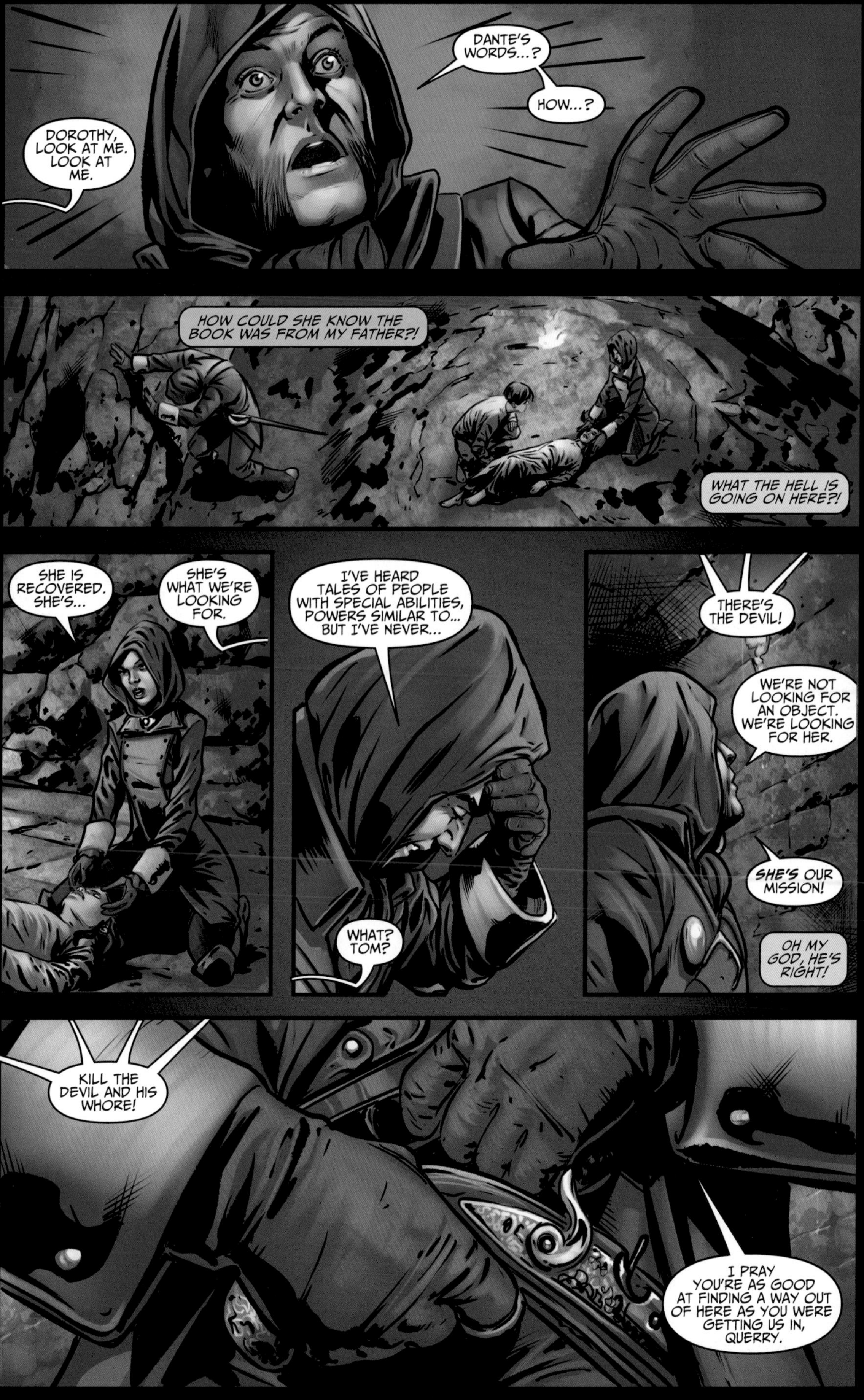
DANTE'S WORDS...?
HOW...?
DOROTHY, LOOK AT ME. LOOK AT ME.
HOW COULD SHE KNOW THE BOOK WAS FROM MY FATHER?!
WHAT THE HELL IS GOING ON HERE?!
SHE IS RECOVERED. SHE'S...
SHE'S WHAT WE'RE LOOKING FOR.
I'VE HEARD TALES OF PEOPLE WITH SPECIAL ABILITIES, POWERS SIMILAR TO... BUT I'VE NEVER...
WHAT? TOM?
THERE'S THE DEVIL!
WE'RE NOT LOOKING FOR AN OBJECT. WE'RE LOOKING FOR HER.
SHE'S OUR MISSION!
OH MY GOD, HE'S RIGHT!
KILL THE DEVIL AND HIS WHORE!
I PRAY YOU'RE AS GOOD AT FINDING A WAY OUT OF HERE AS YOU WERE GETTING US IN, QUERRY.

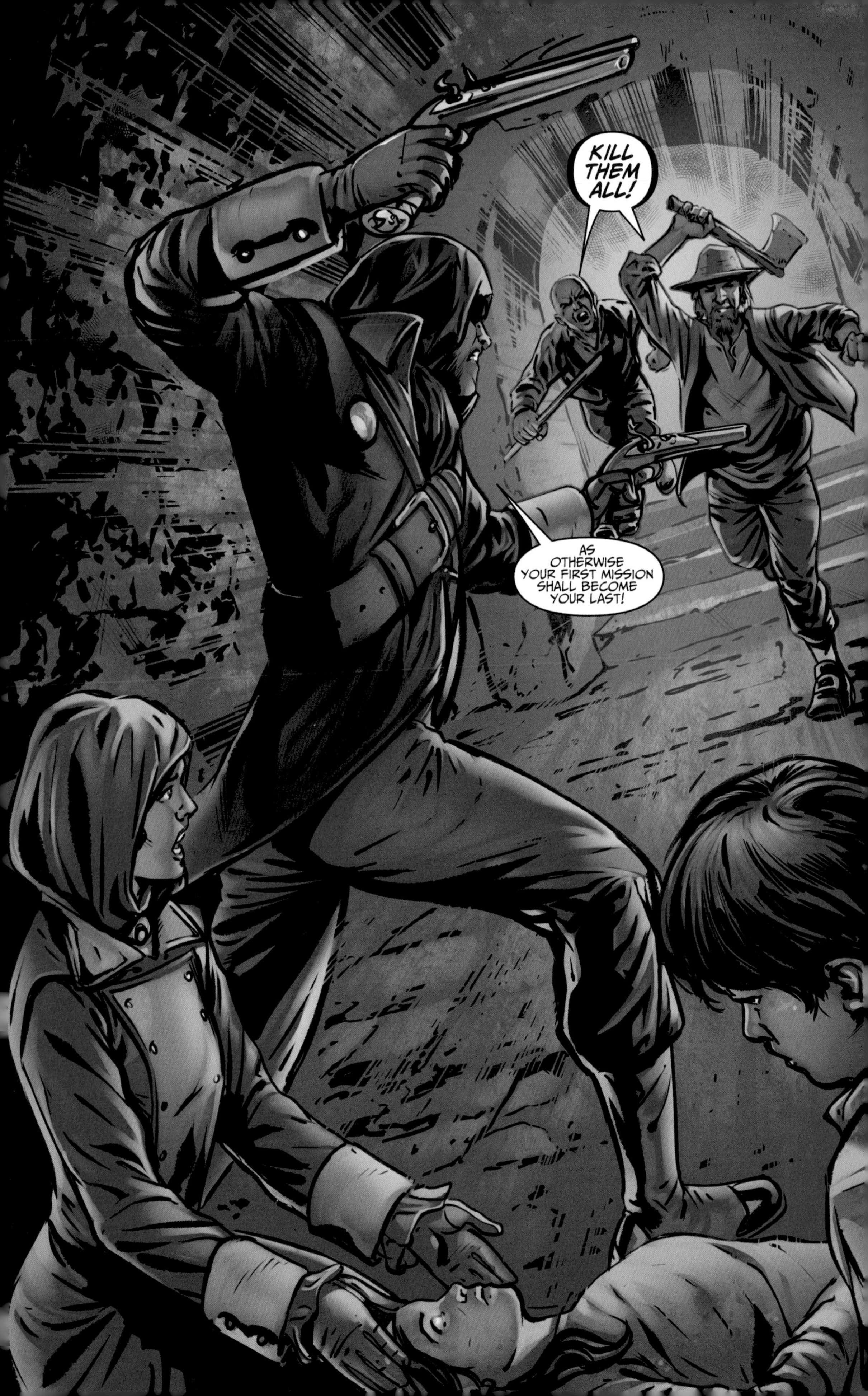
KILL THEM ALL!
AS OTHERWISE YOUR FIRST MISSION SHALL BECOME YOUR LAST!

CHAPTER THREE

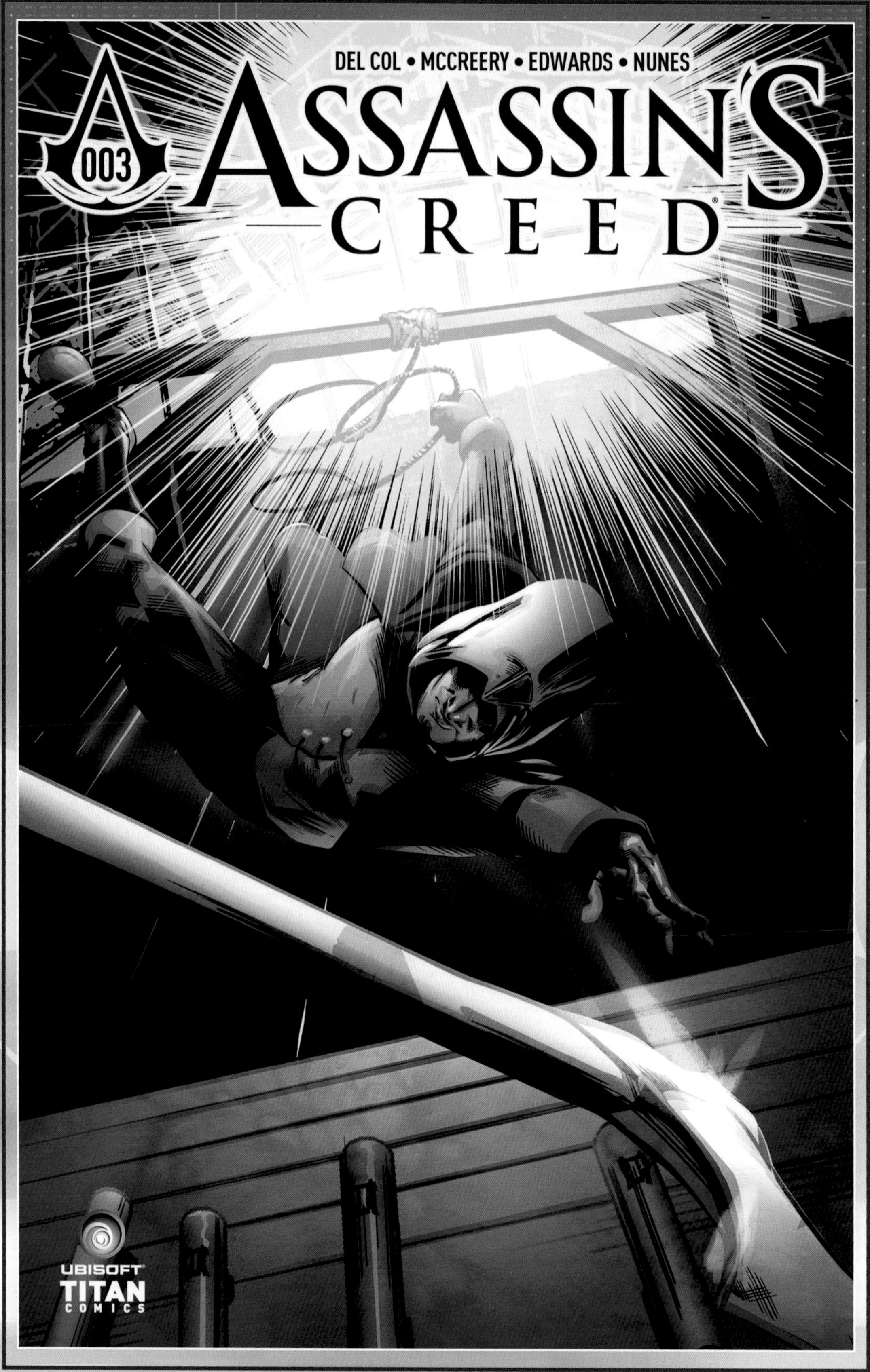
DEL COL • MCCREERY • EDWARDS • NUNES
ASSASSIN'S CREED
003
UBISOFT
TITAN COMICS

COVER A - ISSUE 3
DENNIS CALERO

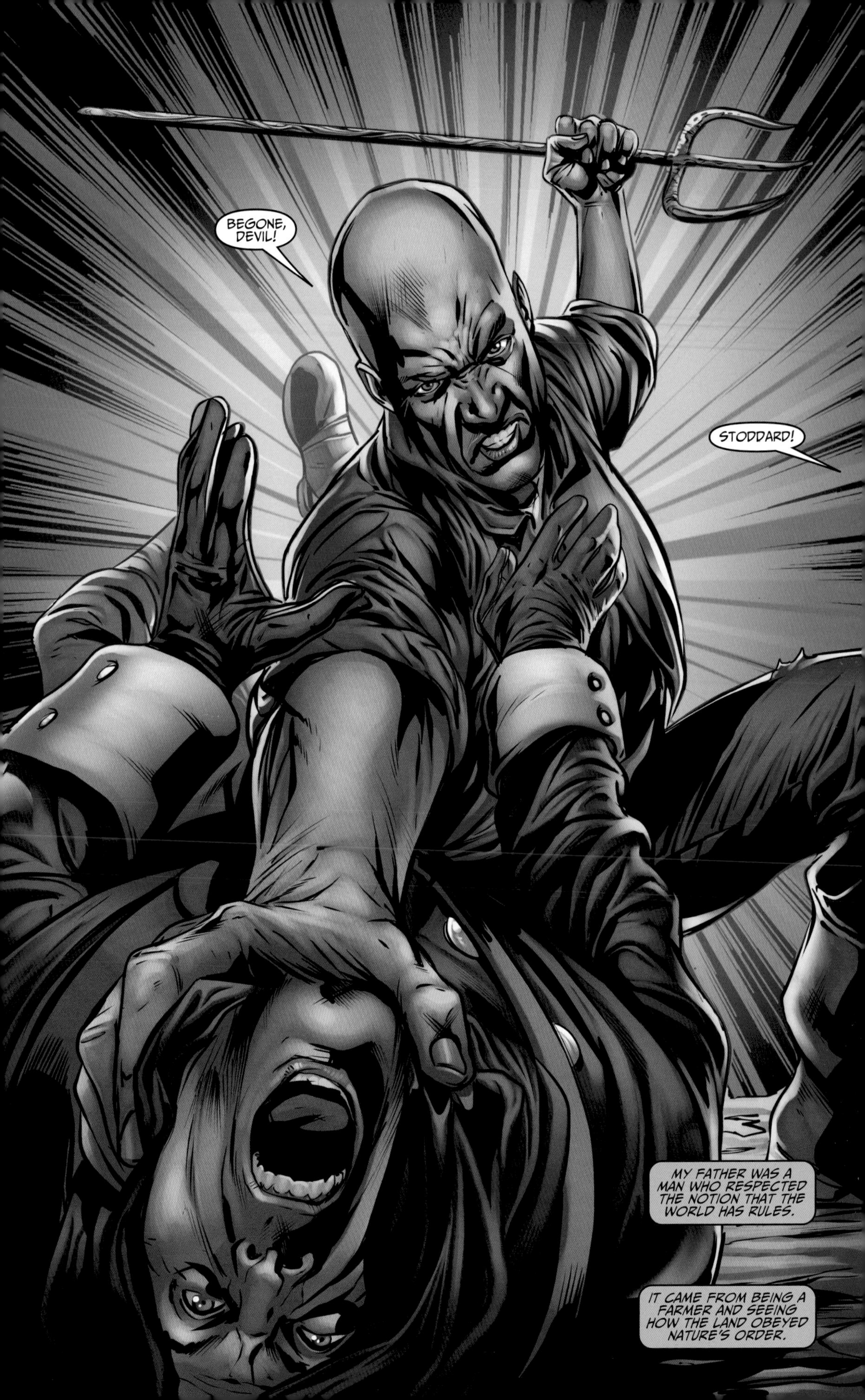
BEGONE, DEVIL!
STODDARD!
MY FATHER WAS A MAN WHO RESPECTED THE NOTION THAT THE WORLD HAS RULES.
IT CAME FROM BEING A FARMER AND SEEING HOW THE LAND OBEYED NATURE'S ORDER.

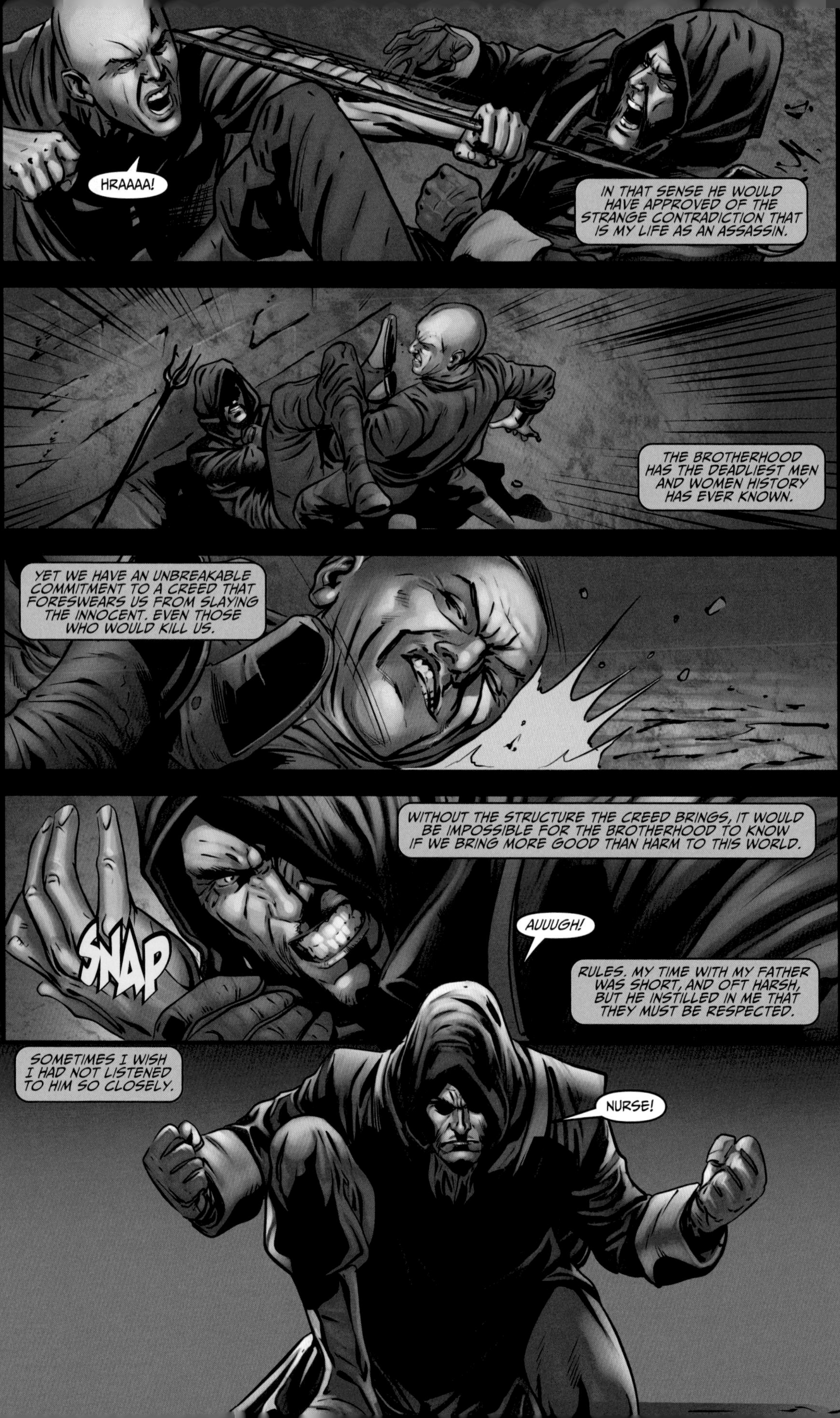
HRAAAA!
IN THAT SENSE HE WOULD HAVE APPROVED OF THE STRANGE CONTRADICTION THAT IS MY LIFE AS AN ASSASSIN.
THE BROTHERHOOD HAS THE DEADLIEST MEN AND WOMEN HISTORY HAS EVER KNOWN.
YET WE HAVE AN UNBREAKABLE COMMITMENT TO A CREED THAT FORESWEARS US FROM SLAYING THE INNOCENT. EVEN THOSE WHO WOULD KILL US.
WITHOUT THE STRUCTURE THE CREED BRINGS, IT WOULD BE IMPOSSIBLE FOR THE BROTHERHOOD TO KNOW IF WE BRING MORE GOOD THAN HARM TO THIS WORLD.
SNAP
AUUUGH!
RULES. MY TIME WITH MY FATHER WAS SHORT, AND OFT HARSH, BUT HE INSTILLED IN ME THAT THEY MUST BE RESPECTED.
SOMETIMES I WISH I HAD NOT LISTENED TO HIM SO CLOSELY.
NURSE!

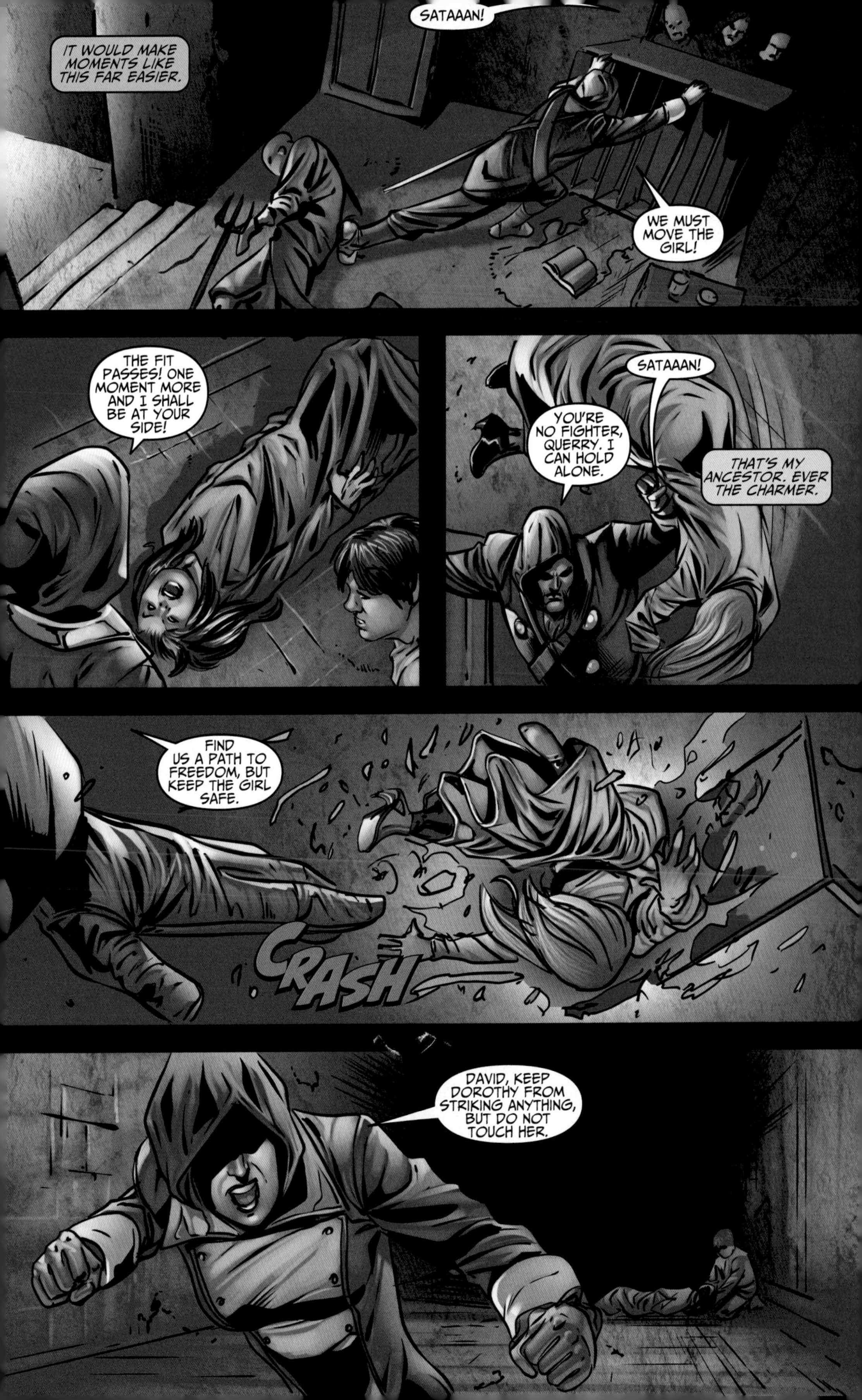
IT WOULD MAKE MOMENTS LIKE THIS FAR EASIER.
SATAAAN!
WE MUST MOVE THE GIRL!
THE FIT PASSES! ONE MOMENT MORE AND I SHALL BE AT YOUR SIDE!
SATAAAN!
YOU'RE NO FIGHTER, QUERRY. I CAN HOLD ALONE.
THAT'S MY ANCESTOR. EVER THE CHARMER.
FIND US A PATH TO FREEDOM, BUT KEEP THE GIRL SAFE.
CRASH
DAVID, KEEP DOROTHY FROM STRIKING ANYTHING, BUT DO NOT TOUCH HER.

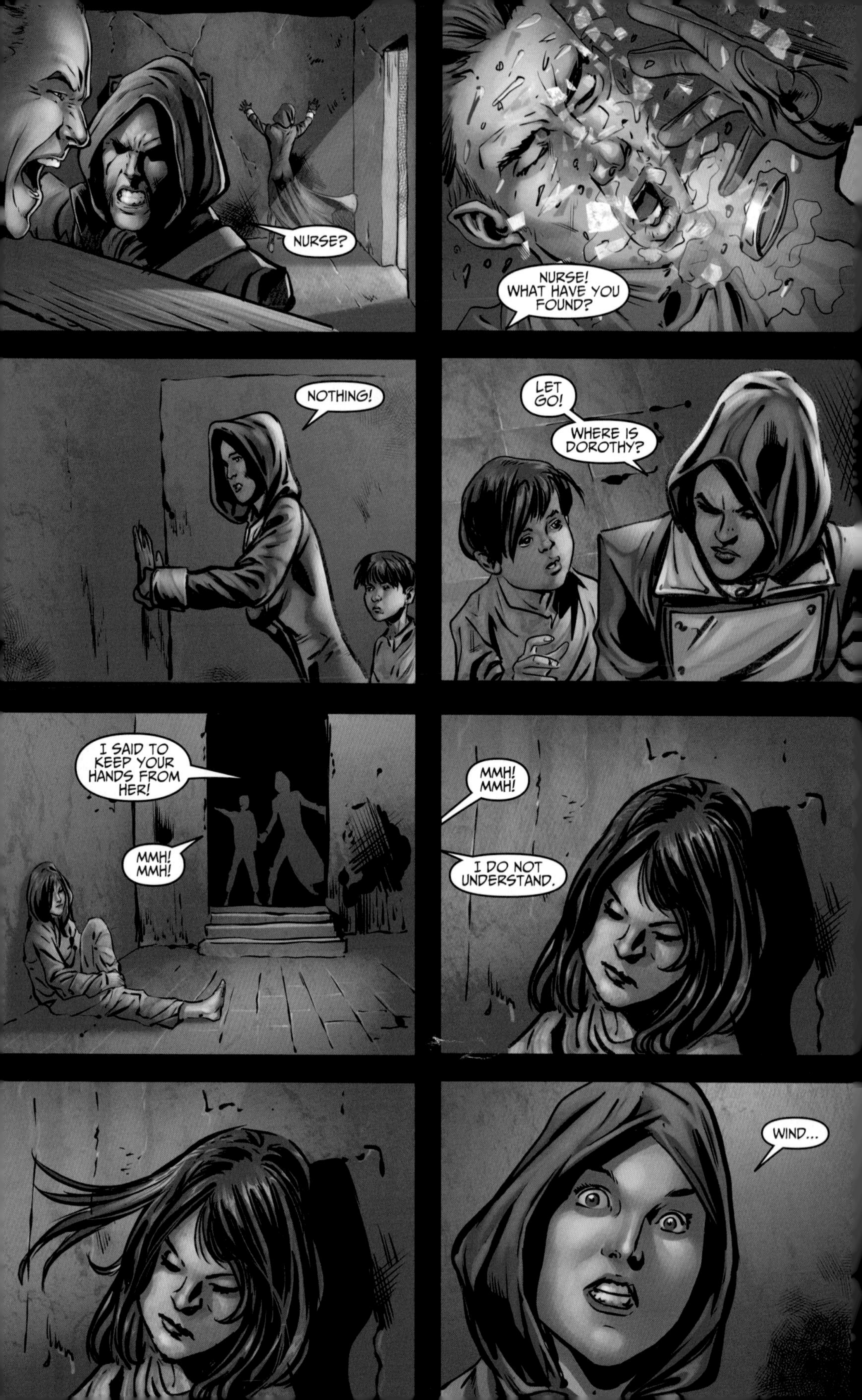
NURSE?
NURSE! WHAT HAVE YOU FOUND?
NOTHING!
LET GO!
WHERE IS DOROTHY?
I SAID TO KEEP YOUR HANDS FROM HER!
MMH! MMH!
MMH! MMH!
I DO NOT UNDERSTAND.
WIND...

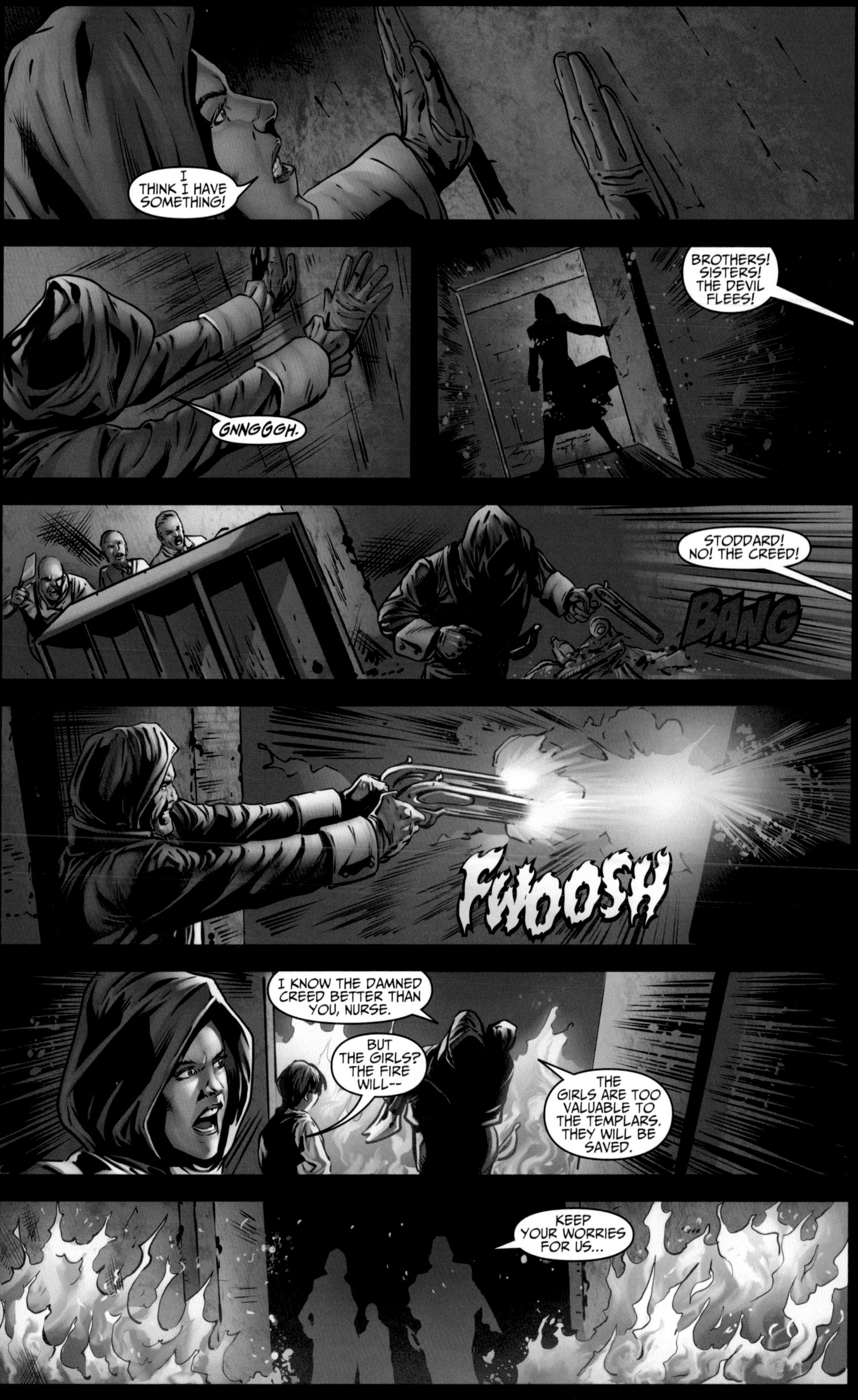
I THINK I HAVE SOMETHING!
GNNGGGH.
BROTHERS! SISTERS! THE DEVIL FLEES!
STODDARD! NO! THE CREED!
BANG
FWOOSH
I KNOW THE DAMNED CREED BETTER THAN YOU, NURSE.
BUT THE GIRLS? THE FIRE WILL--
THE GIRLS ARE TOO VALUABLE TO THE TEMPLARS. THEY WILL BE SAVED.
KEEP YOUR WORRIES FOR US...

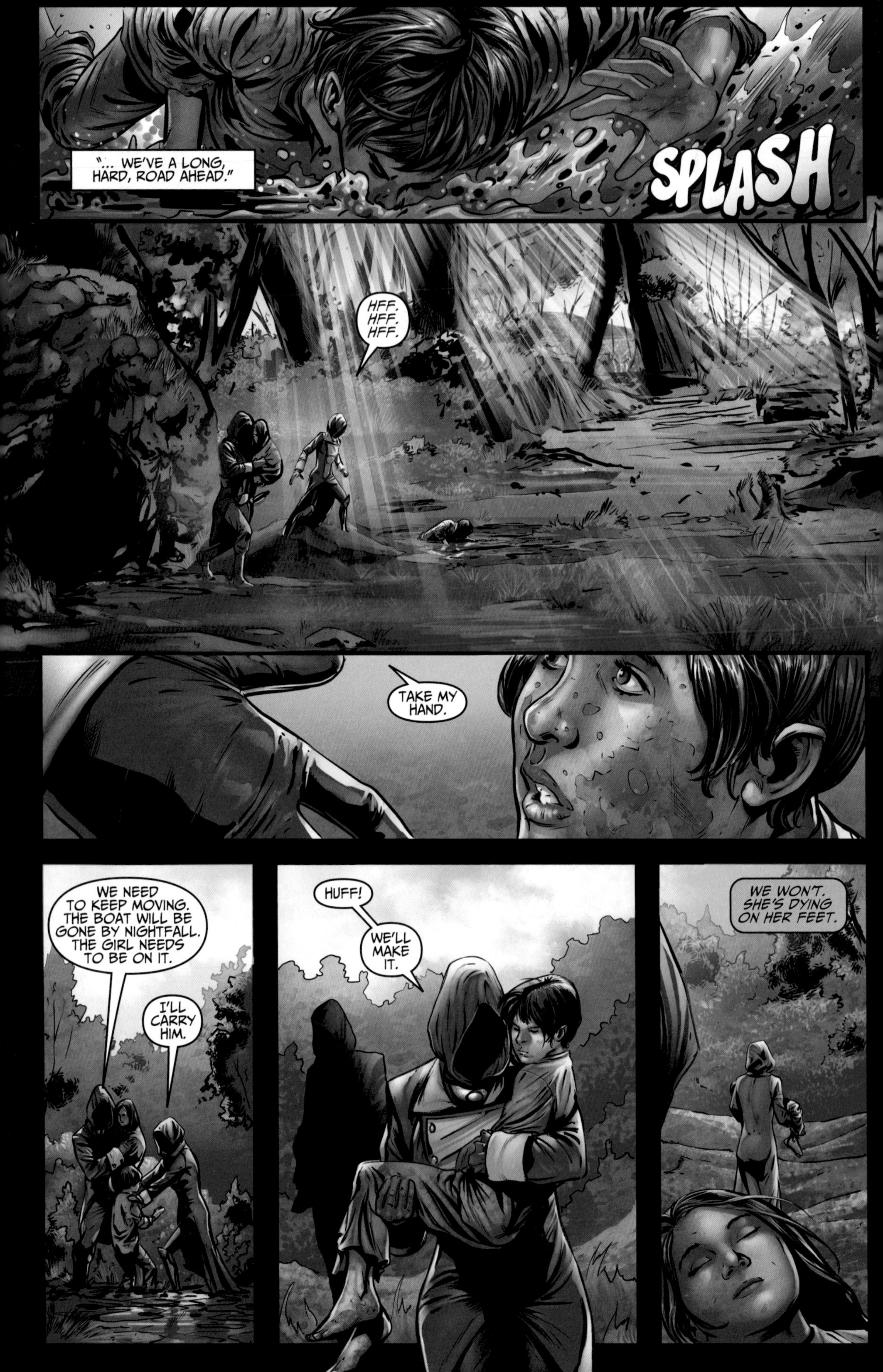
"... WE'VE A LONG, HARD, ROAD AHEAD."
SPLASH
HFF. HFF. HFF.
TAKE MY HAND.
WE NEED TO KEEP MOVING. THE BOAT WILL BE GONE BY NIGHTFALL. THE GIRL NEEDS TO BE ON IT.
I'LL CARRY HIM.
HUFF!
WE'LL MAKE IT.
WE WON'T. SHE'S DYING ON HER FEET.

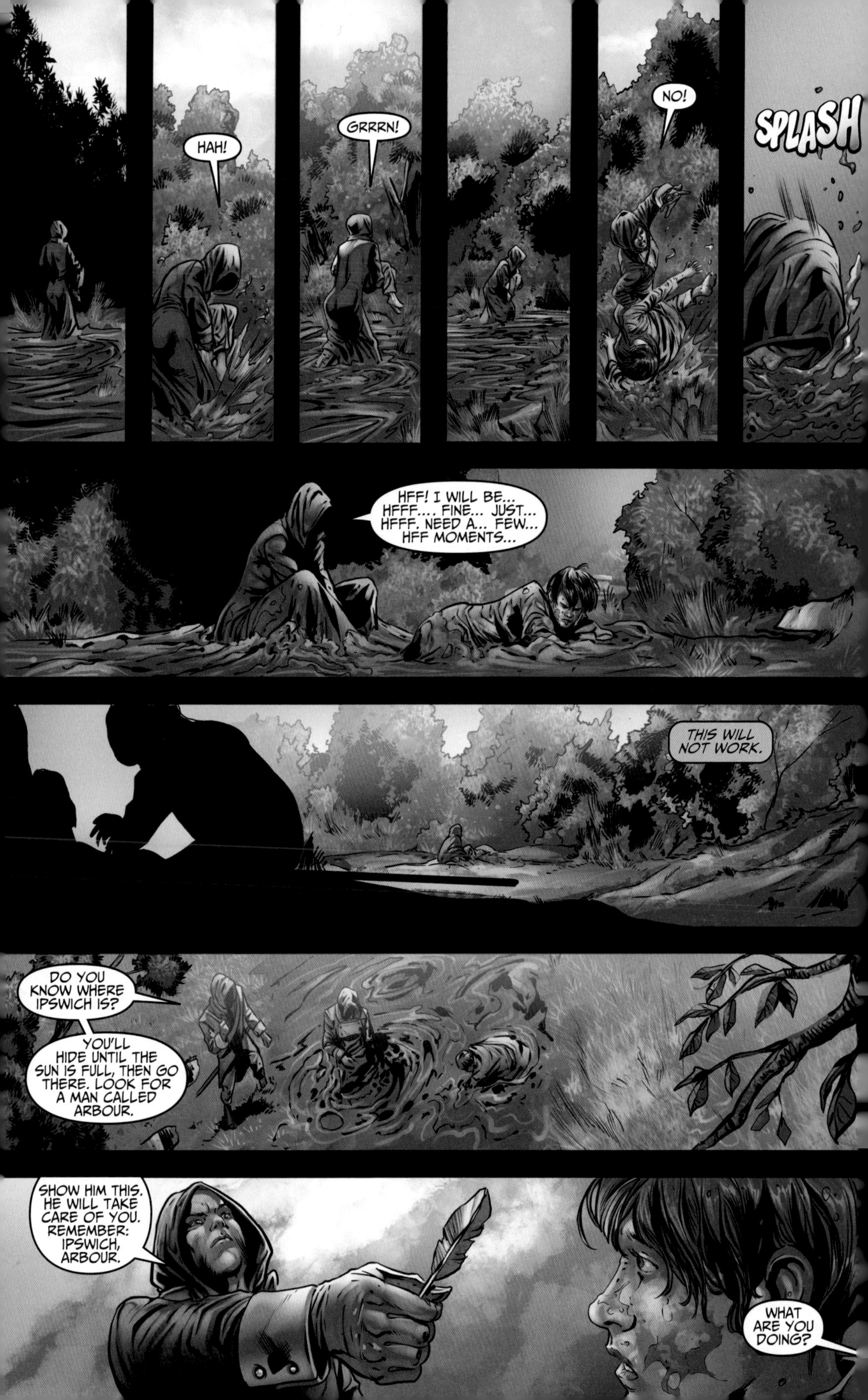
HAH!
GRRRN!
NO!
SPLASH
HFF! I WILL BE... HFFF.... FINE... JUST... HFFF. NEED A... FEW... HFF MOMENTS...
THIS WILL NOT WORK.
DO YOU KNOW WHERE IPSWICH IS?
YOU'LL HIDE UNTIL THE SUN IS FULL, THEN GO THERE. LOOK FOR A MAN CALLED ARBOUR.
SHOW HIM THIS. HE WILL TAKE CARE OF YOU. REMEMBER: IPSWICH, ARBOUR.
WHAT ARE YOU DOING?

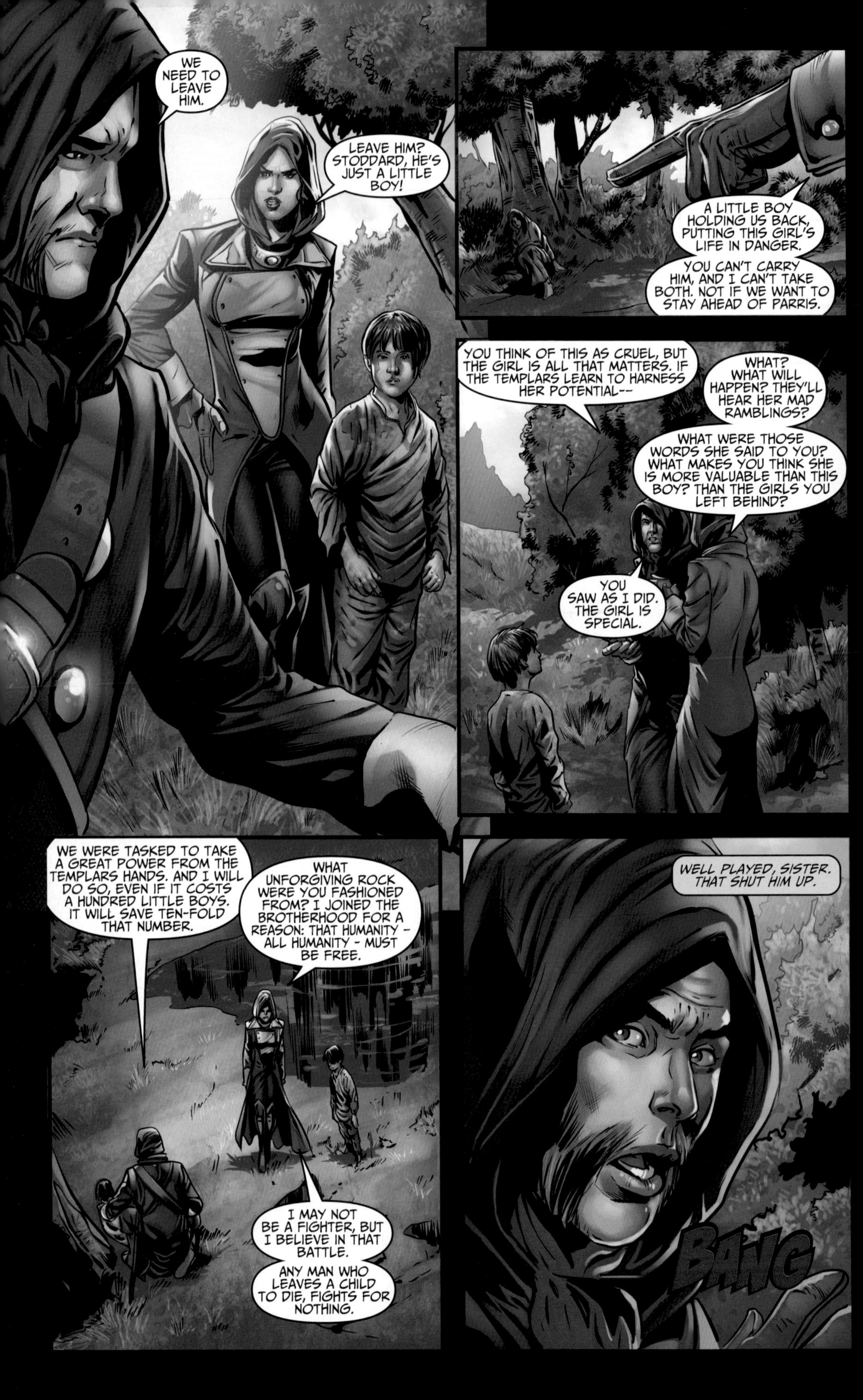
WE NEED TO LEAVE HIM.
LEAVE HIM? STODDARD, HE'S JUST A LITTLE BOY!
A LITTLE BOY HOLDING US BACK, PUTTING THIS GIRL'S LIFE IN DANGER.
YOU CAN'T CARRY HIM, AND I CAN'T TAKE BOTH. NOT IF WE WANT TO STAY AHEAD OF PARRIS.
YOU THINK OF THIS AS CRUEL, BUT THE GIRL IS ALL THAT MATTERS. IF THE TEMPLARS LEARN TO HARNESS HER POTENTIAL--
WHAT? WHAT WILL HAPPEN? THEY'LL HEAR HER MAD RAMBLINGS?
WHAT WERE THOSE WORDS SHE SAID TO YOU? WHAT MAKES YOU THINK SHE IS MORE VALUABLE THAN THIS BOY? THAN THE GIRLS YOU LEFT BEHIND?
YOU SAW AS I DID. THE GIRL IS SPECIAL.
WE WERE TASKED TO TAKE A GREAT POWER FROM THE TEMPLARS HANDS. AND I WILL DO SO, EVEN IF IT COSTS A HUNDRED LITTLE BOYS. IT WILL SAVE TEN-FOLD THAT NUMBER.
WHAT UNFORGIVING ROCK WERE YOU FASHIONED FROM? I JOINED THE BROTHERHOOD FOR A REASON: THAT HUMANITY - ALL HUMANITY - MUST BE FREE.
I MAY NOT BE A FIGHTER, BUT I BELIEVE IN THAT BATTLE.
ANY MAN WHO LEAVES A CHILD TO DIE, FIGHTS FOR NOTHING.
WELL PLAYED, SISTER. THAT SHUT HIM UP.
BANG

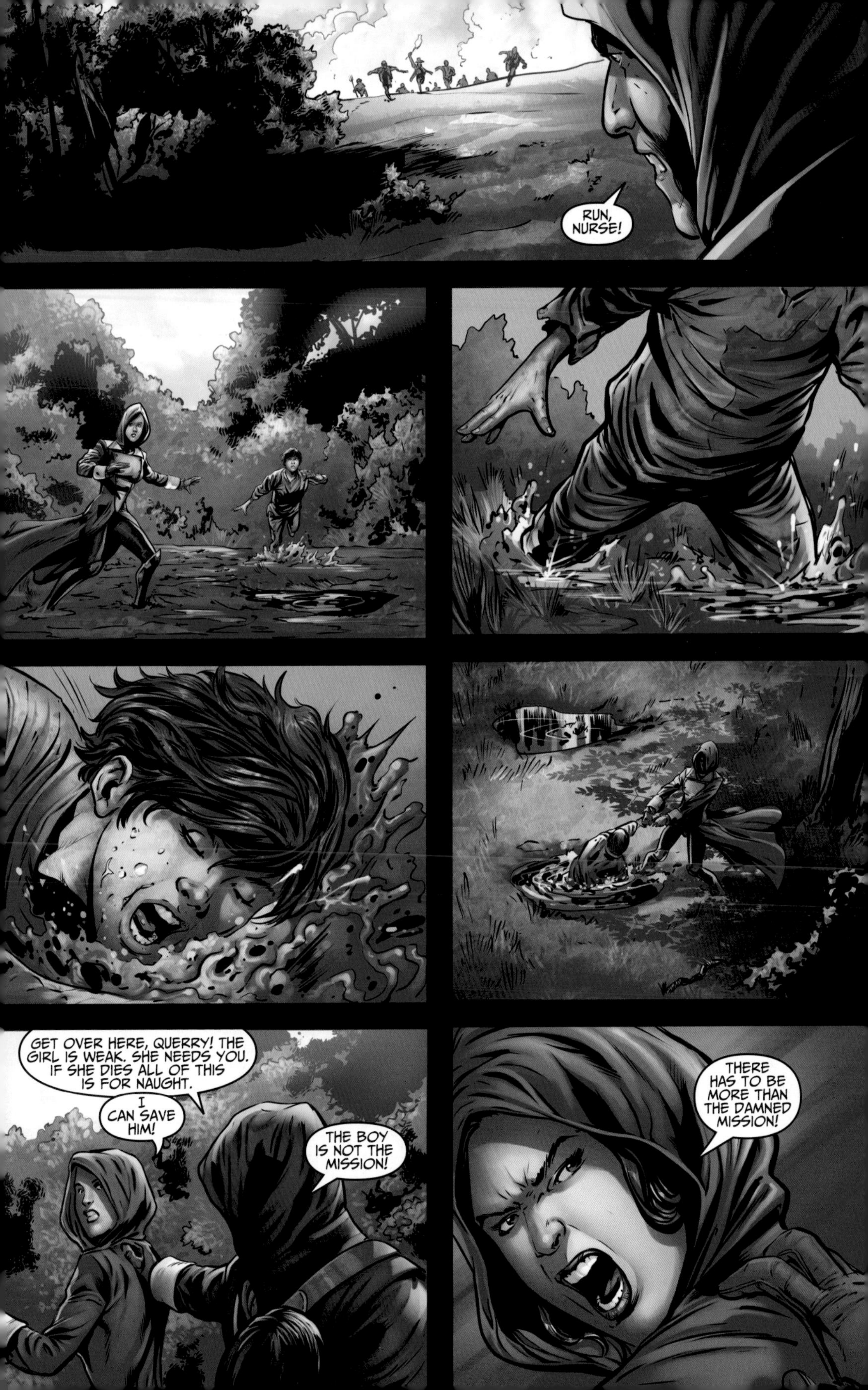
RUN, NURSE!
GET OVER HERE, QUERRY! THE GIRL IS WEAK. SHE NEEDS YOU. IF SHE DIES ALL OF THIS IS FOR NAUGHT.
I CAN SAVE HIM!
THE BOY IS NOT THE MISSION!
THERE HAS TO BE MORE THAN THE DAMNED MISSION!

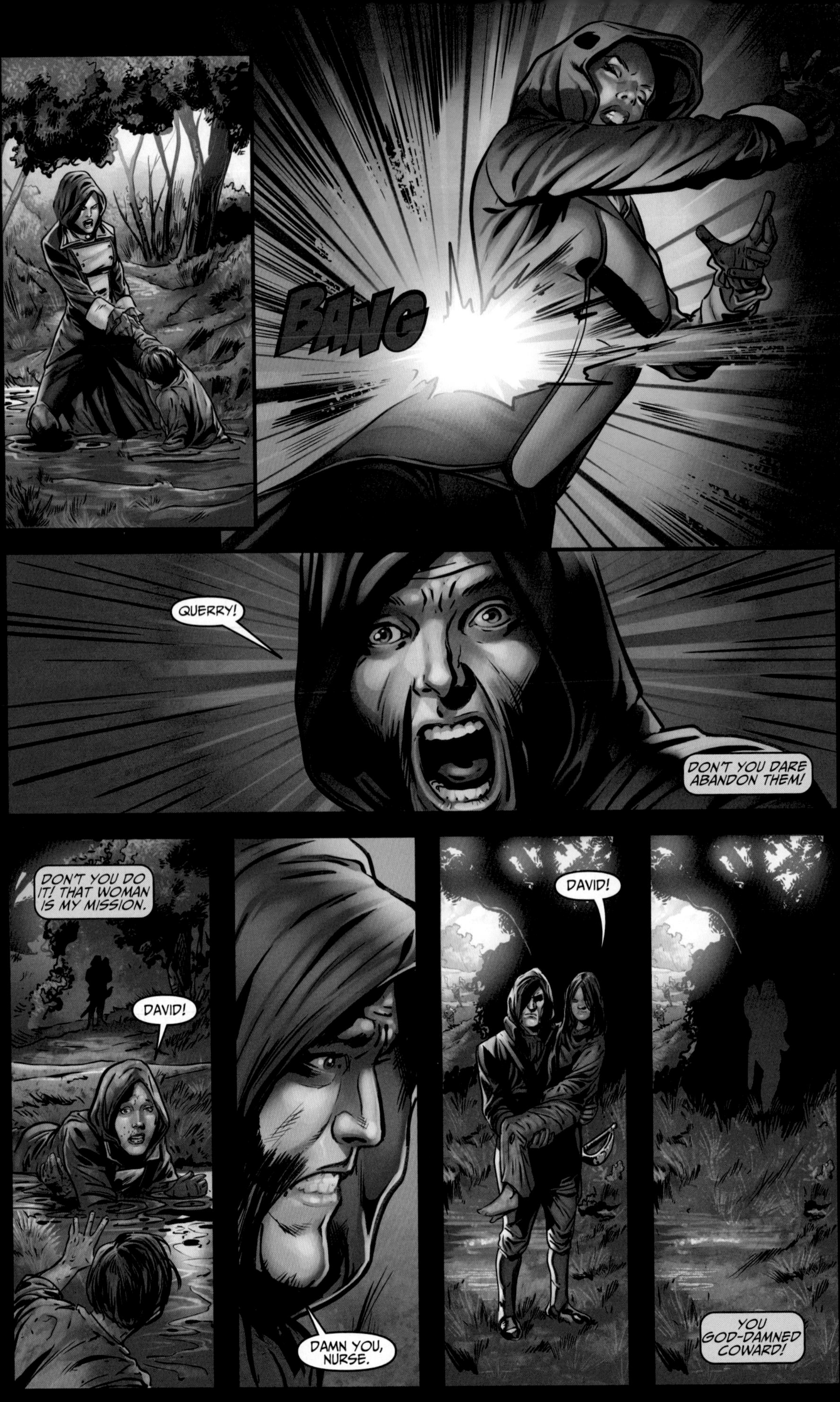
BANG
QUERRY!
DON'T YOU DARE ABANDON THEM!
DON'T YOU DO IT! THAT WOMAN IS MY MISSION.
DAVID!
DAMN YOU, NURSE.
DAVID!
YOU GOD-DAMNED COWARD!

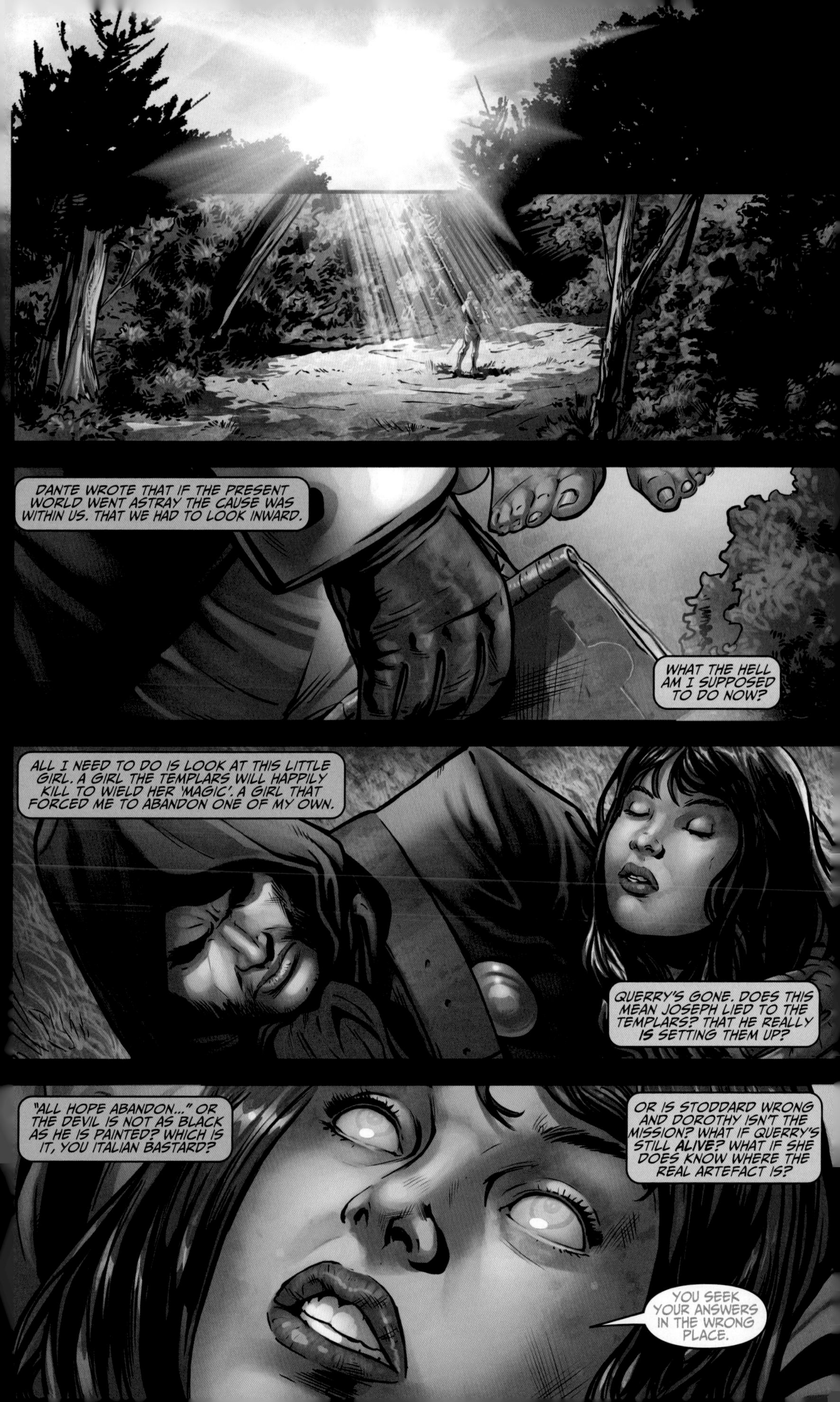
DANTE WROTE THAT IF THE PRESENT WORLD WENT ASTRAY THE CAUSE WAS WITHIN US. THAT WE HAD TO LOOK INWARD.
WHAT THE HELL AM I SUPPOSED TO DO NOW?
ALL I NEED TO DO IS LOOK AT THIS LITTLE GIRL. A GIRL THE TEMPLARS WILL HAPPILY KILL TO WIELD HER 'MAGIC'. A GIRL THAT FORCED ME TO ABANDON ONE OF MY OWN.
QUERRY'S GONE. DOES THIS MEAN JOSEPH LIED TO THE TEMPLARS? THAT HE REALLY IS SETTING THEM UP?
"ALL HOPE ABANDON..." OR THE DEVIL IS NOT AS BLACK AS HE IS PAINTED? WHICH IS IT, YOU ITALIAN BASTARD?
OR IS STODDARD WRONG AND DOROTHY ISN'T THE MISSION? WHAT IF QUERRY'S STILL ALIVE? WHAT IF SHE DOES KNOW WHERE THE REAL ARTEFACT IS?
YOU SEEK YOUR ANSWERS IN THE WRONG PLACE.

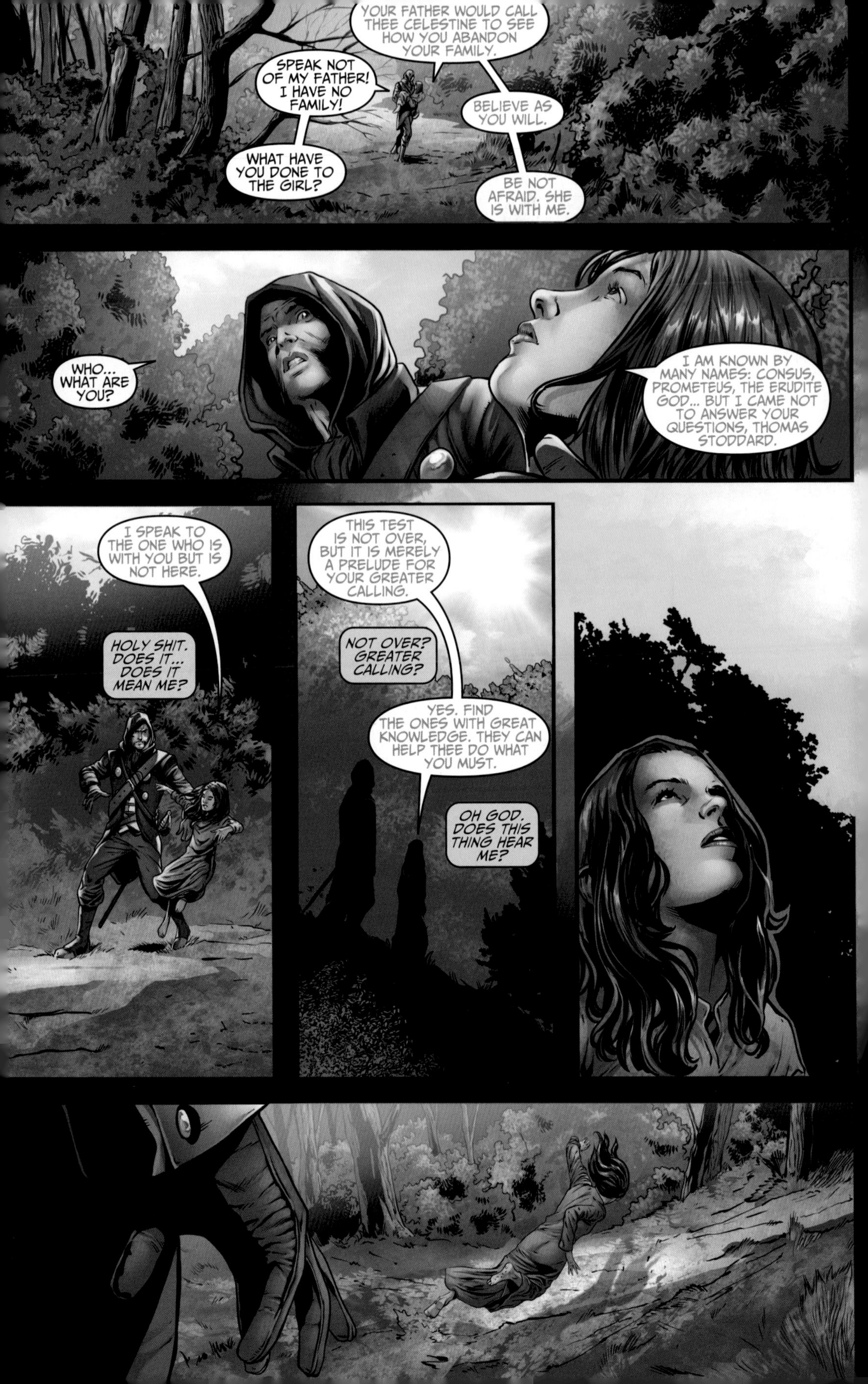
YOUR FATHER WOULD CALL THEE CELESTINE TO SEE HOW YOU ABANDON YOUR FAMILY.
SPEAK NOT OF MY FATHER! I HAVE NO FAMILY!
BELIEVE AS YOU WILL.
WHAT HAVE YOU DONE TO THE GIRL?
BE NOT AFRAID. SHE IS WITH ME.
WHO... WHAT ARE YOU?
I AM KNOWN BY MANY NAMES: CONSUS, PROMETEUS, THE ERUDITE GOD... BUT I CAME NOT TO ANSWER YOUR QUESTIONS, THOMAS STODDARD.
I SPEAK TO THE ONE WHO IS WITH YOU BUT IS NOT HERE.
HOLY SHIT. DOES IT... DOES IT MEAN ME?
THIS TEST IS NOT OVER, BUT IT IS MERELY A PRELUDE FOR YOUR GREATER CALLING.
NOT OVER? GREATER CALLING?
YES. FIND THE ONES WITH GREAT KNOWLEDGE. THEY CAN HELP THEE DO WHAT YOU MUST.
OH GOD. DOES THIS THING HEAR ME?

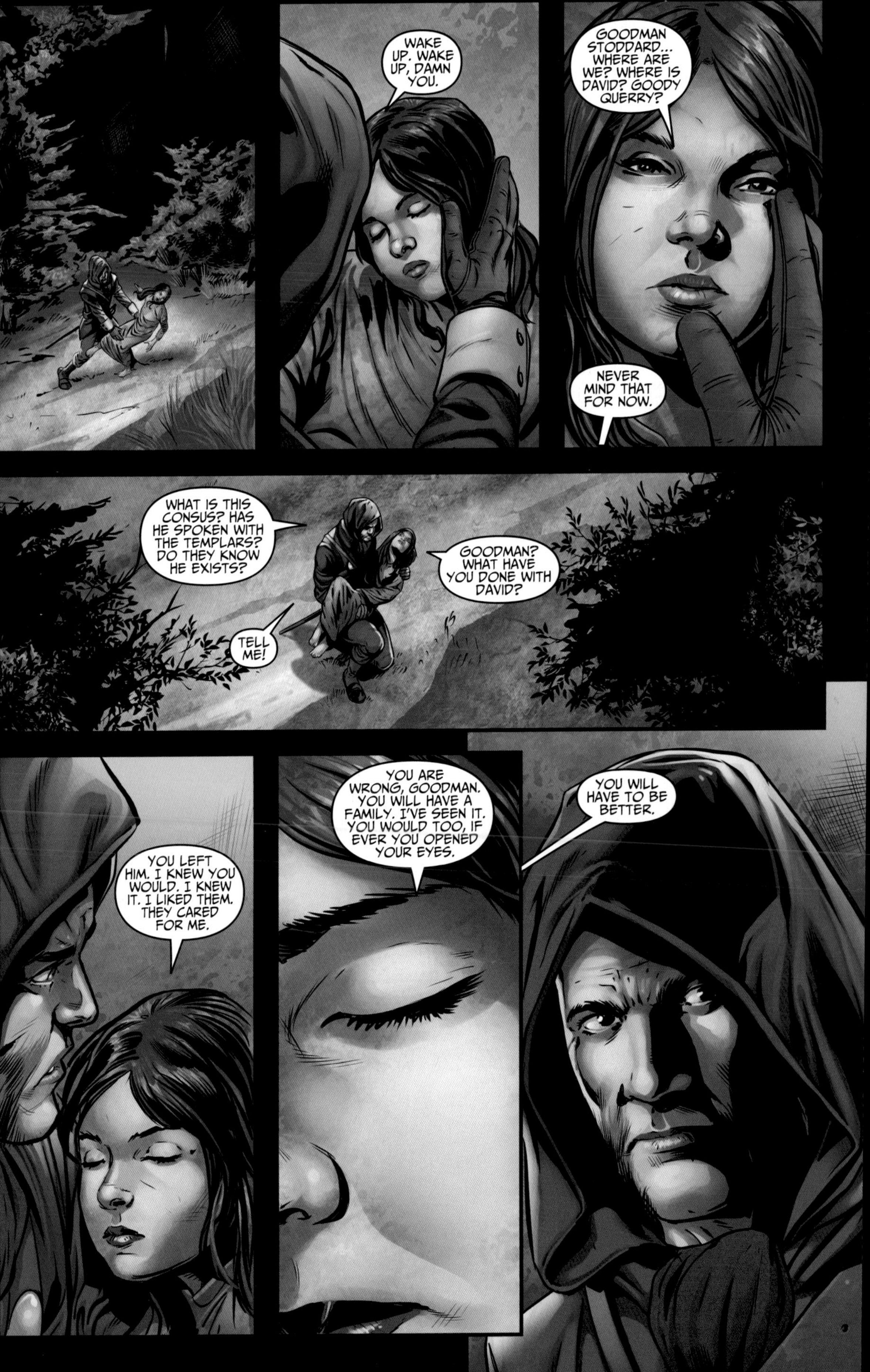
WAKE UP. WAKE UP, DAMN YOU.
GOODMAN STODDARD... WHERE ARE WE? WHERE IS DAVID? GOODY QUERRY?
NEVER MIND THAT FOR NOW.
WHAT IS THIS CONSUS? HAS HE SPOKEN WITH THE TEMPLARS? DO THEY KNOW HE EXISTS?
TELL ME!
GOODMAN? WHAT HAVE YOU DONE WITH DAVID?
YOU LEFT HIM. I KNEW YOU WOULD. I KNEW IT. I LIKED THEM. THEY CARED FOR ME.
YOU ARE WRONG, GOODMAN. YOU WILL HAVE A FAMILY. I'VE SEEN IT. YOU WOULD TOO, IF EVER YOU OPENED YOUR EYES.
YOU WILL HAVE TO BE BETTER.

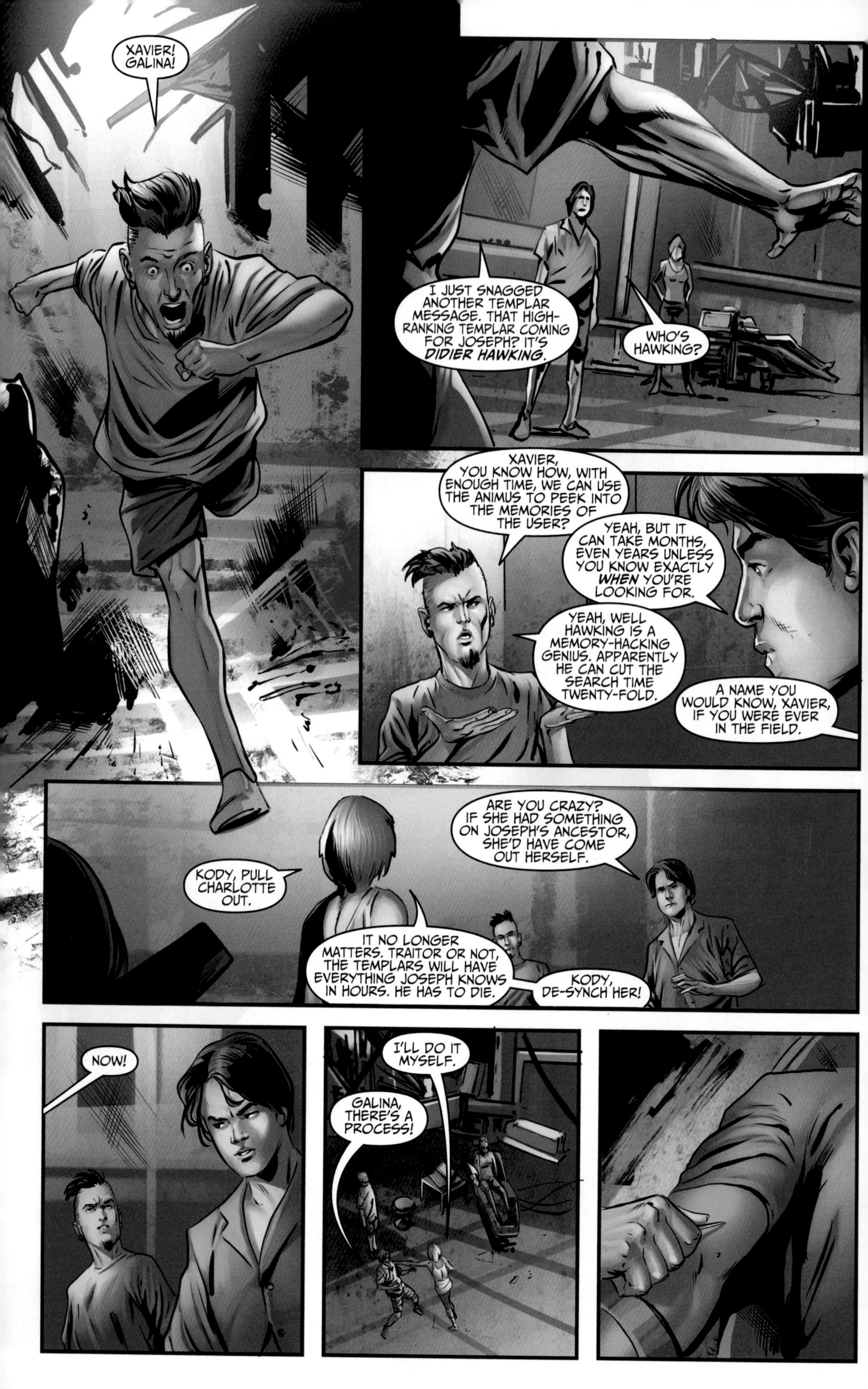
XAVIER! GALINA!
I JUST SNAGGED ANOTHER TEMPLAR MESSAGE. THAT HIGH-RANKING TEMPLAR COMING FOR JOSEPH? IT'S *DIDIER HAWKING*.
WHO'S HAWKING?
XAVIER, YOU KNOW HOW, WITH ENOUGH TIME, WE CAN USE THE ANIMUS TO PEEK INTO THE MEMORIES OF THE USER?
YEAH, BUT IT CAN TAKE MONTHS, EVEN YEARS UNLESS YOU KNOW EXACTLY *WHEN* YOU'RE LOOKING FOR.
YEAH, WELL HAWKING IS A MEMORY-HACKING GENIUS. APPARENTLY HE CAN CUT THE SEARCH TIME TWENTY-FOLD.
A NAME YOU WOULD KNOW, XAVIER, IF YOU WERE EVER IN THE FIELD.
KODY, PULL CHARLOTTE OUT.
ARE YOU CRAZY? IF SHE HAD SOMETHING ON JOSEPH'S ANCESTOR, SHE'D HAVE COME OUT HERSELF.
IT NO LONGER MATTERS. TRAITOR OR NOT, THE TEMPLARS WILL HAVE EVERYTHING JOSEPH KNOWS IN HOURS. HE HAS TO DIE.
KODY, DE-SYNCH HER!
NOW!
I'LL DO IT MYSELF.
GALINA, THERE'S A PROCESS!

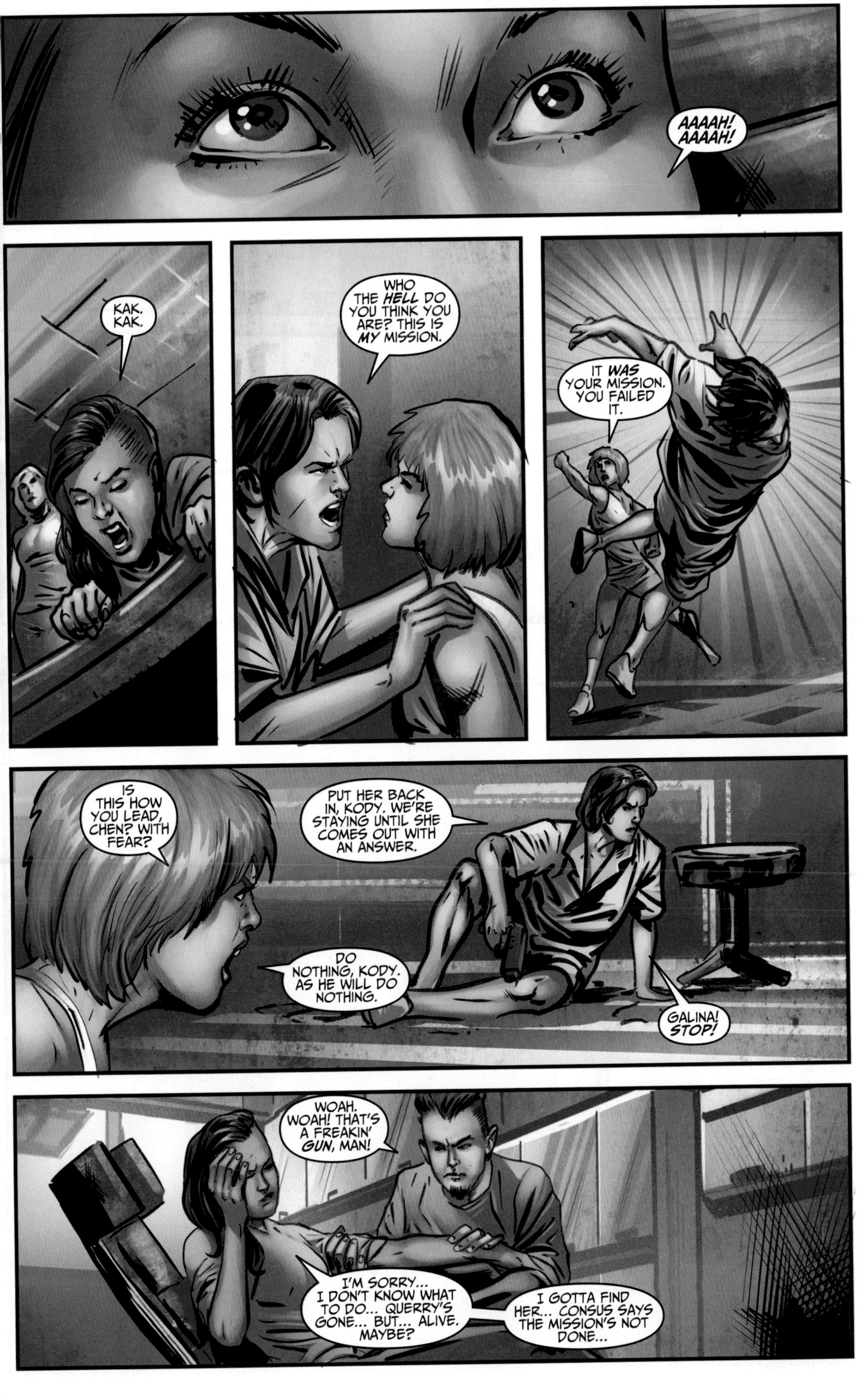
AAAAH! AAAAH!
KAK. KAK.
WHO THE HELL DO YOU THINK YOU ARE? THIS IS MY MISSION.
IT WAS YOUR MISSION. YOU FAILED IT.
IS THIS HOW YOU LEAD, CHEN? WITH FEAR?
PUT HER BACK IN, KODY. WE'RE STAYING UNTIL SHE COMES OUT WITH AN ANSWER.
DO NOTHING, KODY. AS HE WILL DO NOTHING.
GALINA! STOP!
WOAH. WOAH! THAT'S A FREAKIN' GUN, MAN!
I'M SORRY... I DON'T KNOW WHAT TO DO... QUERRY'S GONE... BUT... ALIVE. MAYBE?
I GOTTA FIND HER... CONSUS SAYS THE MISSION'S NOT DONE...

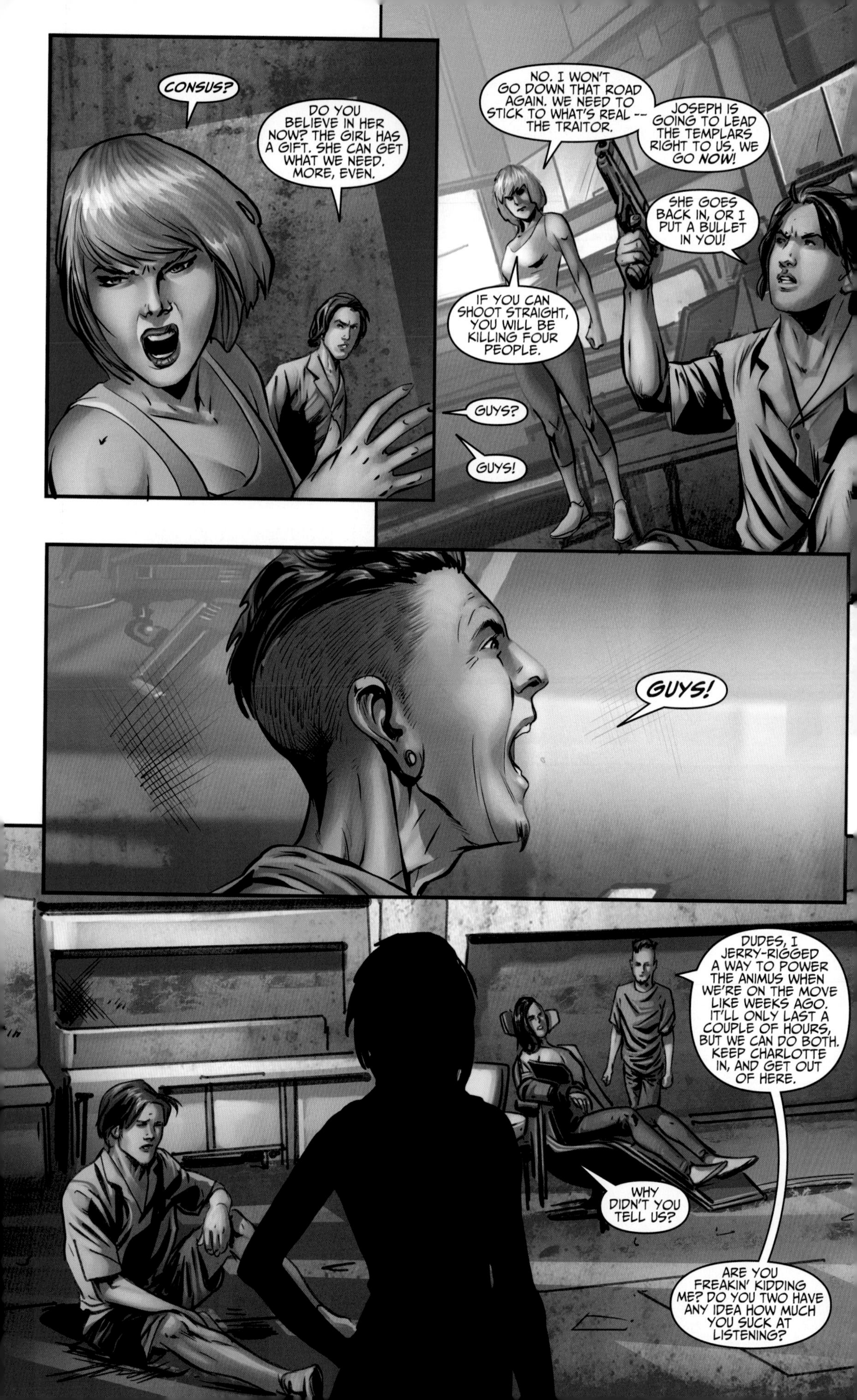
CONSUS?
DO YOU BELIEVE IN HER NOW? THE GIRL HAS A GIFT. SHE CAN GET WHAT WE NEED. MORE, EVEN.
NO. I WON'T GO DOWN THAT ROAD AGAIN. WE NEED TO STICK TO WHAT'S REAL -- THE TRAITOR.
JOSEPH IS GOING TO LEAD THE TEMPLARS RIGHT TO US. WE GO NOW!
SHE GOES BACK IN, OR I PUT A BULLET IN YOU!
IF YOU CAN SHOOT STRAIGHT, YOU WILL BE KILLING FOUR PEOPLE.
GUYS?
GUYS!
GUYS!
DUDES, I JERRY-RIGGED A WAY TO POWER THE ANIMUS WHEN WE'RE ON THE MOVE LIKE WEEKS AGO. IT'LL ONLY LAST A COUPLE OF HOURS, BUT WE CAN DO BOTH. KEEP CHARLOTTE IN, AND GET OUT OF HERE.
WHY DIDN'T YOU TELL US?
ARE YOU FREAKIN' KIDDING ME? DO YOU TWO HAVE ANY IDEA HOW MUCH YOU SUCK AT LISTENING?

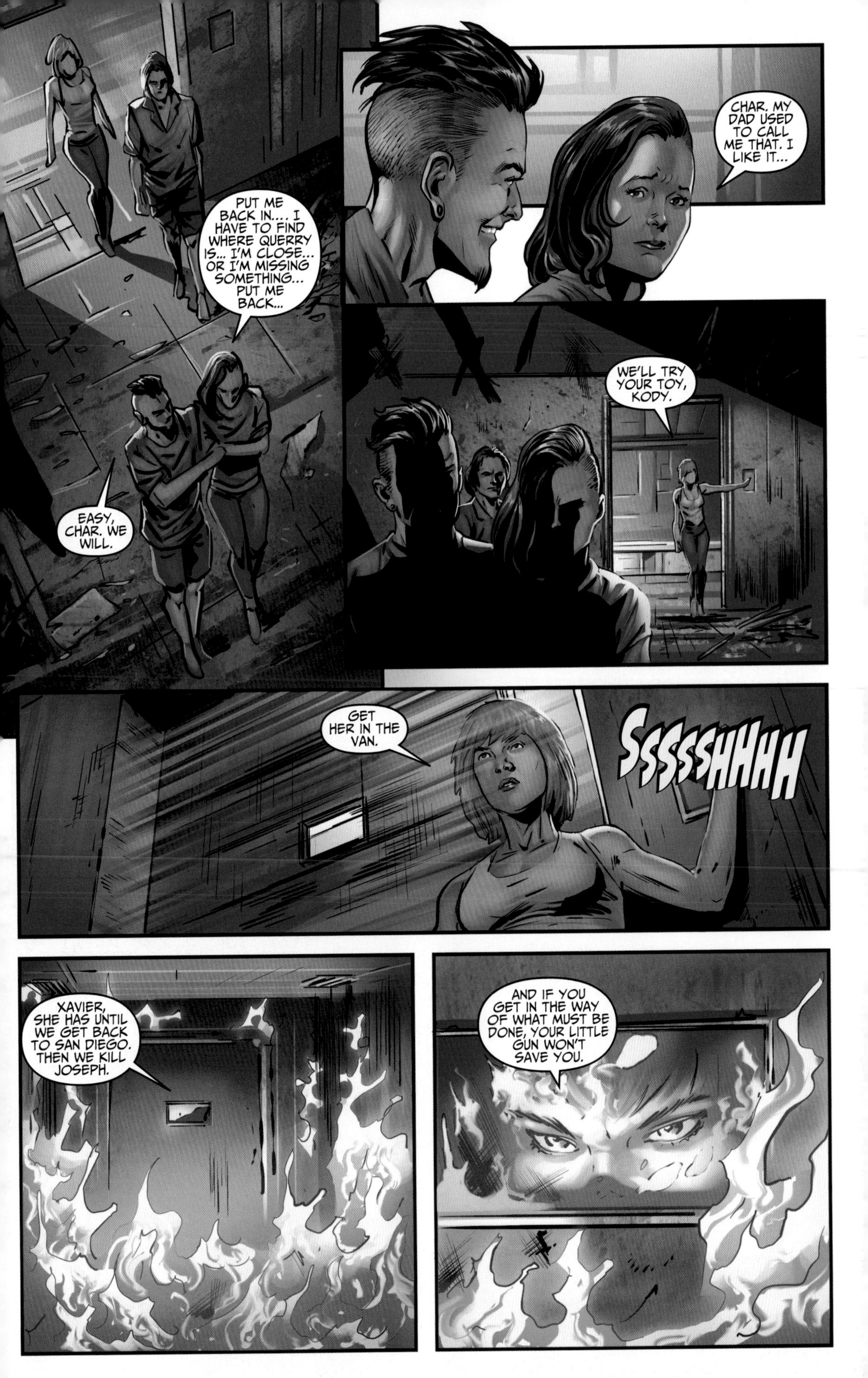
PUT ME BACK IN.... I HAVE TO FIND WHERE QUERRY IS... I'M CLOSE... OR I'M MISSING SOMETHING... PUT ME BACK...
EASY, CHAR. WE WILL.
CHAR. MY DAD USED TO CALL ME THAT. I LIKE IT...
WE'LL TRY YOUR TOY, KODY.
GET HER IN THE VAN.
SSSSSHHHH
XAVIER, SHE HAS UNTIL WE GET BACK TO SAN DIEGO. THEN WE KILL JOSEPH.
AND IF YOU GET IN THE WAY OF WHAT MUST BE DONE, YOUR LITTLE GUN WON'T SAVE YOU.

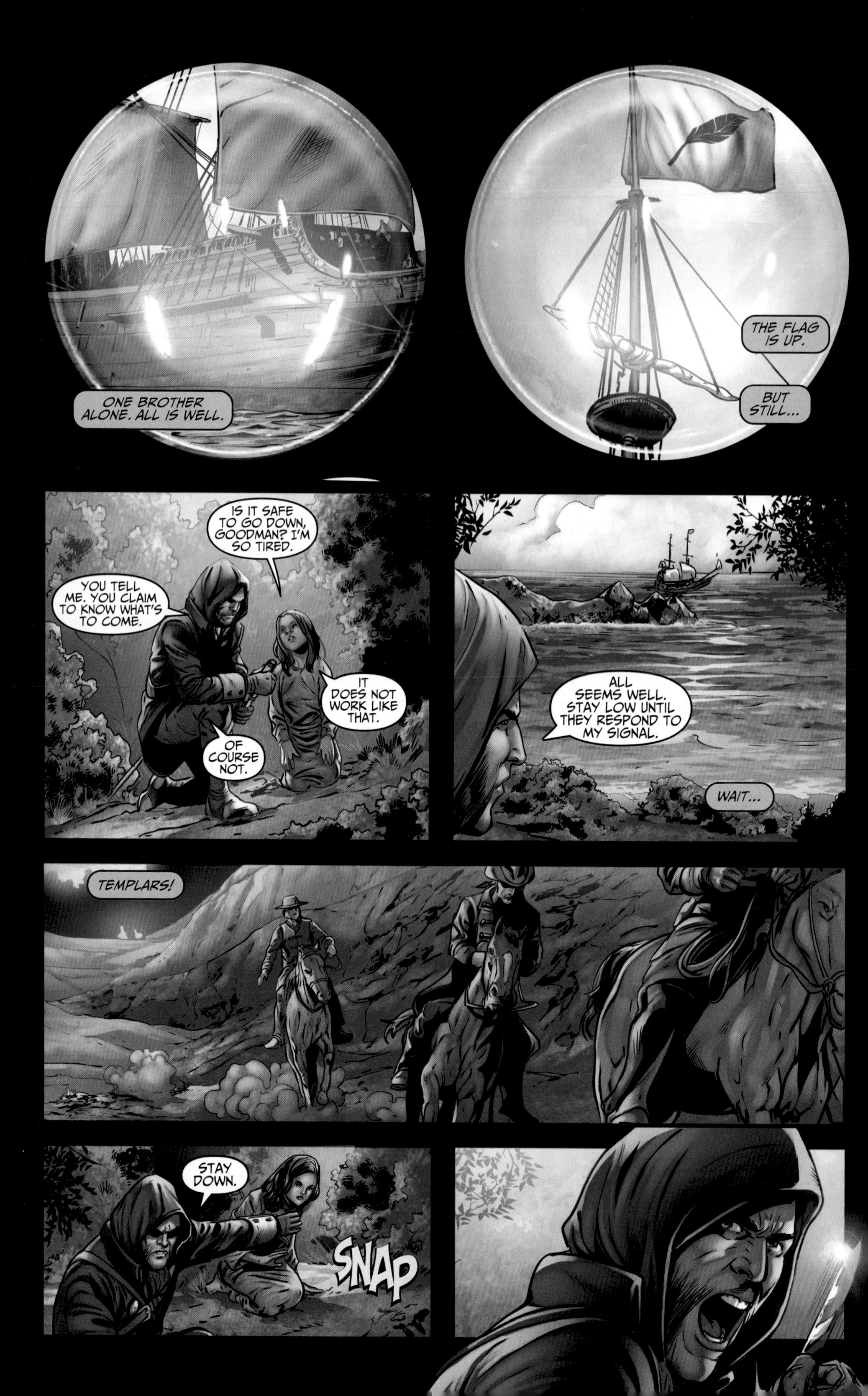
ONE BROTHER ALONE. ALL IS WELL.
THE FLAG IS UP.
BUT STILL...
IS IT SAFE TO GO DOWN, GOODMAN? I'M SO TIRED.
YOU TELL ME. YOU CLAIM TO KNOW WHAT'S TO COME.
IT DOES NOT WORK LIKE THAT.
OF COURSE NOT.
ALL SEEMS WELL. STAY LOW UNTIL THEY RESPOND TO MY SIGNAL.
WAIT...
TEMPLARS!
STAY DOWN.
SNAP

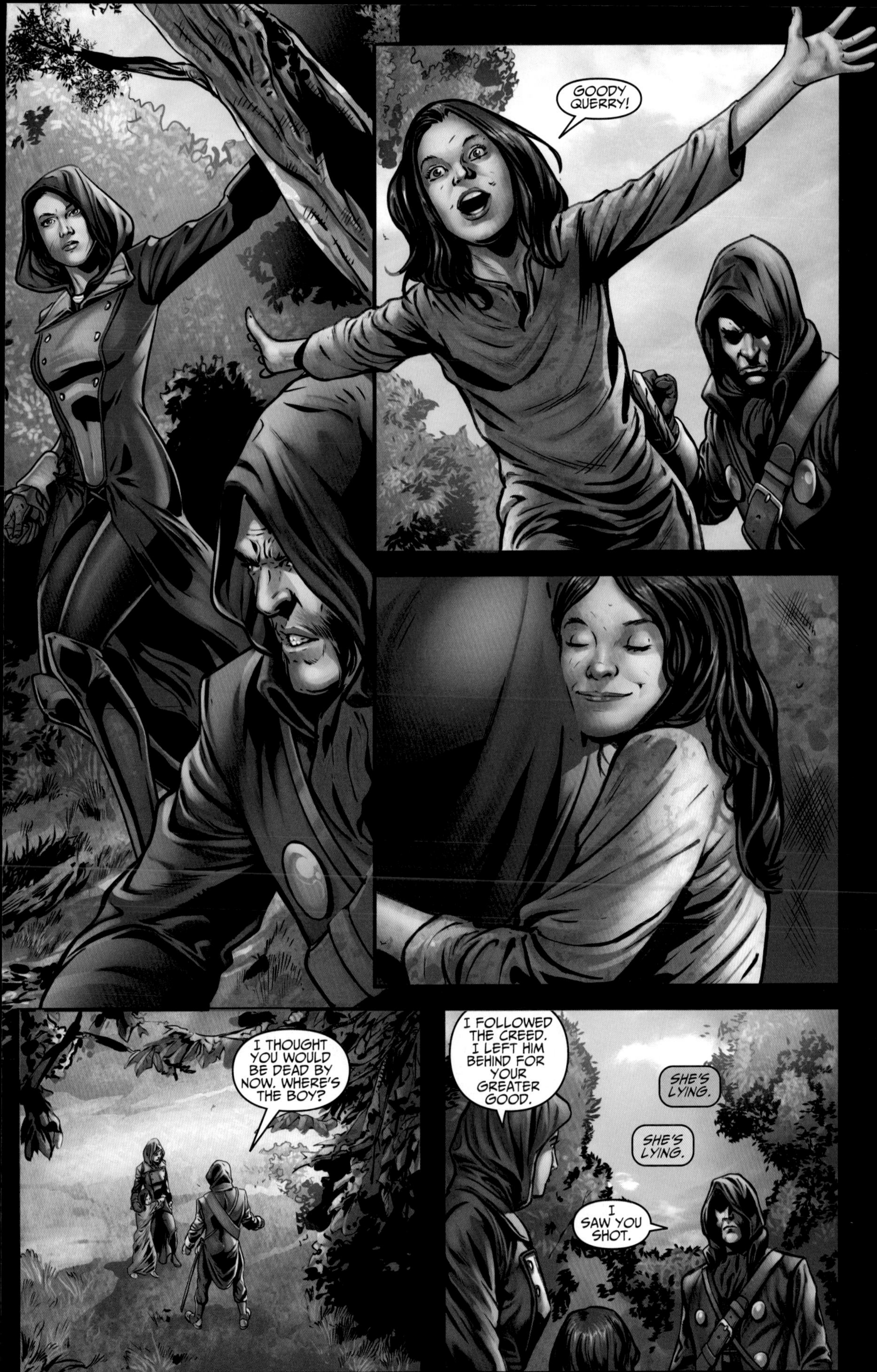
GOODY QUERRY!
I THOUGHT YOU WOULD BE DEAD BY NOW. WHERE'S THE BOY?
I FOLLOWED THE CREED. I LEFT HIM BEHIND FOR YOUR GREATER GOOD.
SHE'S LYING.
SHE'S LYING.
I SAW YOU SHOT.

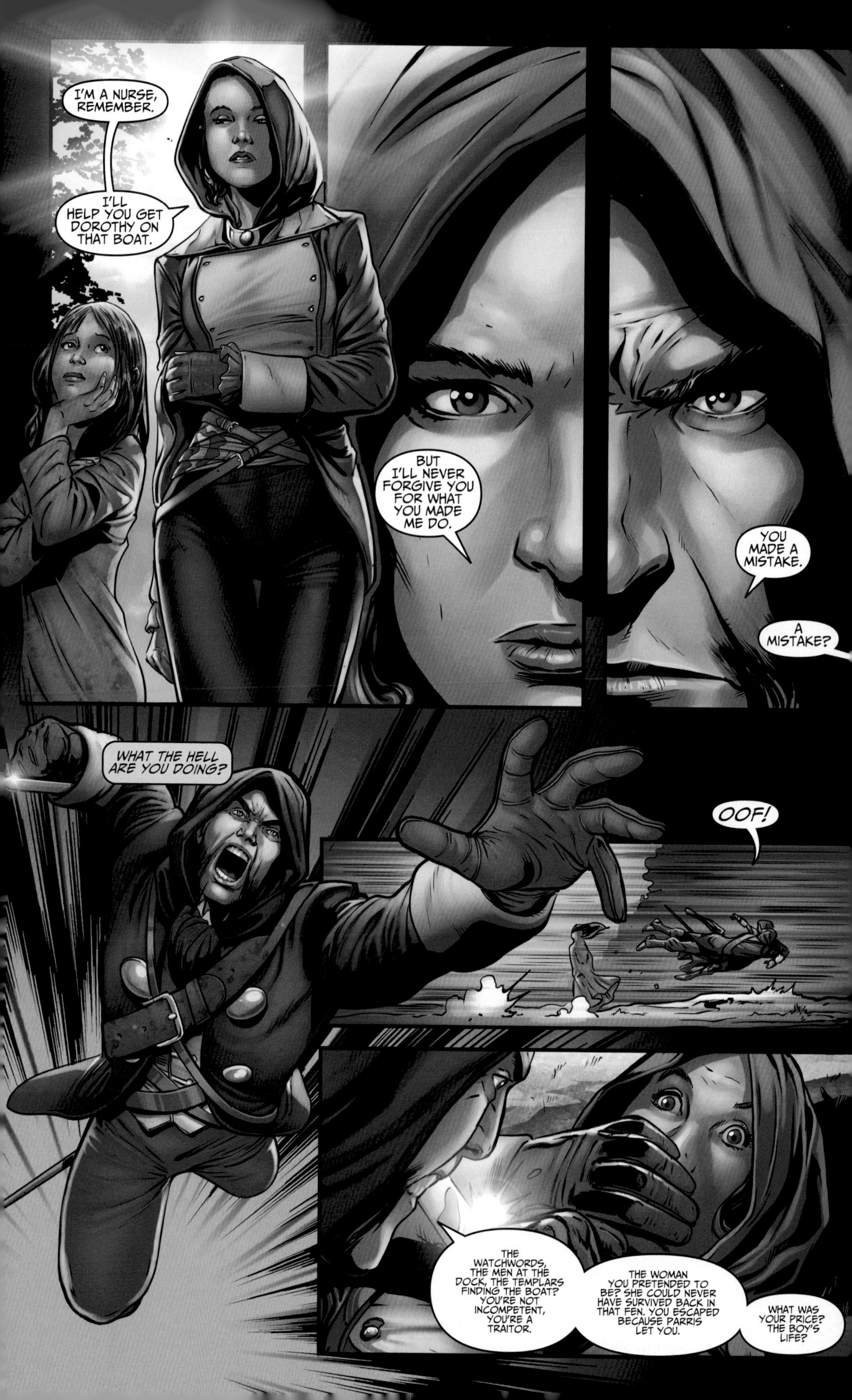
I'M A NURSE, REMEMBER.
I'LL HELP YOU GET DOROTHY ON THAT BOAT.
BUT I'LL NEVER FORGIVE YOU FOR WHAT YOU MADE ME DO.
YOU MADE A MISTAKE.
A MISTAKE?
WHAT THE HELL ARE YOU DOING?
OOF!
THE WATCHWORDS, THE MEN AT THE DOCK, THE TEMPLARS FINDING THE BOAT? YOU'RE NOT INCOMPETENT, YOU'RE A TRAITOR.
THE WOMAN YOU PRETENDED TO BE? SHE COULD NEVER HAVE SURVIVED BACK IN THAT FEN. YOU ESCAPED BECAUSE PARRIS LET YOU.
WHAT WAS YOUR PRICE? THE BOY'S LIFE?

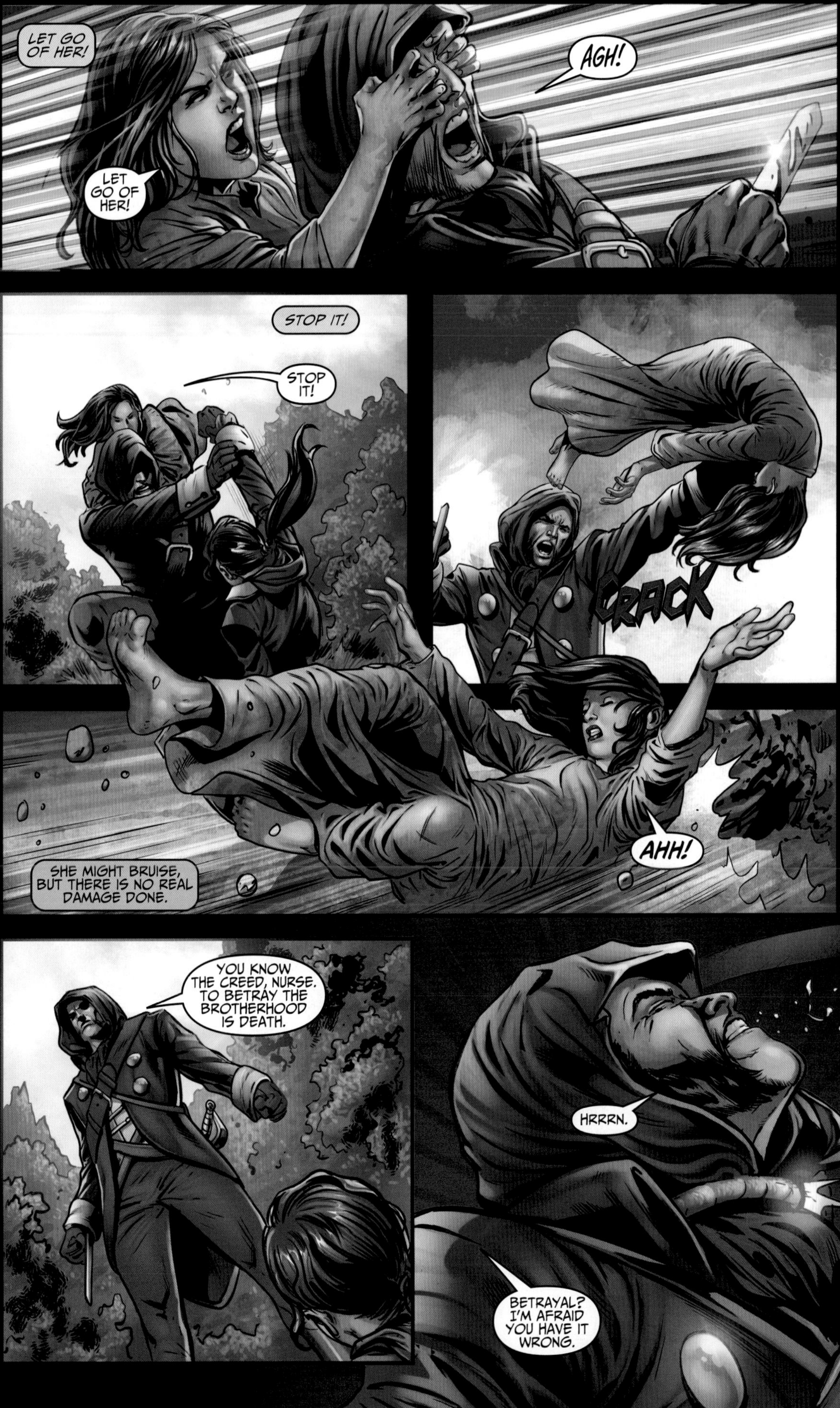
LET GO OF HER!
LET GO OF HER!
AGH!
STOP IT!
STOP IT!
CRACK
AHH!
SHE MIGHT BRUISE, BUT THERE IS NO REAL DAMAGE DONE.
YOU KNOW THE CREED, NURSE. TO BETRAY THE BROTHERHOOD IS DEATH.
HRRRN.
BETRAYAL? I'M AFRAID YOU HAVE IT WRONG.

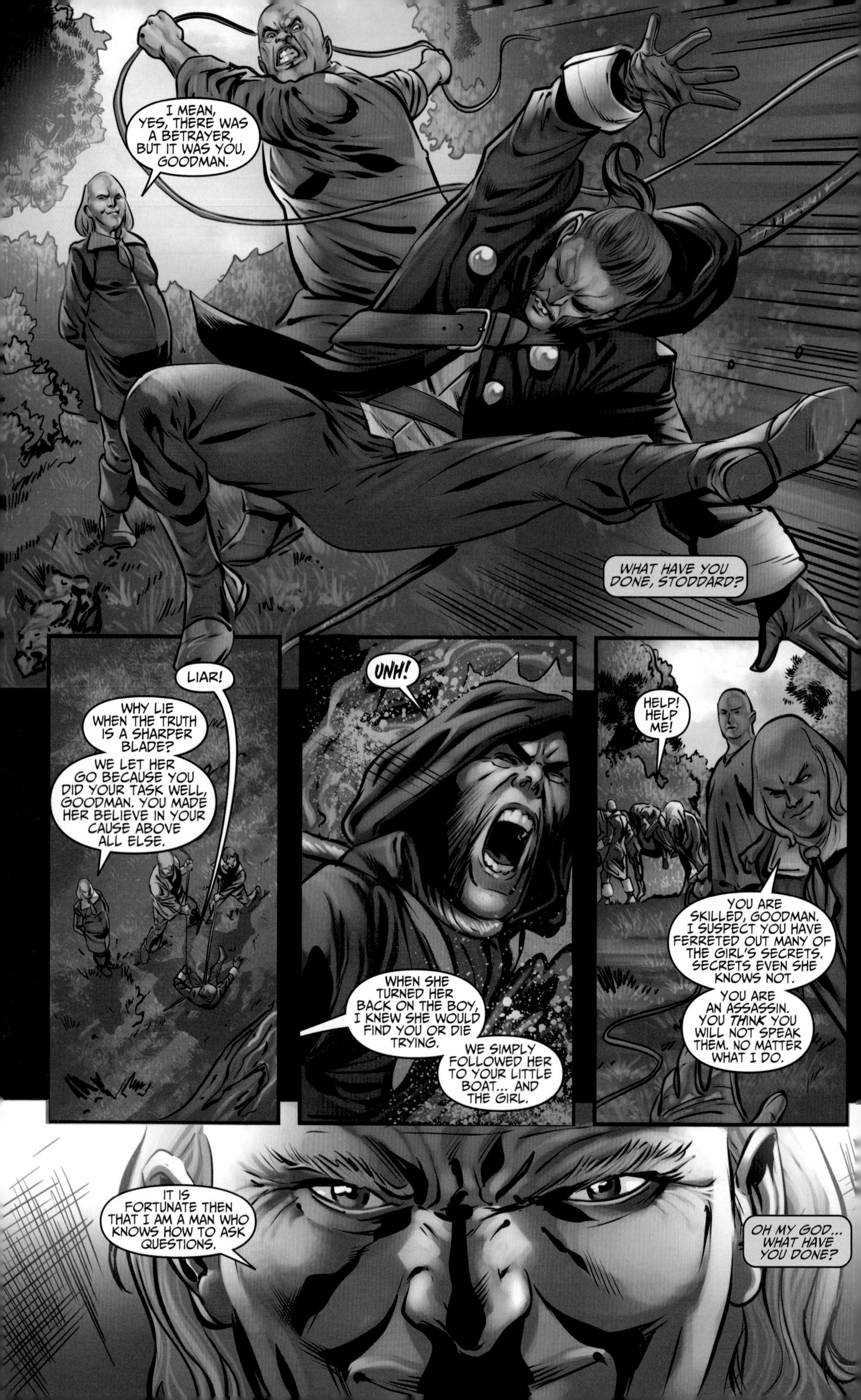
I MEAN, YES, THERE WAS A BETRAYER, BUT IT WAS YOU, GOODMAN.
WHAT HAVE YOU DONE, STODDARD?
LIAR!
WHY LIE WHEN THE TRUTH IS A SHARPER BLADE?
WE LET HER GO BECAUSE YOU DID YOUR TASK WELL, GOODMAN. YOU MADE HER BELIEVE IN YOUR CAUSE ABOVE ALL ELSE.
UNH!
WHEN SHE TURNED HER BACK ON THE BOY, I KNEW SHE WOULD FIND YOU OR DIE TRYING.
WE SIMPLY FOLLOWED HER TO YOUR LITTLE BOAT... AND THE GIRL.
HELP! HELP ME!
YOU ARE SKILLED, GOODMAN. I SUSPECT YOU HAVE FERRETED OUT MANY OF THE GIRL'S SECRETS. SECRETS EVEN SHE KNOWS NOT.
YOU ARE AN ASSASSIN. YOU THINK YOU WILL NOT SPEAK THEM. NO MATTER WHAT I DO.
IT IS FORTUNATE THEN THAT I AM A MAN WHO KNOWS HOW TO ASK QUESTIONS.
OH MY GOD... WHAT HAVE YOU DONE?

CHAPTER
FOUR

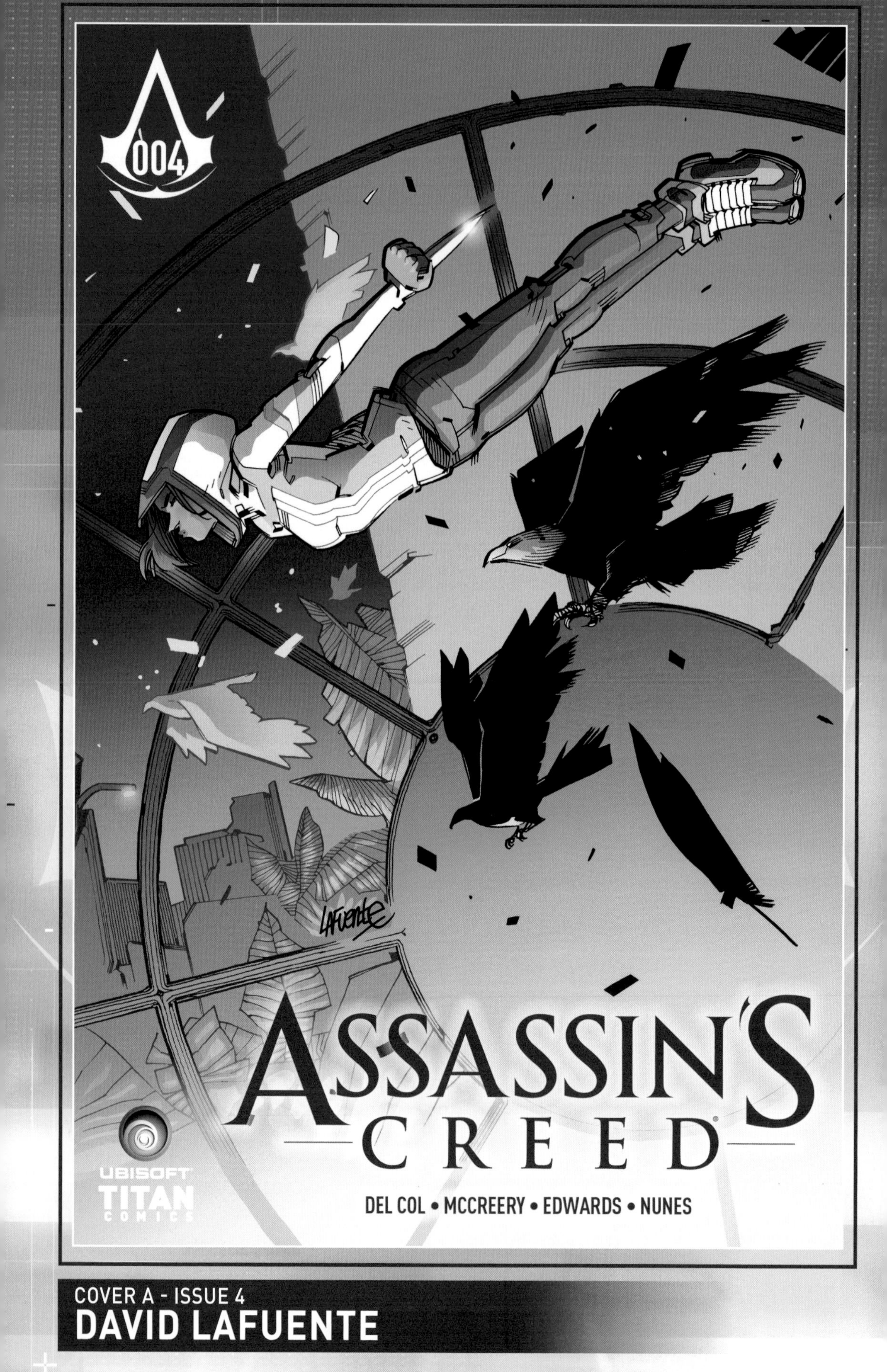
004
LAFUENTE
ASSASSIN'S CREED
UBISOFT
TITAN COMICS
DEL COL • MCCREERY • EDWARDS • NUNES

COVER A - ISSUE 4
DAVID LAFUENTE

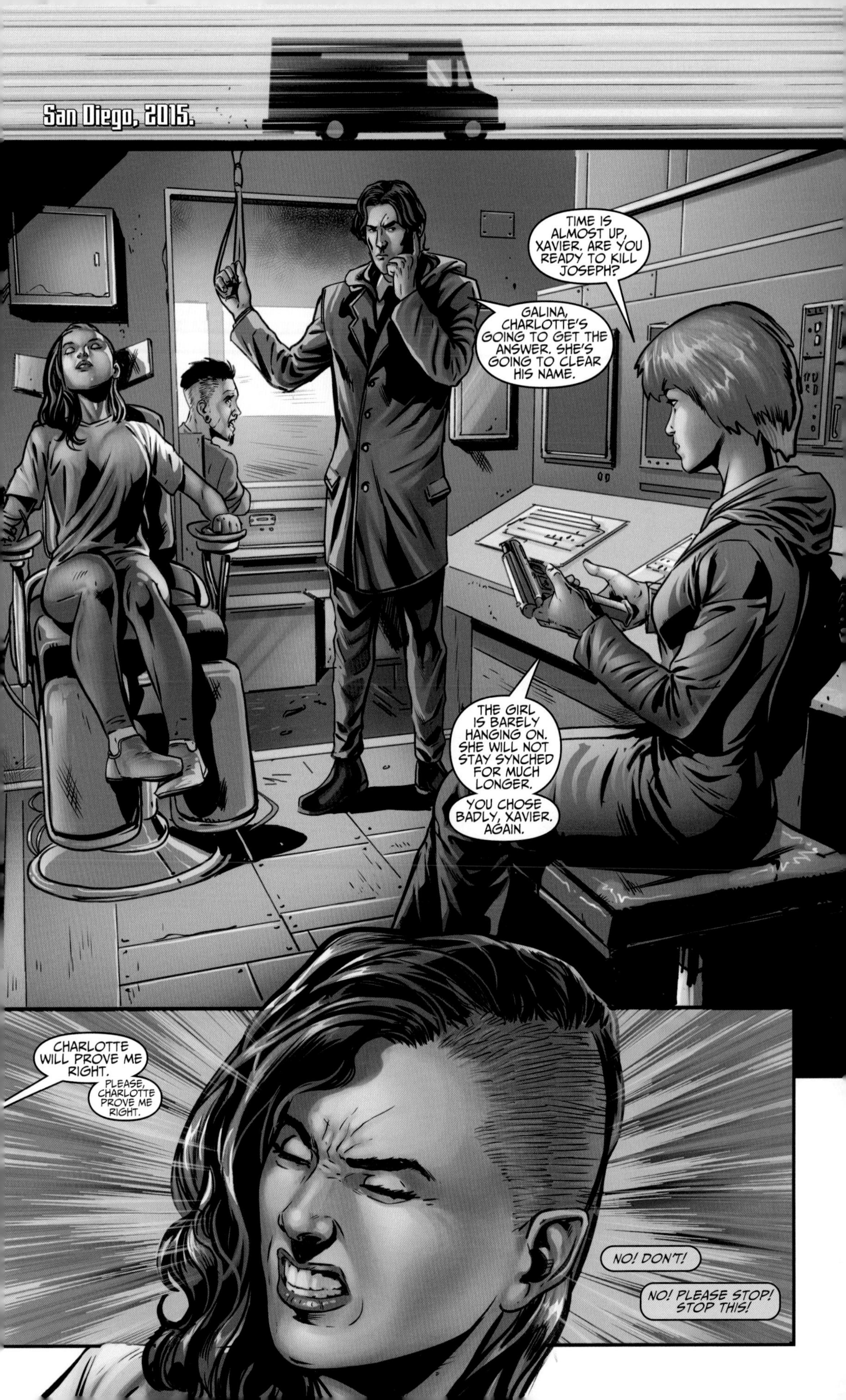
San Diego, 2015.
TIME IS ALMOST UP, XAVIER. ARE YOU READY TO KILL JOSEPH?
GALINA, CHARLOTTE'S GOING TO GET THE ANSWER. SHE'S GOING TO CLEAR HIS NAME.
THE GIRL IS BARELY HANGING ON. SHE WILL NOT STAY SYNCHED FOR MUCH LONGER.
YOU CHOSE BADLY, XAVIER. AGAIN.
CHARLOTTE WILL PROVE ME RIGHT.
PLEASE, CHARLOTTE PROVE ME RIGHT.
NO! DON'T!
NO! PLEASE STOP! STOP THIS!

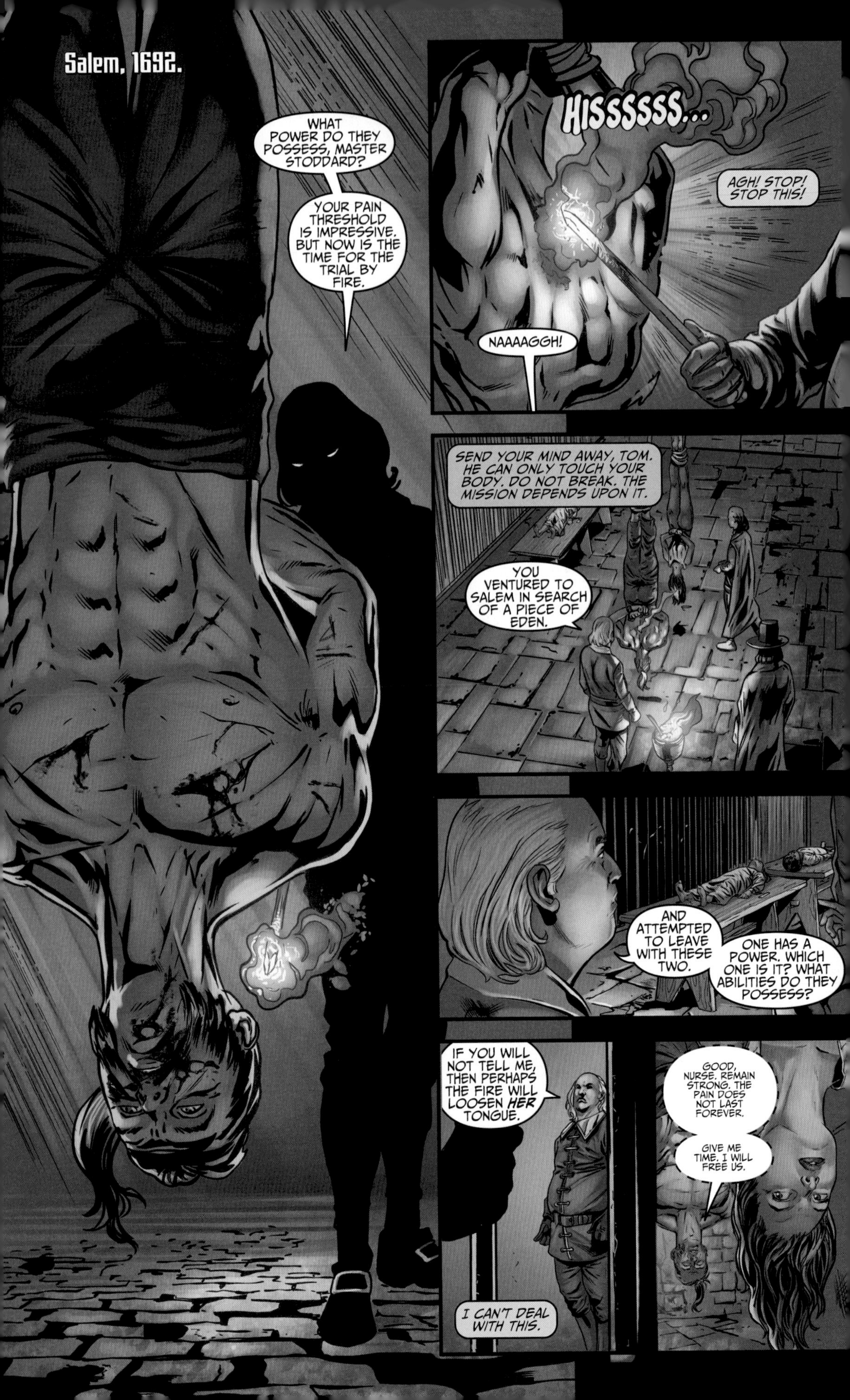
Salem, 1692.
WHAT POWER DO THEY POSSESS, MASTER STODDARD?
YOUR PAIN THRESHOLD IS IMPRESSIVE. BUT NOW IS THE TIME FOR THE TRIAL BY FIRE.
HISSSSSS...
AGH! STOP! STOP THIS!
NAAAAGGH!
SEND YOUR MIND AWAY, TOM. HE CAN ONLY TOUCH YOUR BODY. DO NOT BREAK. THE MISSION DEPENDS UPON IT.
YOU VENTURED TO SALEM IN SEARCH OF A PIECE OF EDEN.
AND ATTEMPTED TO LEAVE WITH THESE TWO.
ONE HAS A POWER. WHICH ONE IS IT? WHAT ABILITIES DO THEY POSSESS?
IF YOU WILL NOT TELL ME, THEN PERHAPS THE FIRE WILL LOOSEN HER TONGUE.
I CAN'T DEAL WITH THIS.
GOOD, NURSE. REMAIN STRONG. THE PAIN DOES NOT LAST FOREVER.
GIVE ME TIME. I WILL FREE US.

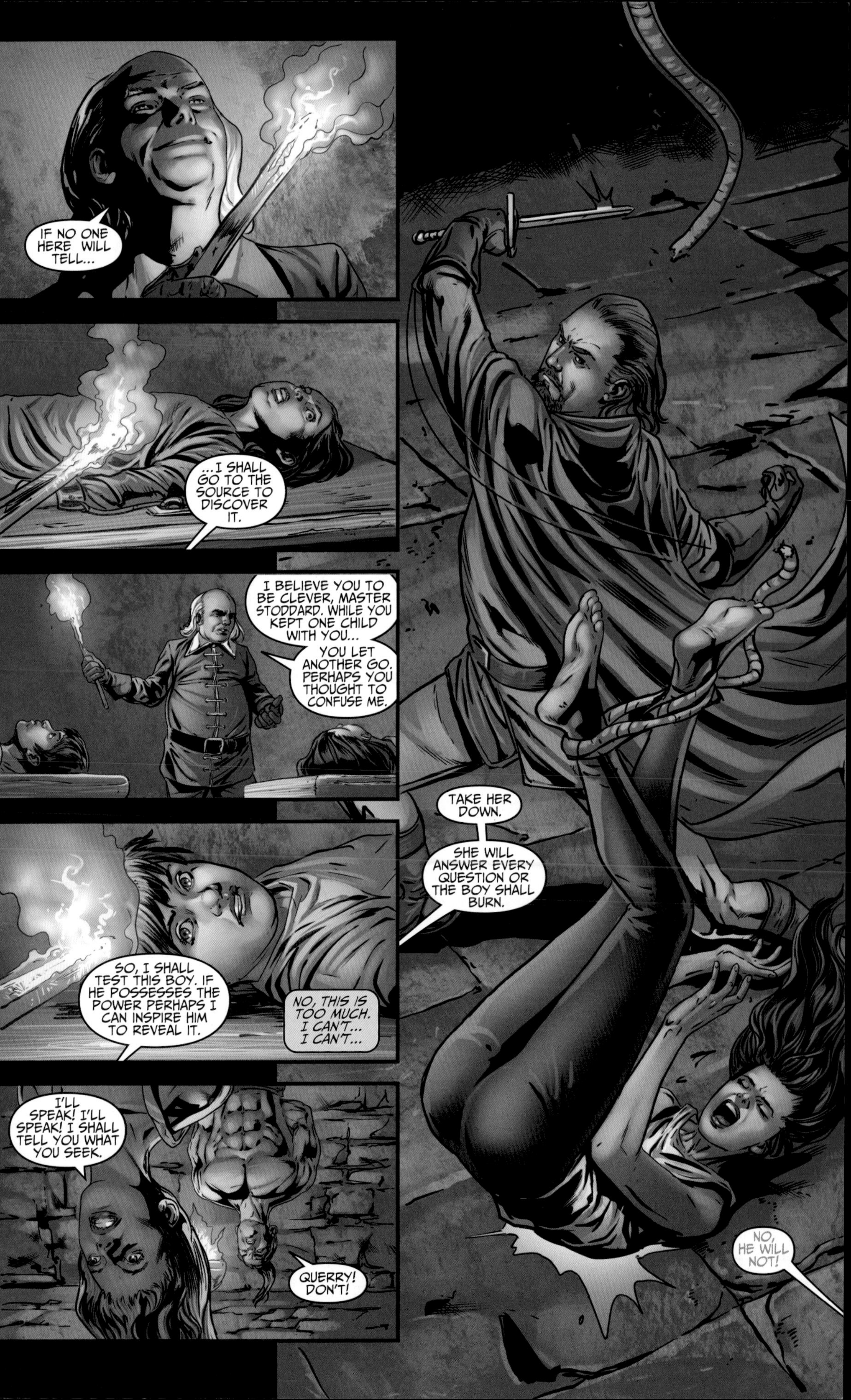
IF NO ONE HERE WILL TELL...
...I SHALL GO TO THE SOURCE TO DISCOVER IT.
I BELIEVE YOU TO BE CLEVER, MASTER STODDARD. WHILE YOU KEPT ONE CHILD WITH YOU...
YOU LET ANOTHER GO. PERHAPS YOU THOUGHT TO CONFUSE ME.
SO, I SHALL TEST THIS BOY. IF HE POSSESSES THE POWER PERHAPS I CAN INSPIRE HIM TO REVEAL IT.
NO, THIS IS TOO MUCH. I CAN'T... I CAN'T...
I'LL SPEAK! I'LL SPEAK! I SHALL TELL YOU WHAT YOU SEEK.
QUERRY! DON'T!
TAKE HER DOWN.
SHE WILL ANSWER EVERY QUESTION OR THE BOY SHALL BURN.
NO, HE WILL NOT!

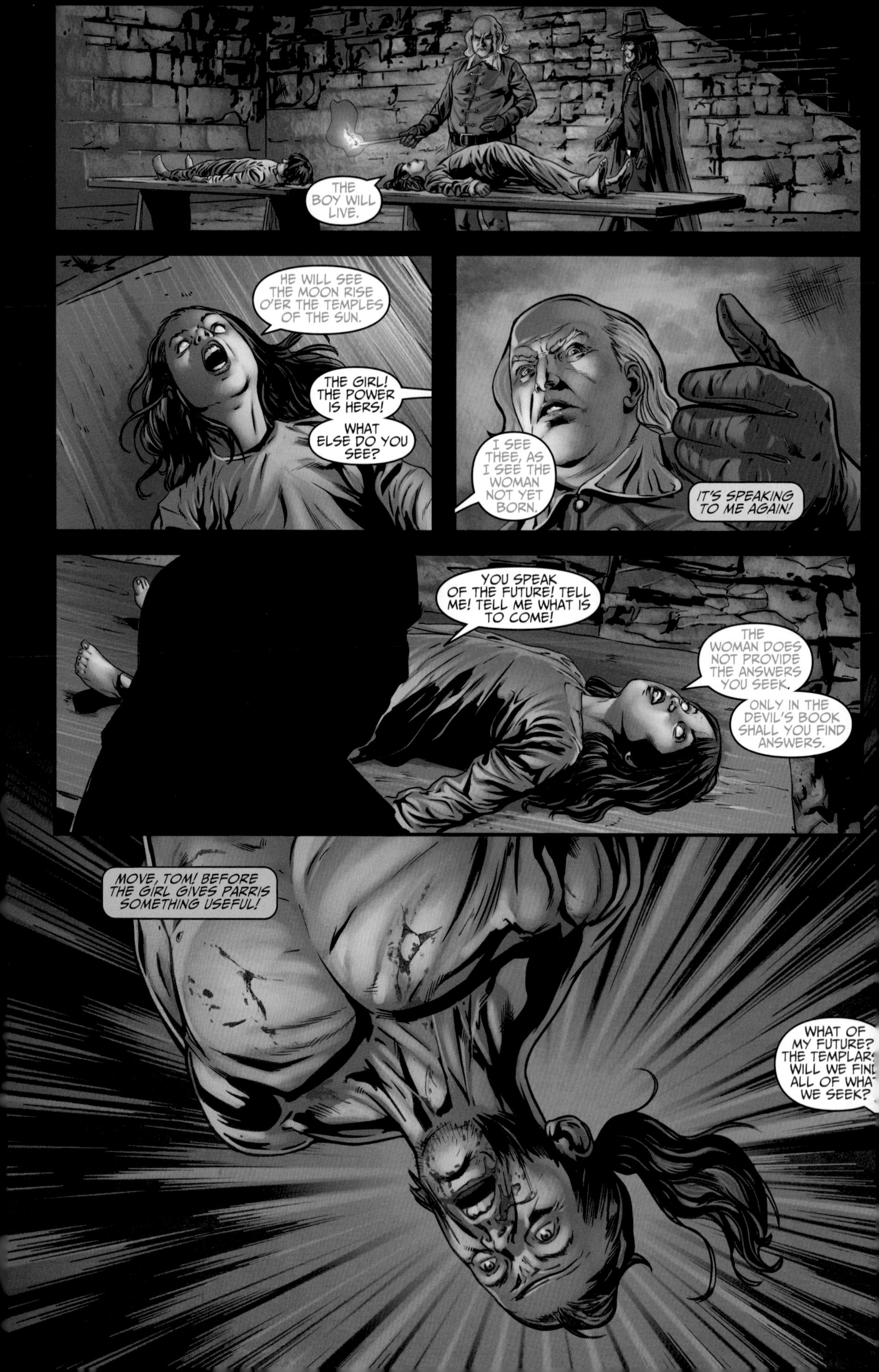
THE BOY WILL LIVE.
HE WILL SEE THE MOON RISE O'ER THE TEMPLES OF THE SUN.
THE GIRL! THE POWER IS HERS!
WHAT ELSE DO YOU SEE?
I SEE THEE, AS I SEE THE WOMAN NOT YET BORN.
IT'S SPEAKING TO ME AGAIN!
YOU SPEAK OF THE FUTURE! TELL ME! TELL ME WHAT IS TO COME!
THE WOMAN DOES NOT PROVIDE THE ANSWERS YOU SEEK.
ONLY IN THE DEVIL'S BOOK SHALL YOU FIND ANSWERS.
MOVE, TOM! BEFORE THE GIRL GIVES PARRIS SOMETHING USEFUL!

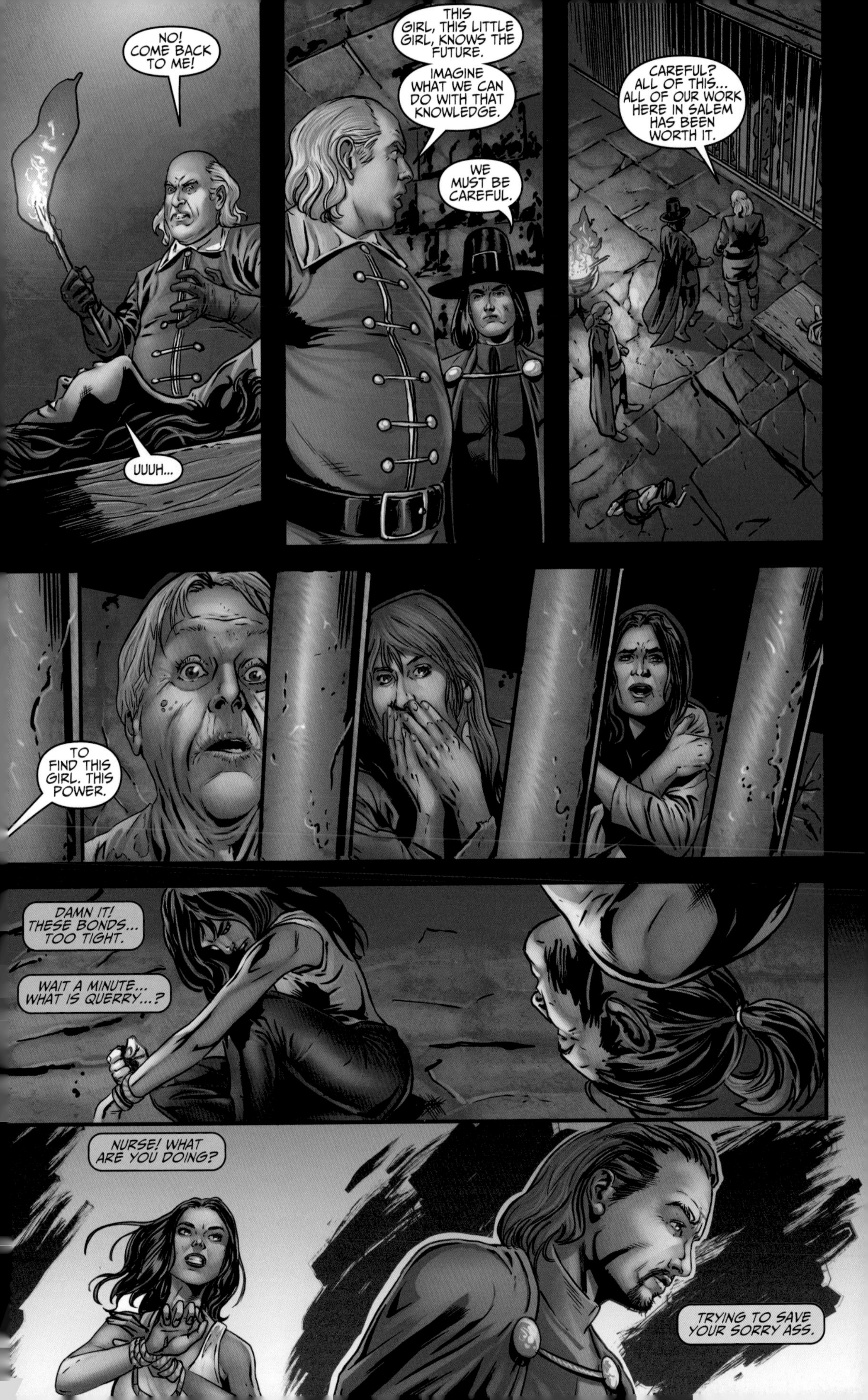
NO! COME BACK TO ME!
UUUH...
THIS GIRL, THIS LITTLE GIRL, KNOWS THE FUTURE.
IMAGINE WHAT WE CAN DO WITH THAT KNOWLEDGE.
WE MUST BE CAREFUL.
CAREFUL? ALL OF THIS... ALL OF OUR WORK HERE IN SALEM HAS BEEN WORTH IT.
TO FIND THIS GIRL. THIS POWER.
DAMN IT! THESE BONDS... TOO TIGHT.
WAIT A MINUTE... WHAT IS QUERRY...?
NURSE! WHAT ARE YOU DOING?
TRYING TO SAVE YOUR SORRY ASS.

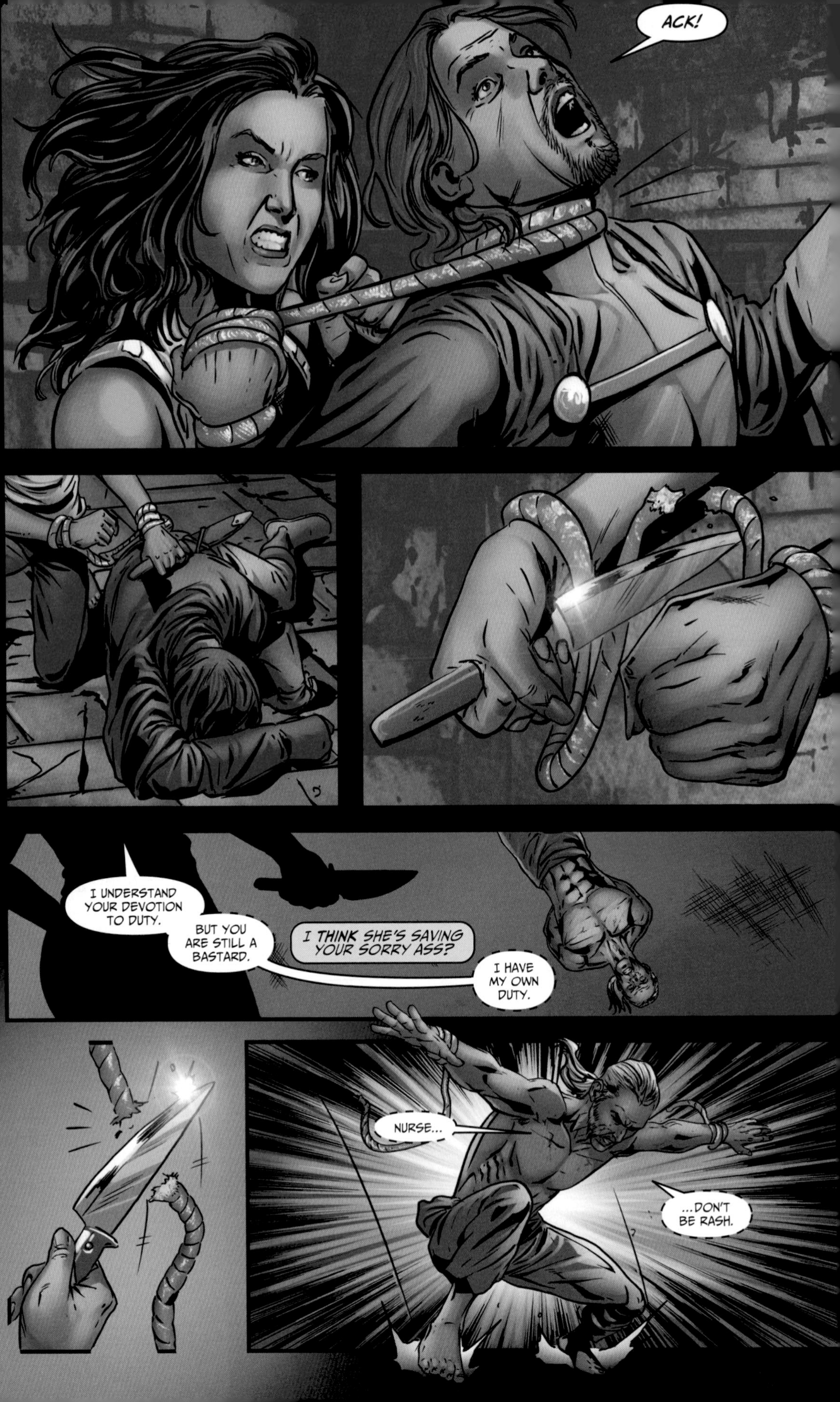
ACK!
I UNDERSTAND YOUR DEVOTION TO DUTY.
BUT YOU ARE STILL A BASTARD.
I THINK SHE'S SAVING YOUR SORRY ASS?
I HAVE MY OWN DUTY.
NURSE...
...DON'T BE RASH.

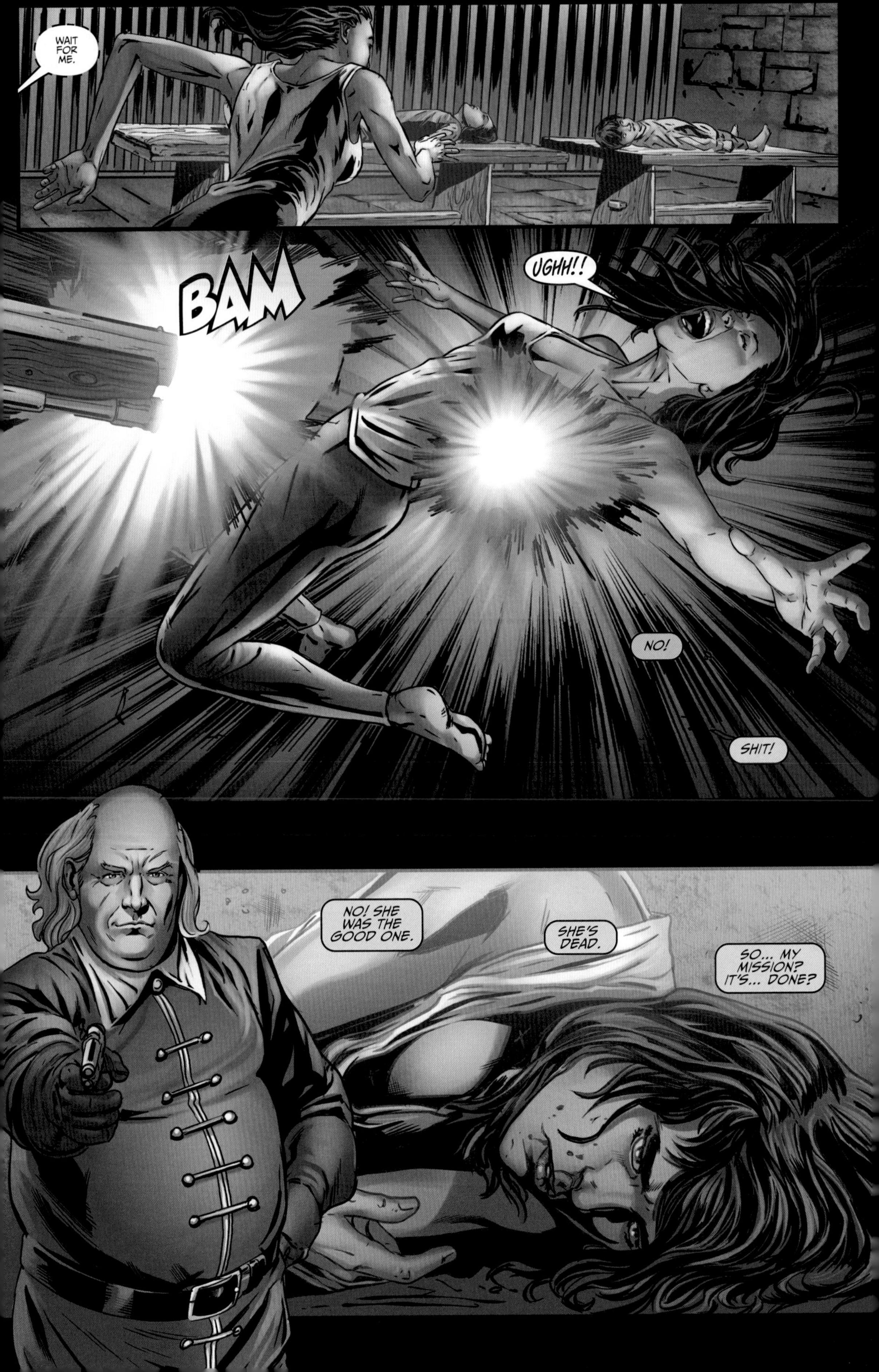
WAIT FOR ME.
BAM
UGHH!!
NO!
SHIT!
NO! SHE WAS THE GOOD ONE.
SHE'S DEAD.
SO... MY MISSION? IT'S... DONE?

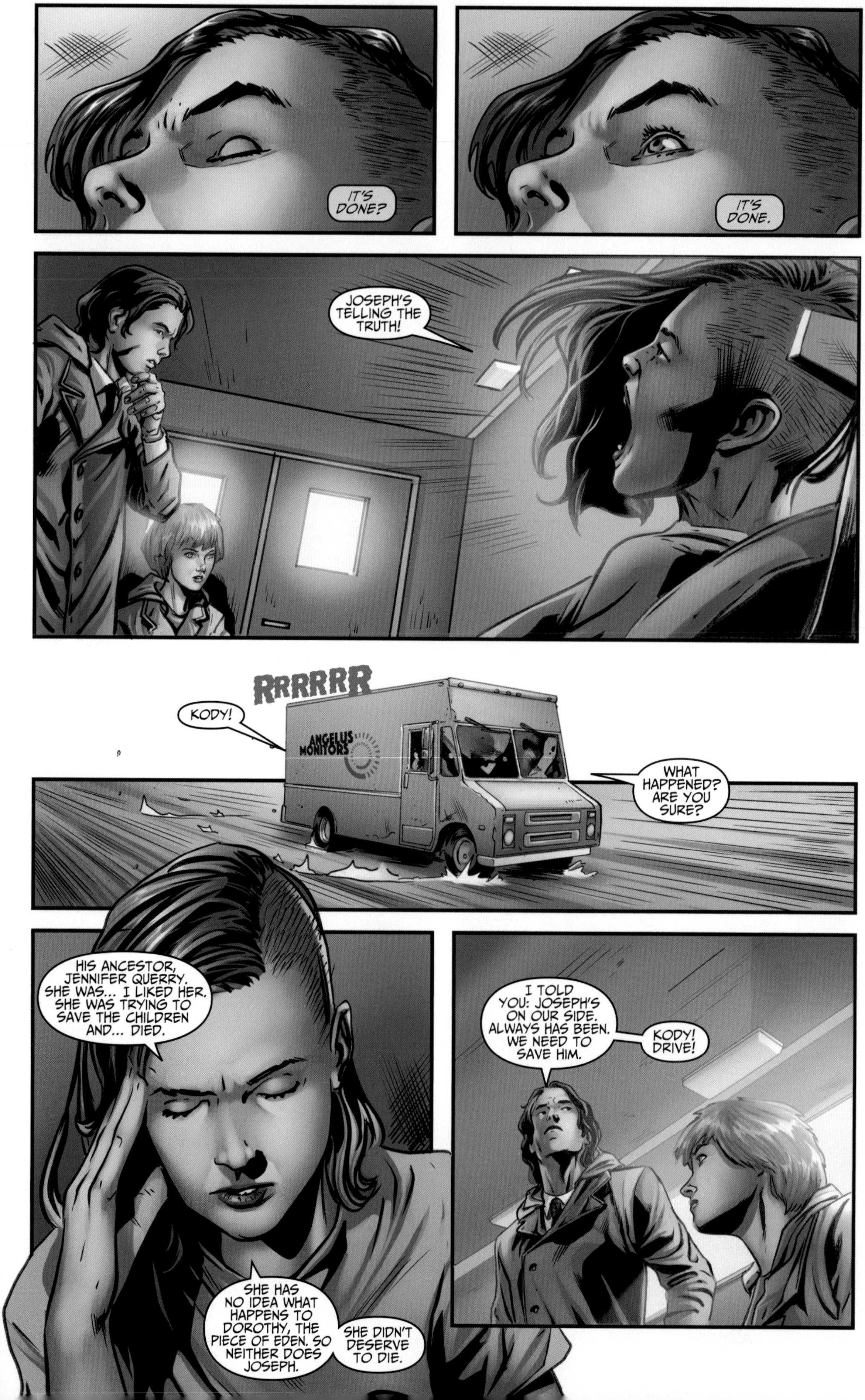
IT'S DONE?
IT'S DONE.
JOSEPH'S TELLING THE TRUTH!
RRRRRR
KODY!
ANGELUS MONITORS
WHAT HAPPENED? ARE YOU SURE?
HIS ANCESTOR, JENNIFER QUERRY. SHE WAS... I LIKED HER. SHE WAS TRYING TO SAVE THE CHILDREN AND... DIED.
SHE HAS NO IDEA WHAT HAPPENS TO DOROTHY, THE PIECE OF EDEN. SO NEITHER DOES JOSEPH.
SHE DIDN'T DESERVE TO DIE.
I TOLD YOU: JOSEPH'S ON OUR SIDE. ALWAYS HAS BEEN. WE NEED TO SAVE HIM.
KODY! DRIVE!

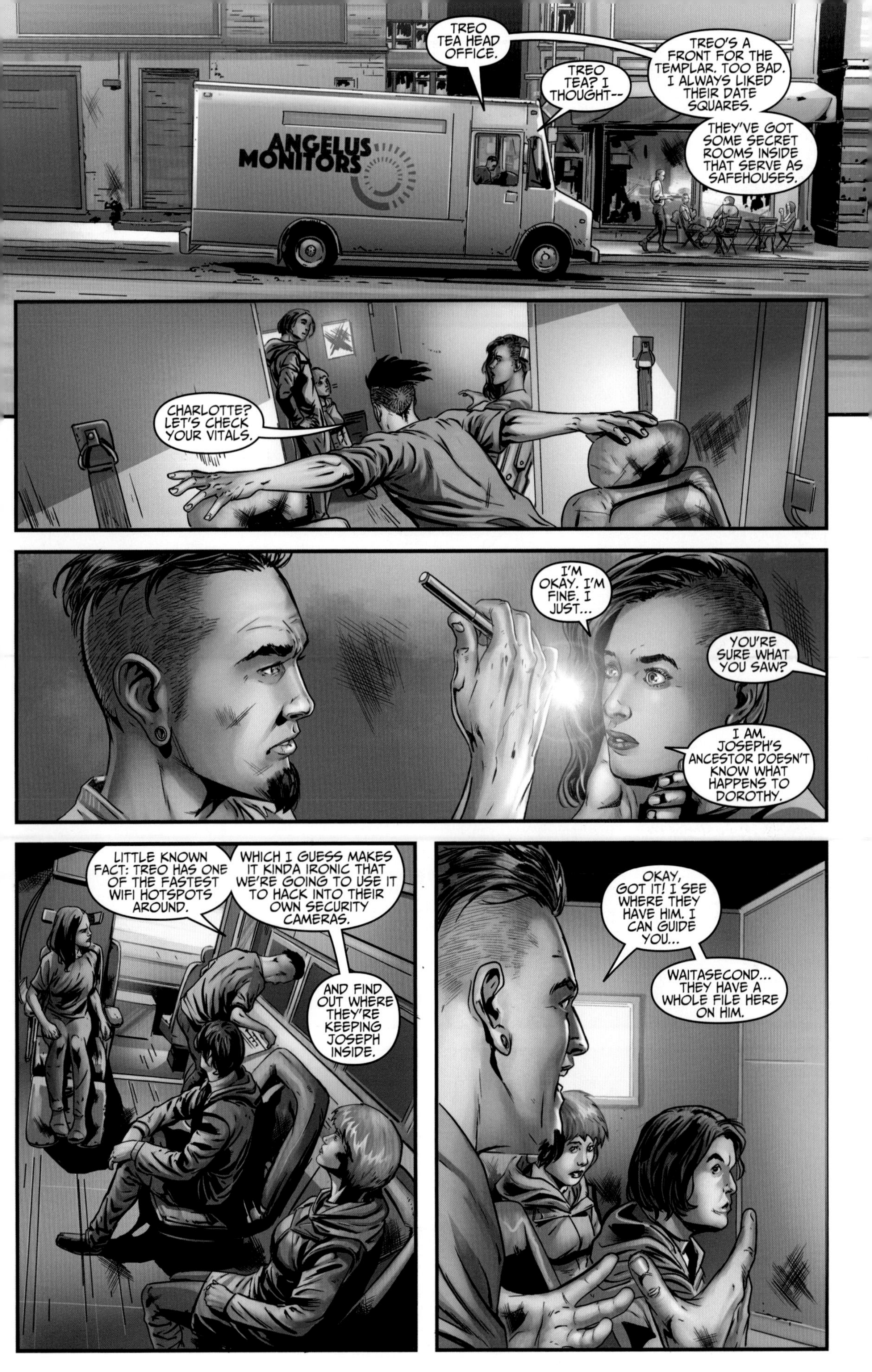
ANGELUS MONITORS
TREO TEA HEAD OFFICE.
TREO TEA? I THOUGHT--
TREO'S A FRONT FOR THE TEMPLAR. TOO BAD. I ALWAYS LIKED THEIR DATE SQUARES.
THEY'VE GOT SOME SECRET ROOMS INSIDE THAT SERVE AS SAFEHOUSES.
CHARLOTTE? LET'S CHECK YOUR VITALS.
I'M OKAY. I'M FINE. I JUST...
YOU'RE SURE WHAT YOU SAW?
I AM. JOSEPH'S ANCESTOR DOESN'T KNOW WHAT HAPPENS TO DOROTHY.
LITTLE KNOWN FACT: TREO HAS ONE OF THE FASTEST WIFI HOTSPOTS AROUND.
WHICH I GUESS MAKES IT KINDA IRONIC THAT WE'RE GOING TO USE IT TO HACK INTO THEIR OWN SECURITY CAMERAS.
AND FIND OUT WHERE THEY'RE KEEPING JOSEPH INSIDE.
OKAY, GOT IT! I SEE WHERE THEY HAVE HIM. I CAN GUIDE YOU...
WAITASECOND... THEY HAVE A WHOLE FILE HERE ON HIM.

XAVIER? YOU OVERSAW THE MISSION HE WENT AWOL FROM? EVERYONE DIED, BUT HIM... AND YOU...?

FINALLY THE TRUTH COMES OUT.

THIS HAS ALWAYS BEEN ABOUT YOUR FEARLESS LEADER MAKING UP FOR HIS PAST FAILURES.

SHUT UP, GALINA!

YOU ALMOST RISKED OUR LIVES BECAUSE OF LOYALTY TO HIM.

GALINA, JOSEPH'S ON OUR SIDE. WE NOW HAVE PROOF.

WHAT EXACTLY DID JOSEPH DO?

IT DOESN'T MATTER. YOU DID YOUR JOB. WE'RE GOOD TO GO.

WHAT DO YOU MEAN, DOESN'T MATTER? DID YOU EVEN NEED TO PUT ME IN THERE?

WE NEEDED YOU, OKAY? BUT I'M THE GODDAMNED LEADER OF THIS MISSION AND I DECIDE WHAT EVERYONE NEEDS TO KNOW.

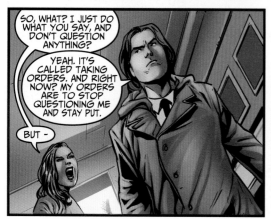

SO, WHAT? I JUST DO WHAT YOU SAY, AND DON'T QUESTION ANYTHING?

YEAH. IT'S CALLED TAKING ORDERS. AND RIGHT NOW? MY ORDERS ARE TO STOP QUESTIONING ME AND STAY PUT.

BUT –

STOP!

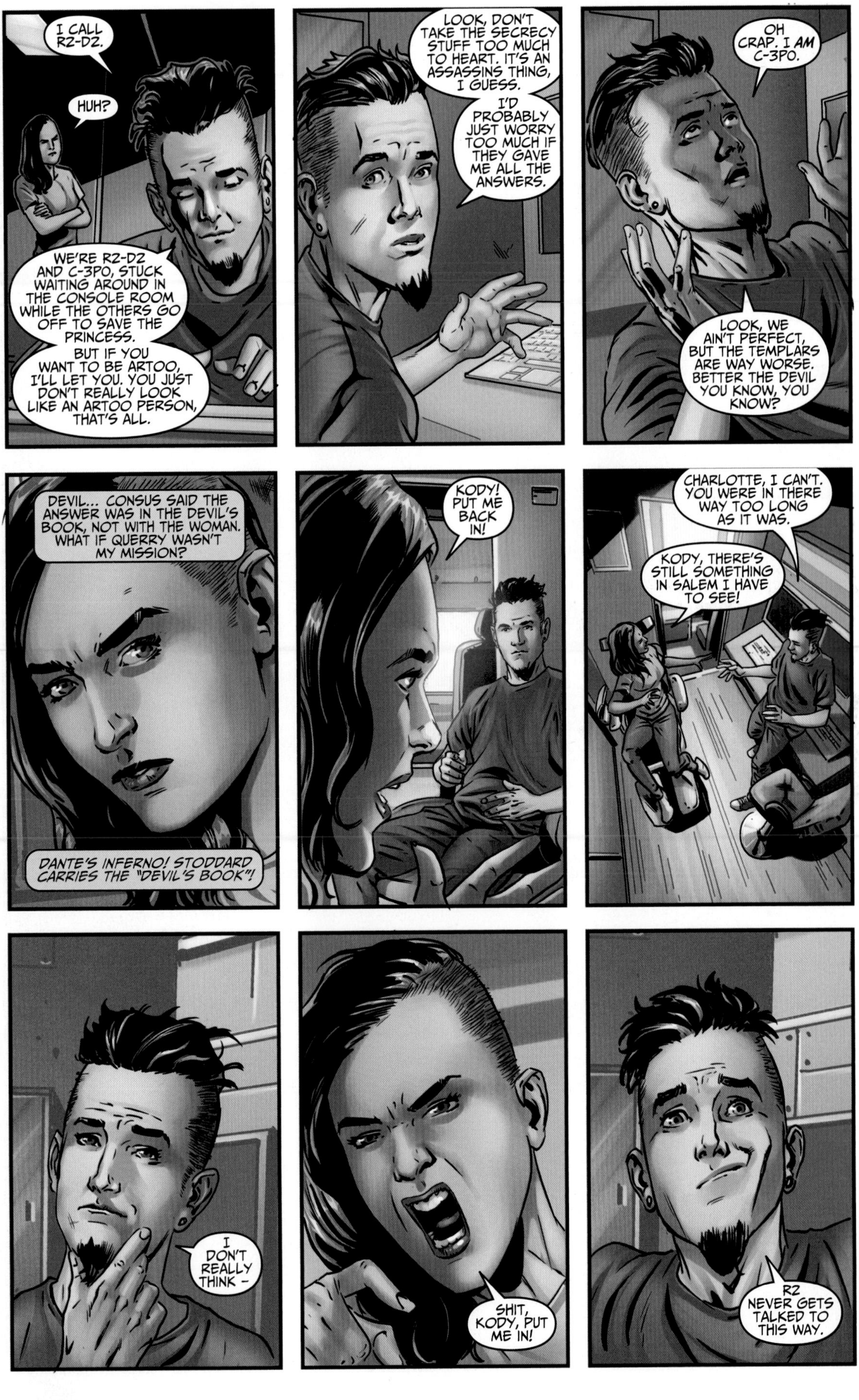
I CALL R2-D2.
HUH?
WE'RE R2-D2 AND C-3PO, STUCK WAITING AROUND IN THE CONSOLE ROOM WHILE THE OTHERS GO OFF TO SAVE THE PRINCESS.
BUT IF YOU WANT TO BE ARTOO, I'LL LET YOU. YOU JUST DON'T REALLY LOOK LIKE AN ARTOO PERSON, THAT'S ALL.
LOOK, DON'T TAKE THE SECRECY STUFF TOO MUCH TO HEART. IT'S AN ASSASSINS THING, I GUESS.
I'D PROBABLY JUST WORRY TOO MUCH IF THEY GAVE ME ALL THE ANSWERS.
OH CRAP. I *AM* C-3PO.
LOOK, WE AIN'T PERFECT, BUT THE TEMPLARS ARE WAY WORSE. BETTER THE DEVIL YOU KNOW, YOU KNOW?
DEVIL... CONSUS SAID THE ANSWER WAS IN THE DEVIL'S BOOK, NOT WITH THE WOMAN. WHAT IF QUERRY WASN'T MY MISSION?
DANTE'S INFERNO! STODDARD CARRIES THE "DEVIL'S BOOK"!
KODY! PUT ME BACK IN!
CHARLOTTE, I CAN'T. YOU WERE IN THERE WAY TOO LONG AS IT WAS.
KODY, THERE'S STILL SOMETHING IN SALEM I HAVE TO SEE!
I DON'T REALLY THINK –
SHIT, KODY, PUT ME IN!
R2 NEVER GETS TALKED TO THIS WAY.

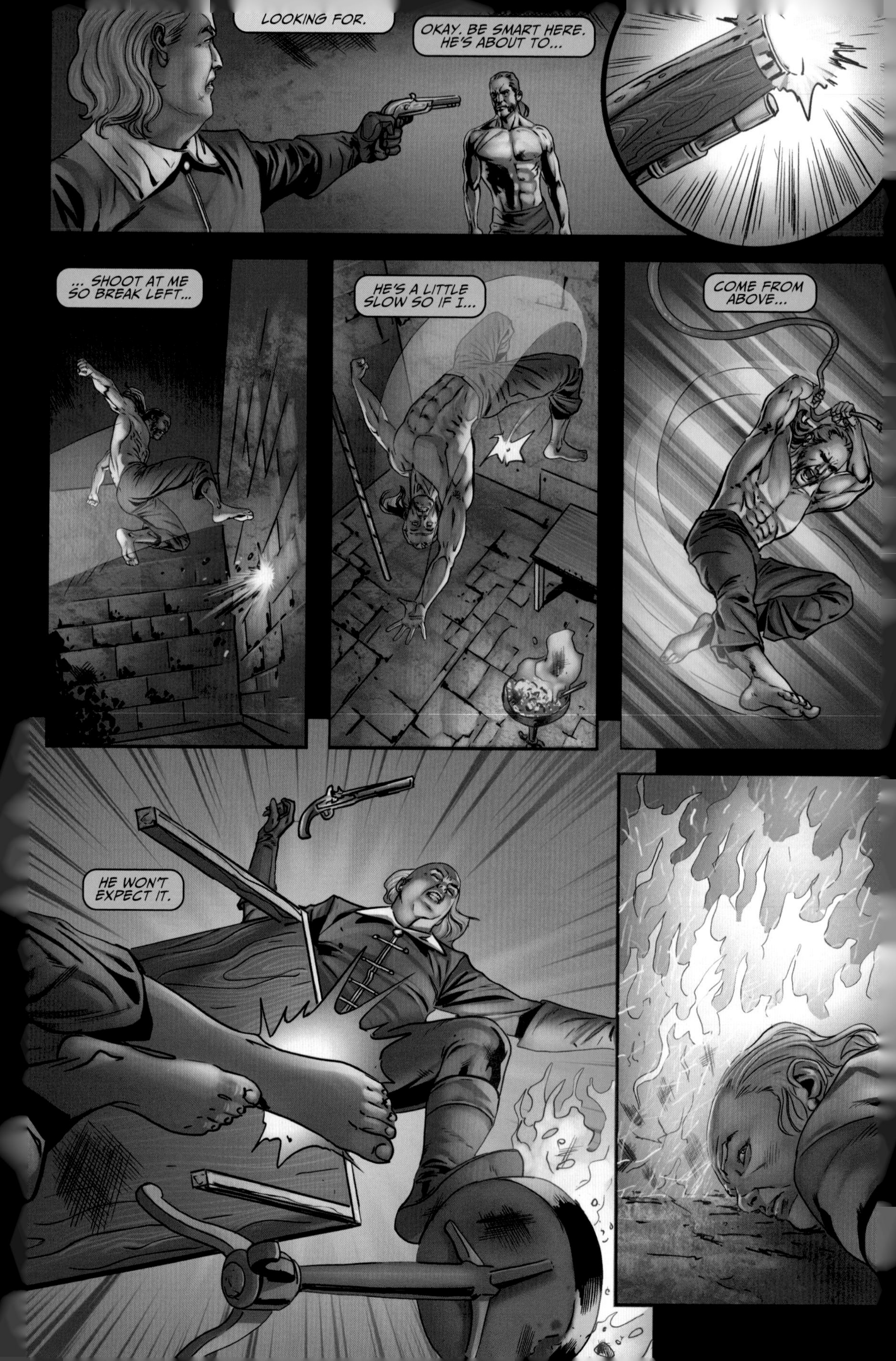
LOOKING FOR.
OKAY. BE SMART HERE. HE'S ABOUT TO...
... SHOOT AT ME SO BREAK LEFT...
HE'S A LITTLE SLOW SO IF I...
COME FROM ABOVE...
HE WON'T EXPECT IT.

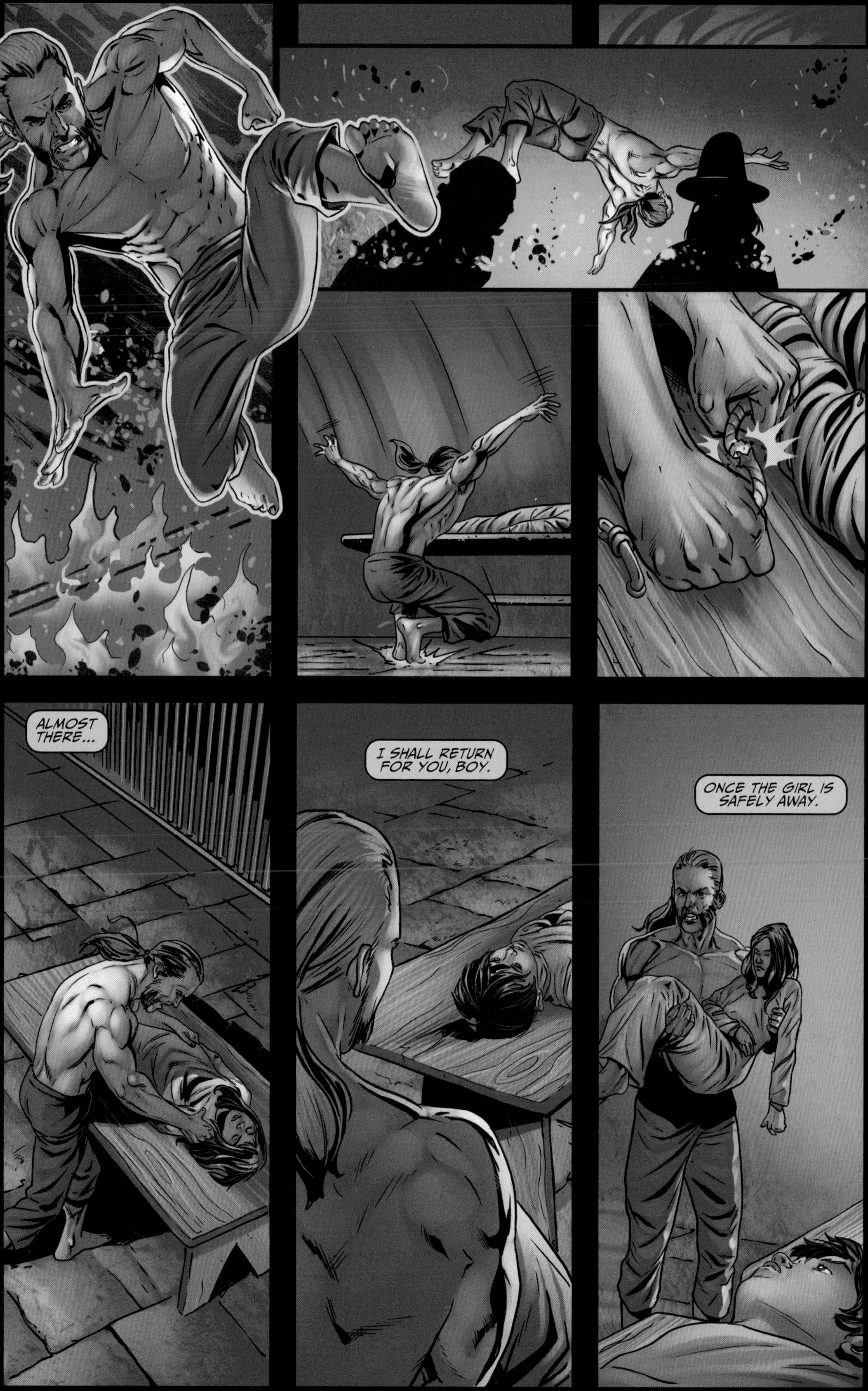
ALMOST THERE...
I SHALL RETURN FOR YOU, BOY.
ONCE THE GIRL IS SAFELY AWAY.

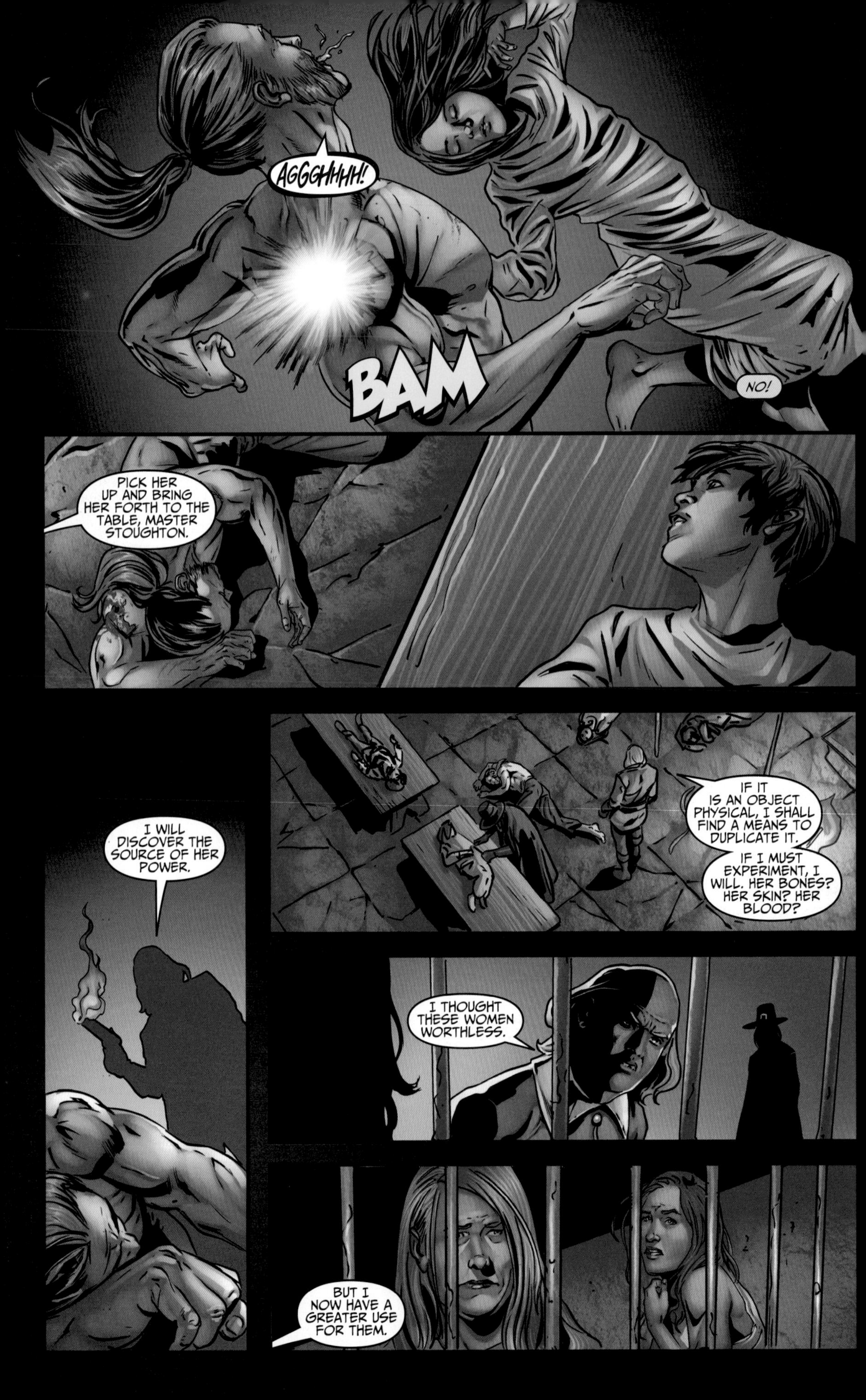
AGGGHHHH!
BAM
NO!
PICK HER UP AND BRING HER FORTH TO THE TABLE, MASTER STOUGHTON.
IF IT IS AN OBJECT PHYSICAL, I SHALL FIND A MEANS TO DUPLICATE IT.
IF I MUST EXPERIMENT, I WILL. HER BONES? HER SKIN? HER BLOOD?
I WILL DISCOVER THE SOURCE OF HER POWER.
I THOUGHT THESE WOMEN WORTHLESS.
BUT I NOW HAVE A GREATER USE FOR THEM.

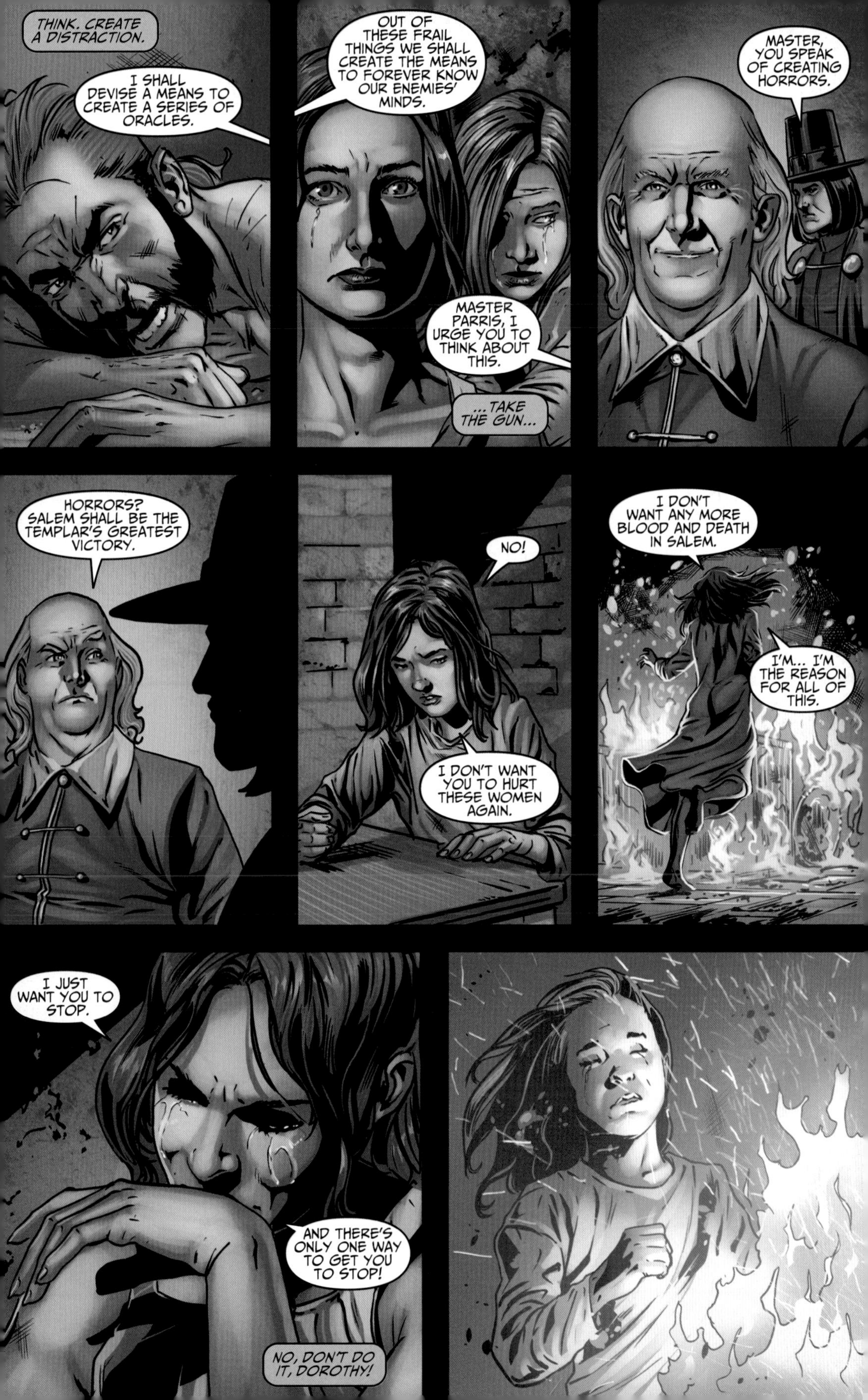
THINK. CREATE A DISTRACTION.
I SHALL DEVISE A MEANS TO CREATE A SERIES OF ORACLES.
OUT OF THESE FRAIL THINGS WE SHALL CREATE THE MEANS TO FOREVER KNOW OUR ENEMIES' MINDS.
MASTER PARRIS, I URGE YOU TO THINK ABOUT THIS.
...TAKE THE GUN...
MASTER, YOU SPEAK OF CREATING HORRORS.
HORRORS? SALEM SHALL BE THE TEMPLAR'S GREATEST VICTORY.
NO!
I DON'T WANT YOU TO HURT THESE WOMEN AGAIN.
I DON'T WANT ANY MORE BLOOD AND DEATH IN SALEM.
I'M... I'M THE REASON FOR ALL OF THIS.
I JUST WANT YOU TO STOP.
AND THERE'S ONLY ONE WAY TO GET YOU TO STOP!
NO, DON'T DO IT, DOROTHY!

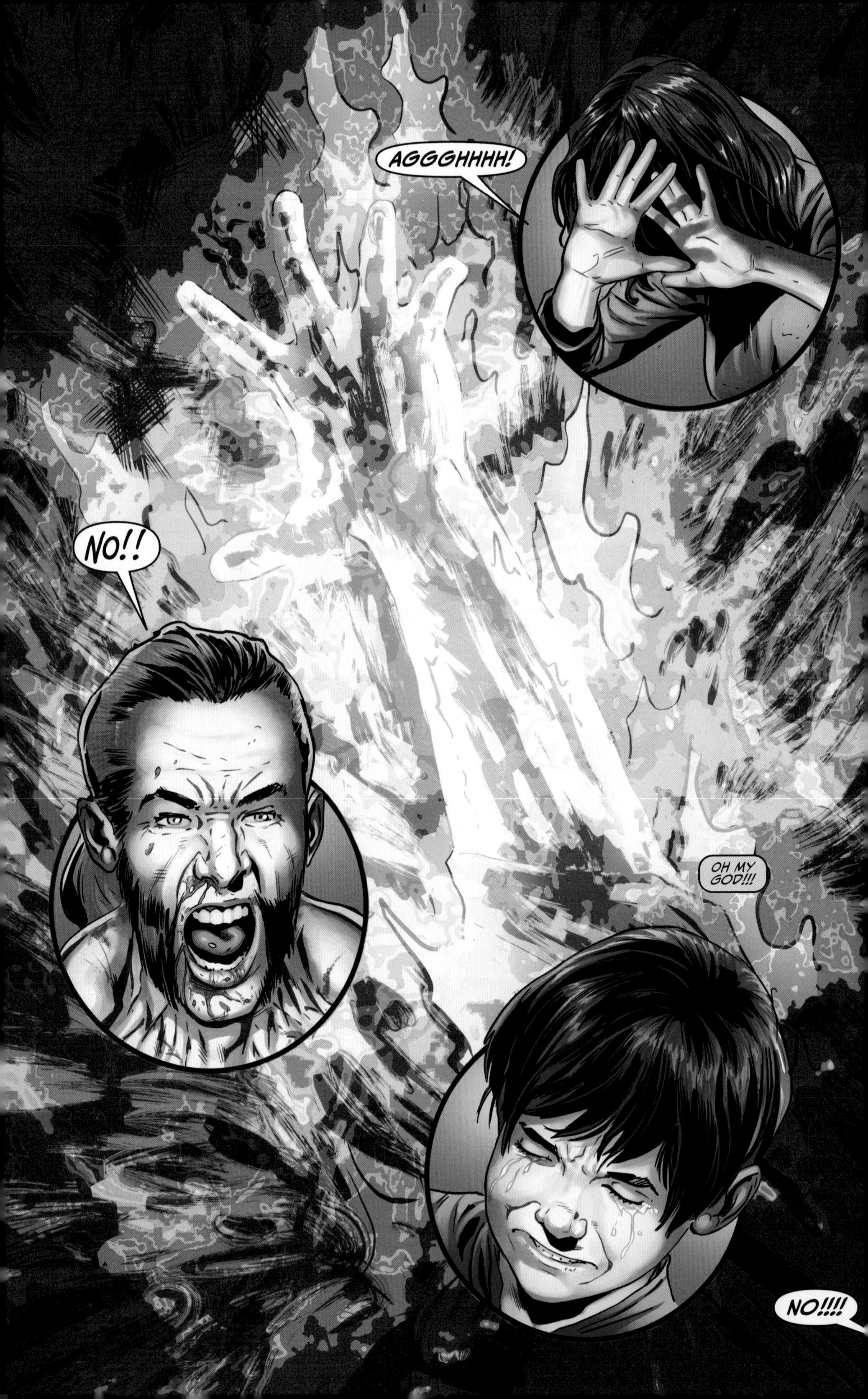
AGGGHHHH!
NO!!
OH MY GOD!!!
NO!!!!

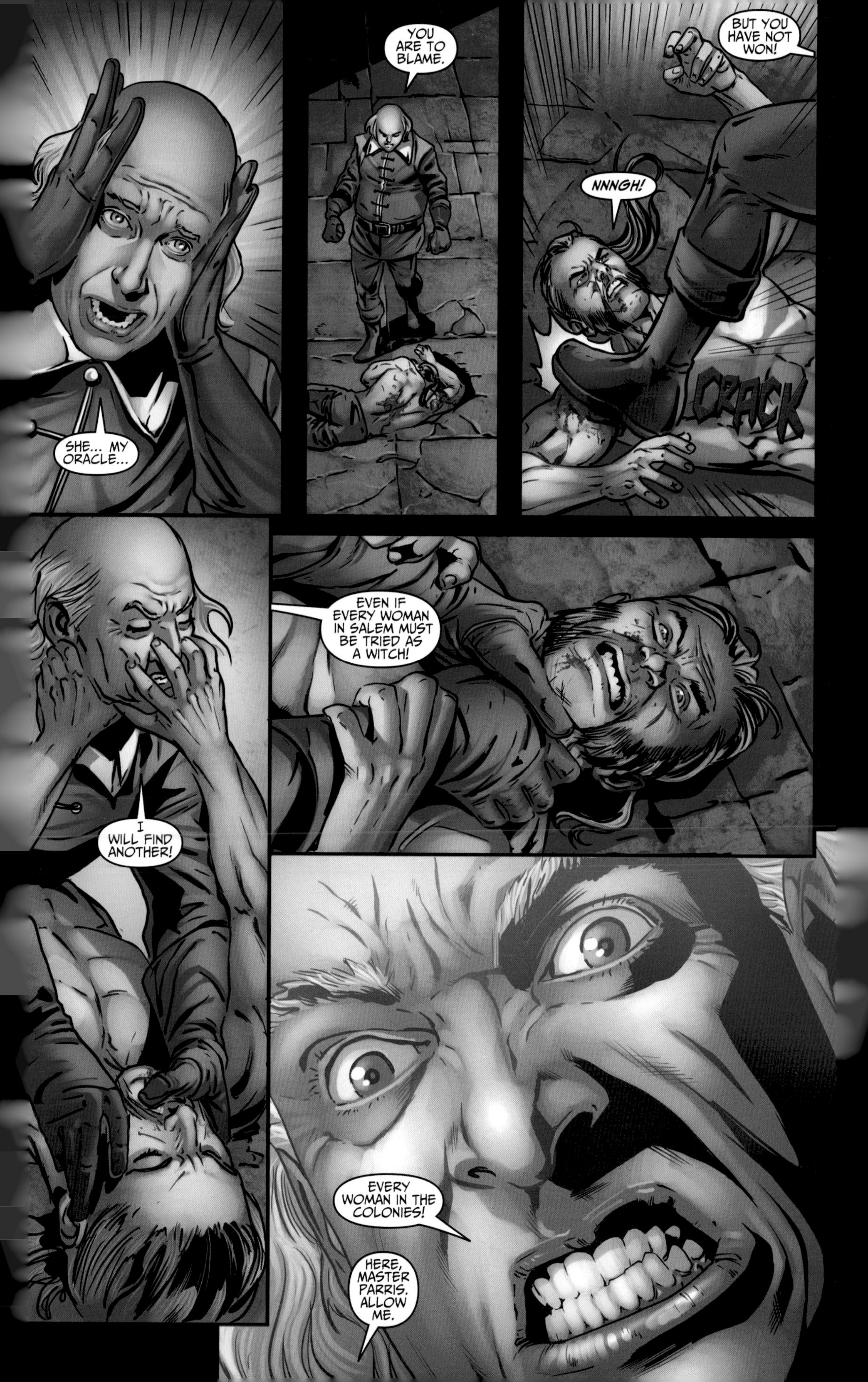
SHE... MY ORACLE...
YOU ARE TO BLAME.
BUT YOU HAVE NOT WON!
NNNGH!
CRACK
I WILL FIND ANOTHER!
EVEN IF EVERY WOMAN IN SALEM MUST BE TRIED AS A WITCH!
EVERY WOMAN IN THE COLONIES!
HERE, MASTER PARRIS. ALLOW ME.

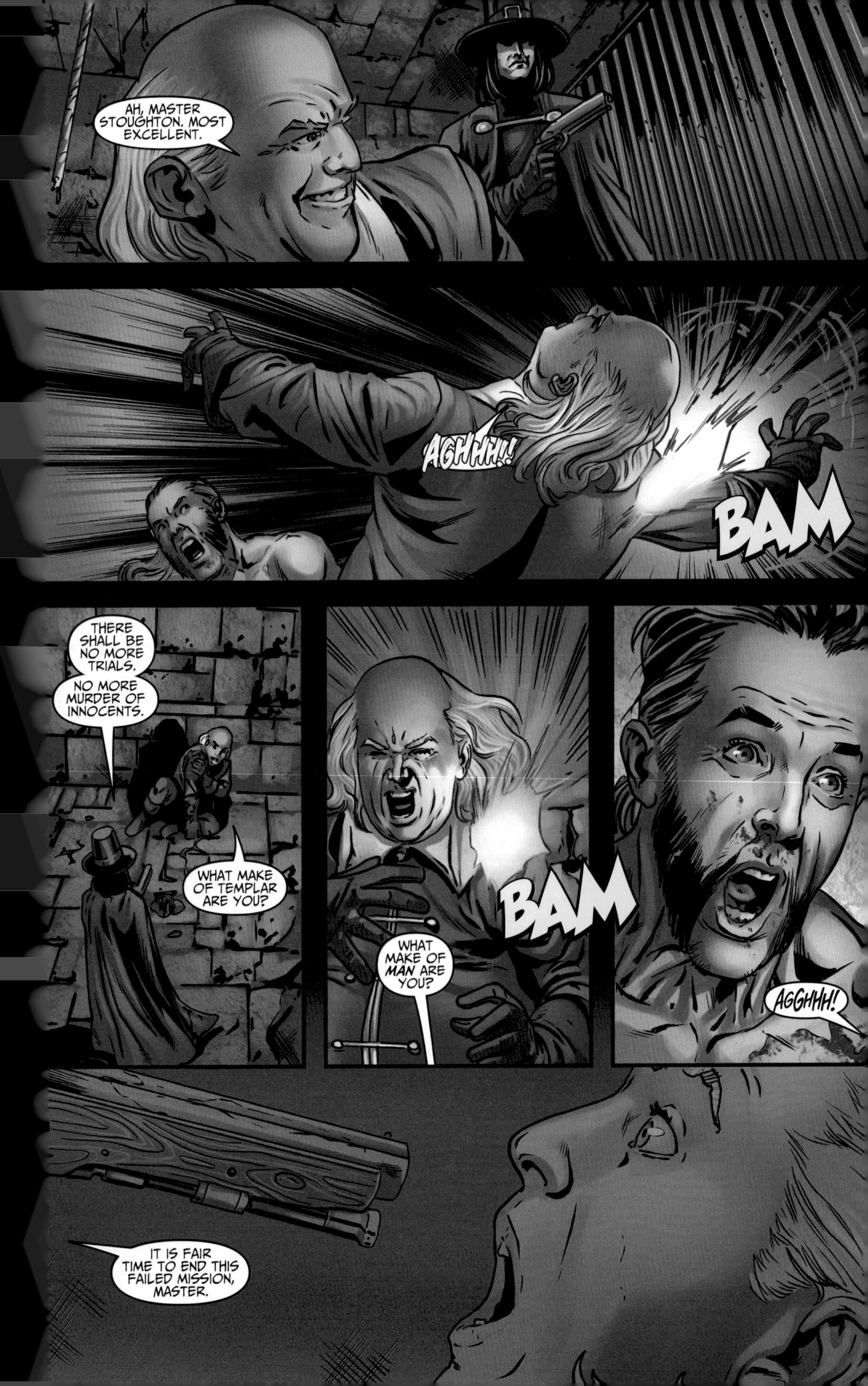
AH, MASTER STOUGHTON. MOST EXCELLENT.
AGHHH!!
BAM
THERE SHALL BE NO MORE TRIALS.
NO MORE MURDER OF INNOCENTS.
WHAT MAKE OF TEMPLAR ARE YOU?
BAM
WHAT MAKE OF MAN ARE YOU?
AGGHHH!
IT IS FAIR TIME TO END THIS FAILED MISSION, MASTER.

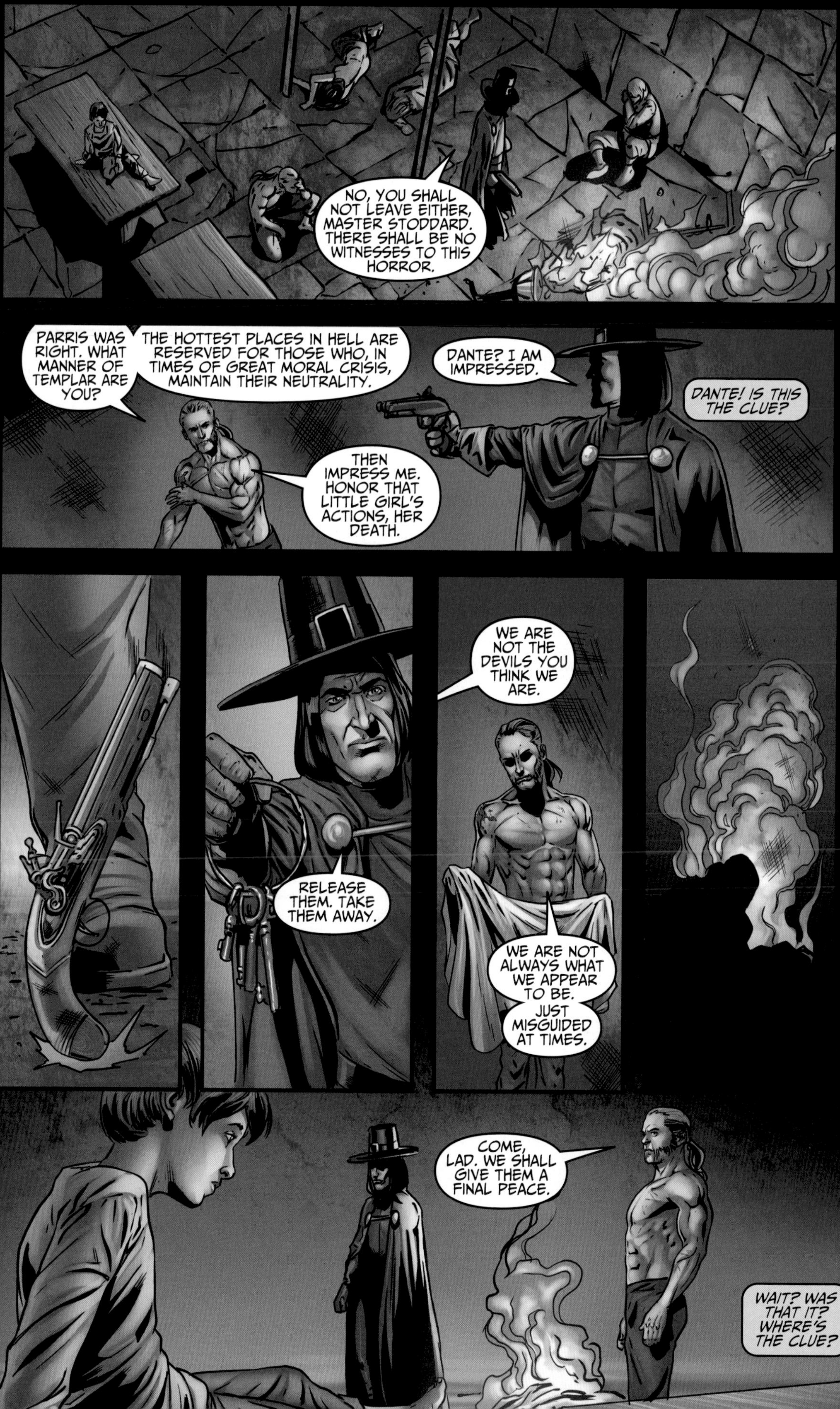
NO, YOU SHALL NOT LEAVE EITHER, MASTER STODDARD. THERE SHALL BE NO WITNESSES TO THIS HORROR.
PARRIS WAS RIGHT. WHAT MANNER OF TEMPLAR ARE YOU?
THE HOTTEST PLACES IN HELL ARE RESERVED FOR THOSE WHO, IN TIMES OF GREAT MORAL CRISIS, MAINTAIN THEIR NEUTRALITY.
DANTE? I AM IMPRESSED.
DANTE! IS THIS THE CLUE?
THEN IMPRESS ME. HONOR THAT LITTLE GIRL'S ACTIONS, HER DEATH.
RELEASE THEM. TAKE THEM AWAY.
WE ARE NOT THE DEVILS YOU THINK WE ARE.
WE ARE NOT ALWAYS WHAT WE APPEAR TO BE. JUST MISGUIDED AT TIMES.
COME, LAD. WE SHALL GIVE THEM A FINAL PEACE.
WAIT? WAS THAT IT? WHERE'S THE CLUE?

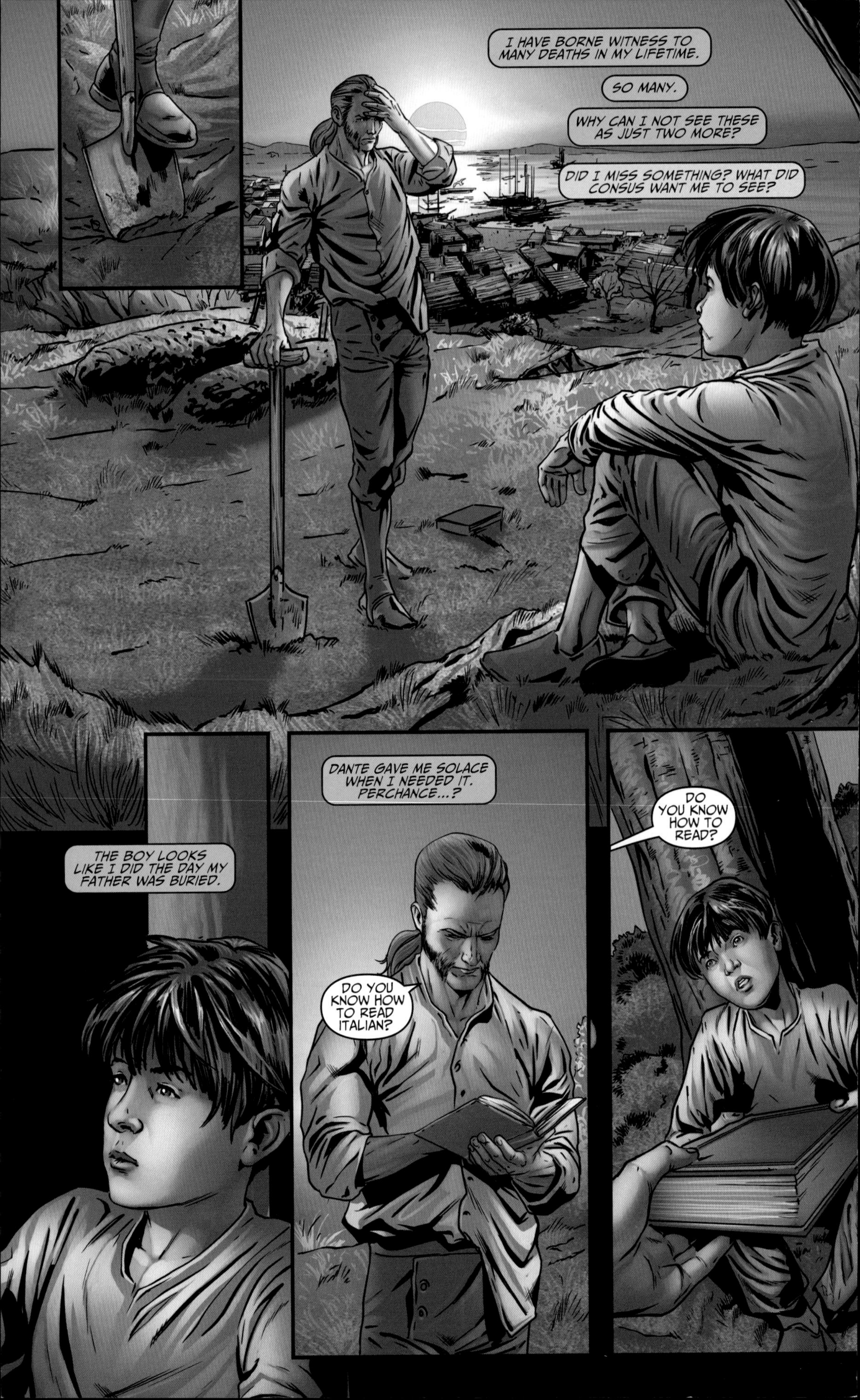
I HAVE BORNE WITNESS TO MANY DEATHS IN MY LIFETIME.
SO MANY.
WHY CAN I NOT SEE THESE AS JUST TWO MORE?
DID I MISS SOMETHING? WHAT DID CONSUS WANT ME TO SEE?
THE BOY LOOKS LIKE I DID THE DAY MY FATHER WAS BURIED.
DANTE GAVE ME SOLACE WHEN I NEEDED IT. PERCHANCE...?
DO YOU KNOW HOW TO READ ITALIAN?
DO YOU KNOW HOW TO READ?

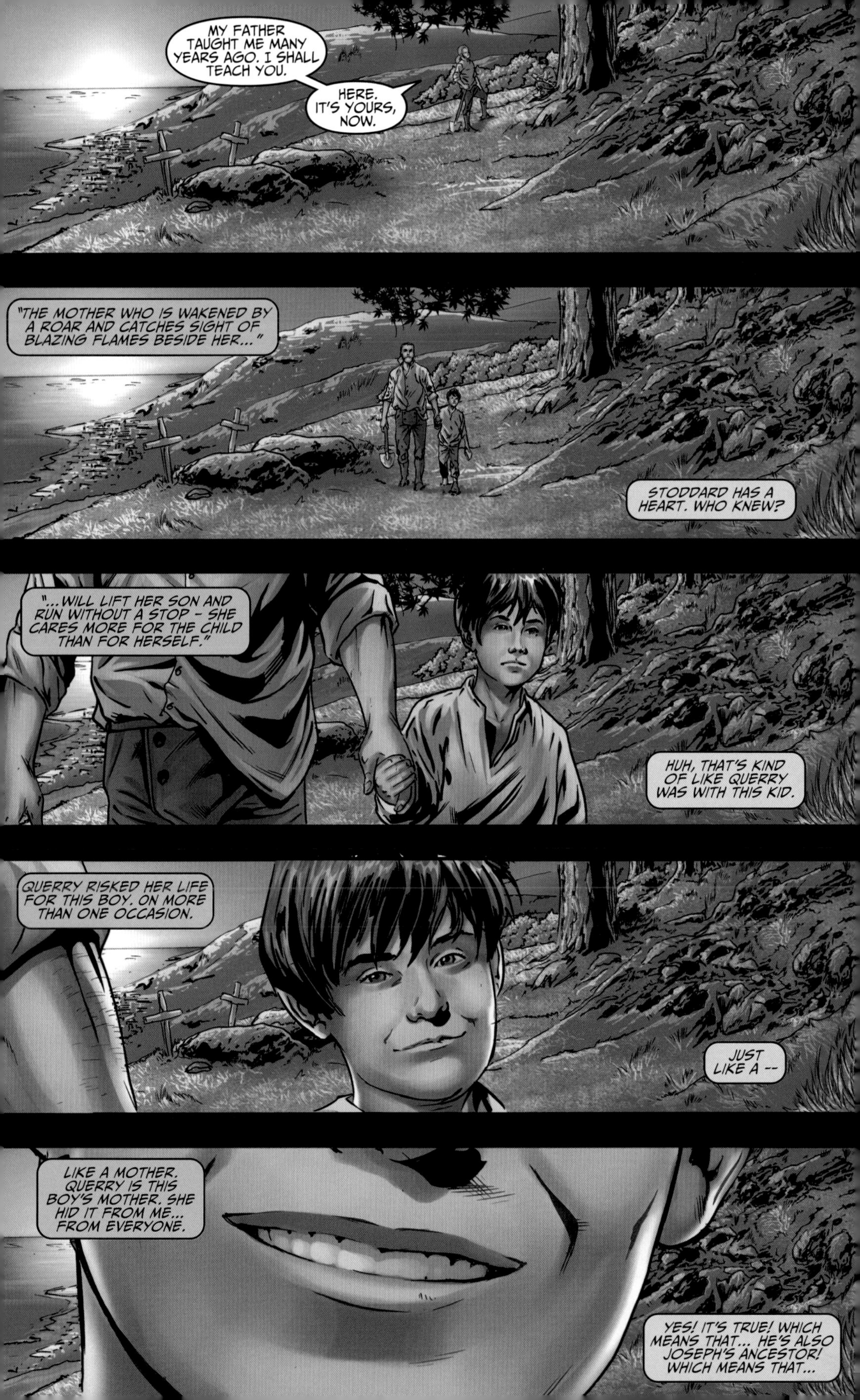
MY FATHER TAUGHT ME MANY YEARS AGO. I SHALL TEACH YOU.
HERE. IT'S YOURS, NOW.
"THE MOTHER WHO IS WAKENED BY A ROAR AND CATCHES SIGHT OF BLAZING FLAMES BESIDE HER..."
STODDARD HAS A HEART. WHO KNEW?
"...WILL LIFT HER SON AND RUN WITHOUT A STOP - SHE CARES MORE FOR THE CHILD THAN FOR HERSELF."
HUH, THAT'S KIND OF LIKE QUERRY WAS WITH THIS KID.
QUERRY RISKED HER LIFE FOR THIS BOY. ON MORE THAN ONE OCCASION.
JUST LIKE A --
LIKE A MOTHER. QUERRY IS THIS BOY'S MOTHER. SHE HID IT FROM ME... FROM EVERYONE.
YES! IT'S TRUE! WHICH MEANS THAT... HE'S ALSO JOSEPH'S ANCESTOR! WHICH MEANS THAT...

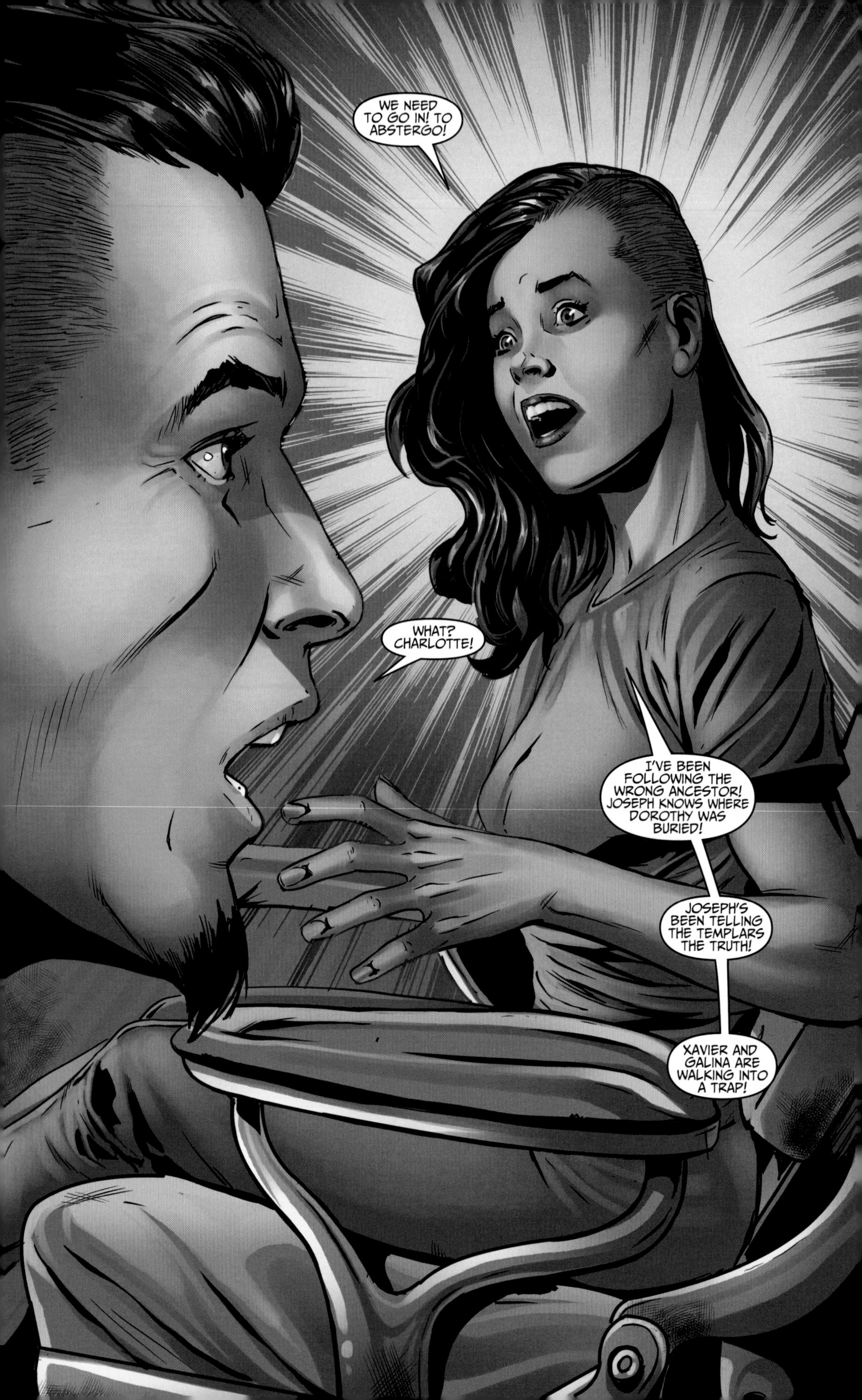
WE NEED TO GO IN! TO ABSTERGO!
WHAT? CHARLOTTE!
I'VE BEEN FOLLOWING THE WRONG ANCESTOR! JOSEPH KNOWS WHERE DOROTHY WAS BURIED!
JOSEPH'S BEEN TELLING THE TEMPLARS THE TRUTH!
XAVIER AND GALINA ARE WALKING INTO A TRAP!

CHAPTER
FIVE

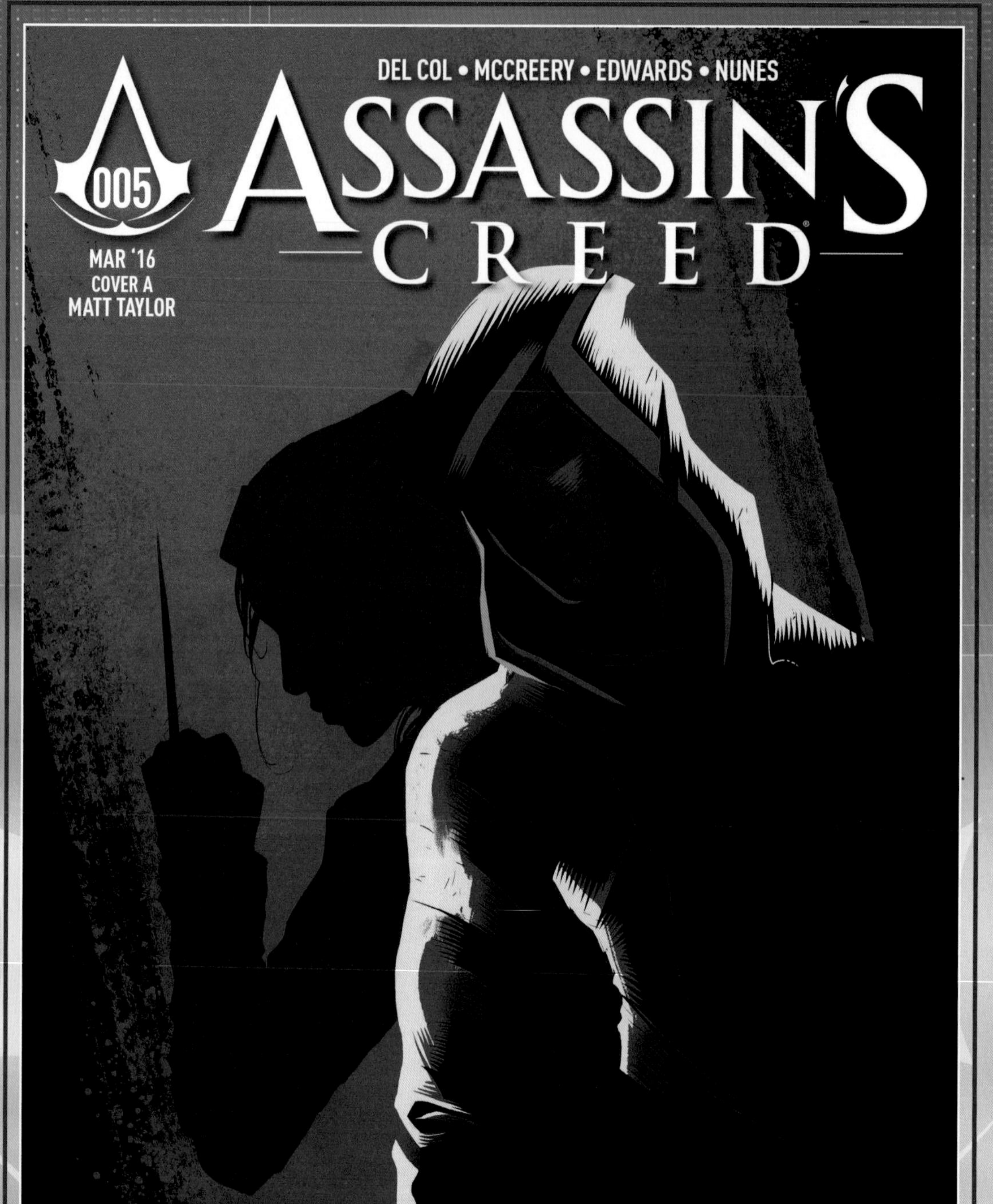
DEL COL • MCCREERY • EDWARDS • NUNES
ASSASSIN'S
CREED
005
MAR '16
COVER A
MATT TAYLOR
UBISOFT
TITAN
COMICS

COVER A - ISSUE 5
MATT TAYLOR

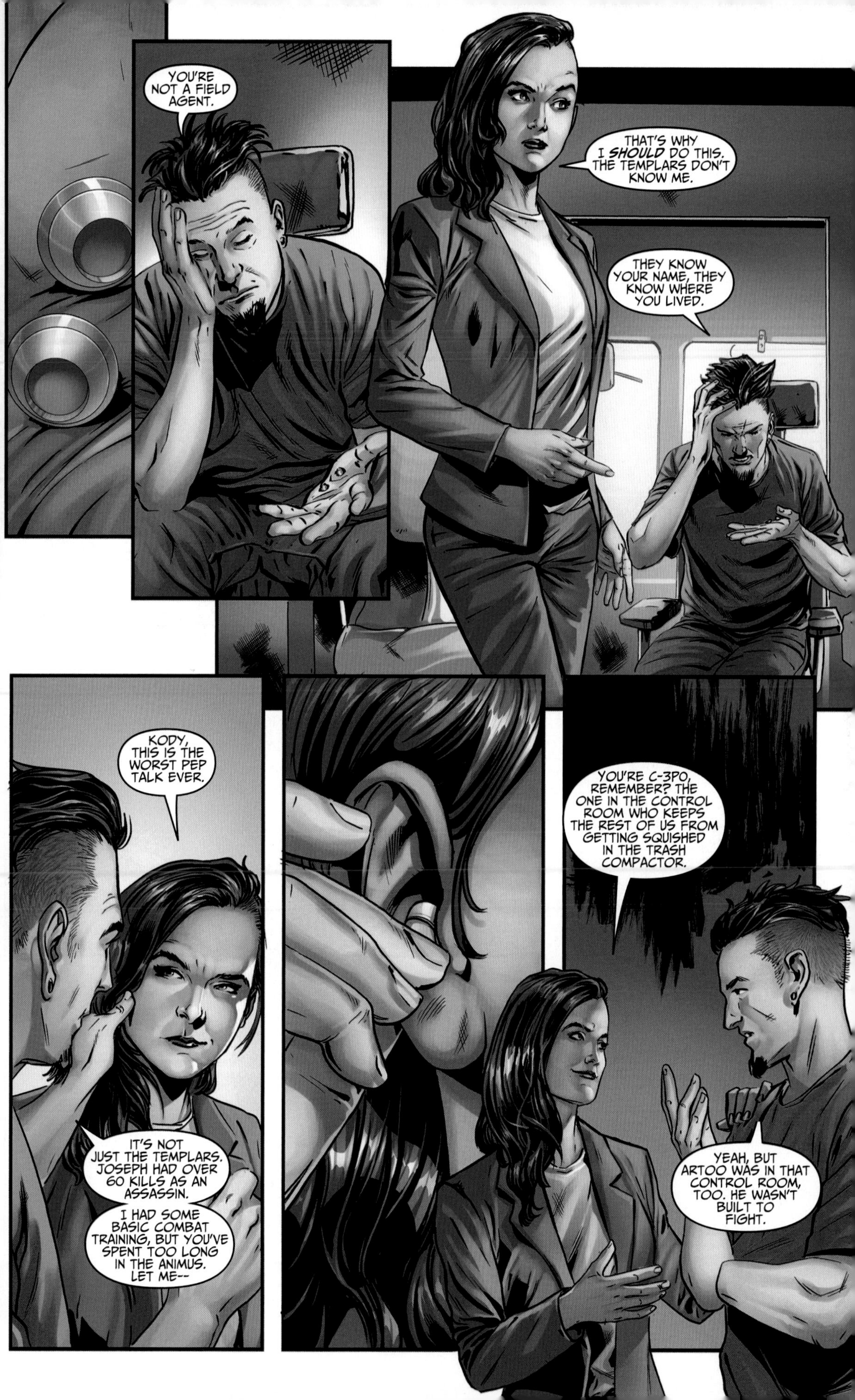
YOU'RE NOT A FIELD AGENT.
THAT'S WHY I *SHOULD* DO THIS. THE TEMPLARS DON'T KNOW ME.
THEY KNOW YOUR NAME, THEY KNOW WHERE YOU LIVED.
KODY, THIS IS THE WORST PEP TALK EVER.
IT'S NOT JUST THE TEMPLARS. JOSEPH HAD OVER 60 KILLS AS AN ASSASSIN.
I HAD SOME BASIC COMBAT TRAINING, BUT YOU'VE SPENT TOO LONG IN THE ANIMUS. LET ME--
YOU'RE C-3PO, REMEMBER? THE ONE IN THE CONTROL ROOM WHO KEEPS THE REST OF US FROM GETTING SQUISHED IN THE TRASH COMPACTOR.
YEAH, BUT ARTOO WAS IN THAT CONTROL ROOM, TOO. HE WASN'T BUILT TO FIGHT.

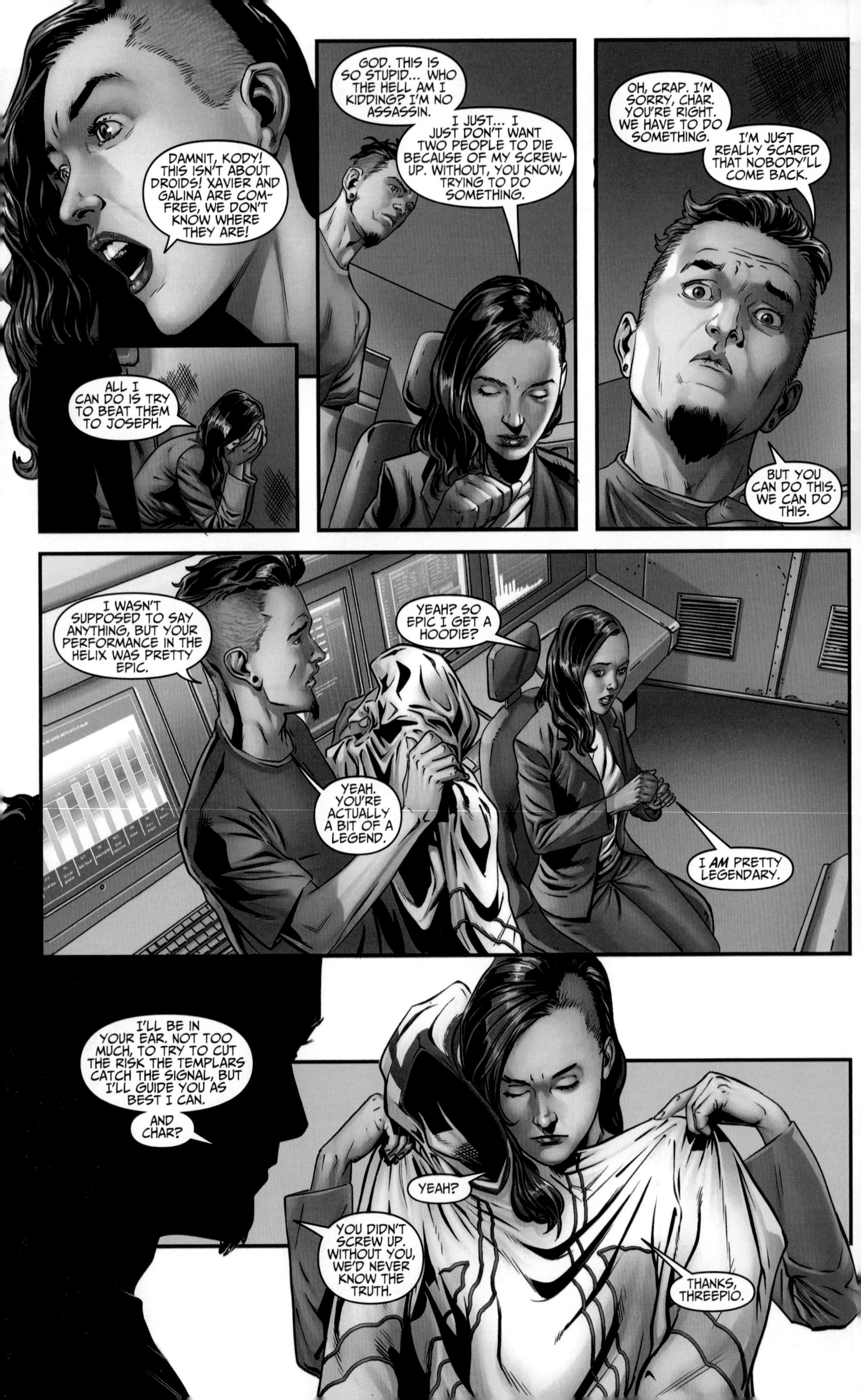
DAMNIT, KODY! THIS ISN'T ABOUT DROIDS! XAVIER AND GALINA ARE COM-FREE, WE DON'T KNOW WHERE THEY ARE!
ALL I CAN DO IS TRY TO BEAT THEM TO JOSEPH.
GOD. THIS IS SO STUPID... WHO THE HELL AM I KIDDING? I'M NO ASSASSIN.
I JUST... I JUST DON'T WANT TWO PEOPLE TO DIE BECAUSE OF MY SCREW-UP. WITHOUT, YOU KNOW, TRYING TO DO SOMETHING.
OH, CRAP. I'M SORRY, CHAR. YOU'RE RIGHT. WE HAVE TO DO SOMETHING.
I'M JUST REALLY SCARED THAT NOBODY'LL COME BACK.
BUT YOU CAN DO THIS. WE CAN DO THIS.
I WASN'T SUPPOSED TO SAY ANYTHING, BUT YOUR PERFORMANCE IN THE HELIX WAS PRETTY EPIC.
YEAH? SO EPIC I GET A HOODIE?
YEAH. YOU'RE ACTUALLY A BIT OF A LEGEND.
I *AM* PRETTY LEGENDARY.
I'LL BE IN YOUR EAR. NOT TOO MUCH, TO TRY TO CUT THE RISK THE TEMPLARS CATCH THE SIGNAL, BUT I'LL GUIDE YOU AS BEST I CAN.
AND CHAR?
YEAH?
YOU DIDN'T SCREW UP. WITHOUT YOU, WE'D NEVER KNOW THE TRUTH.
THANKS, THREEPIO.

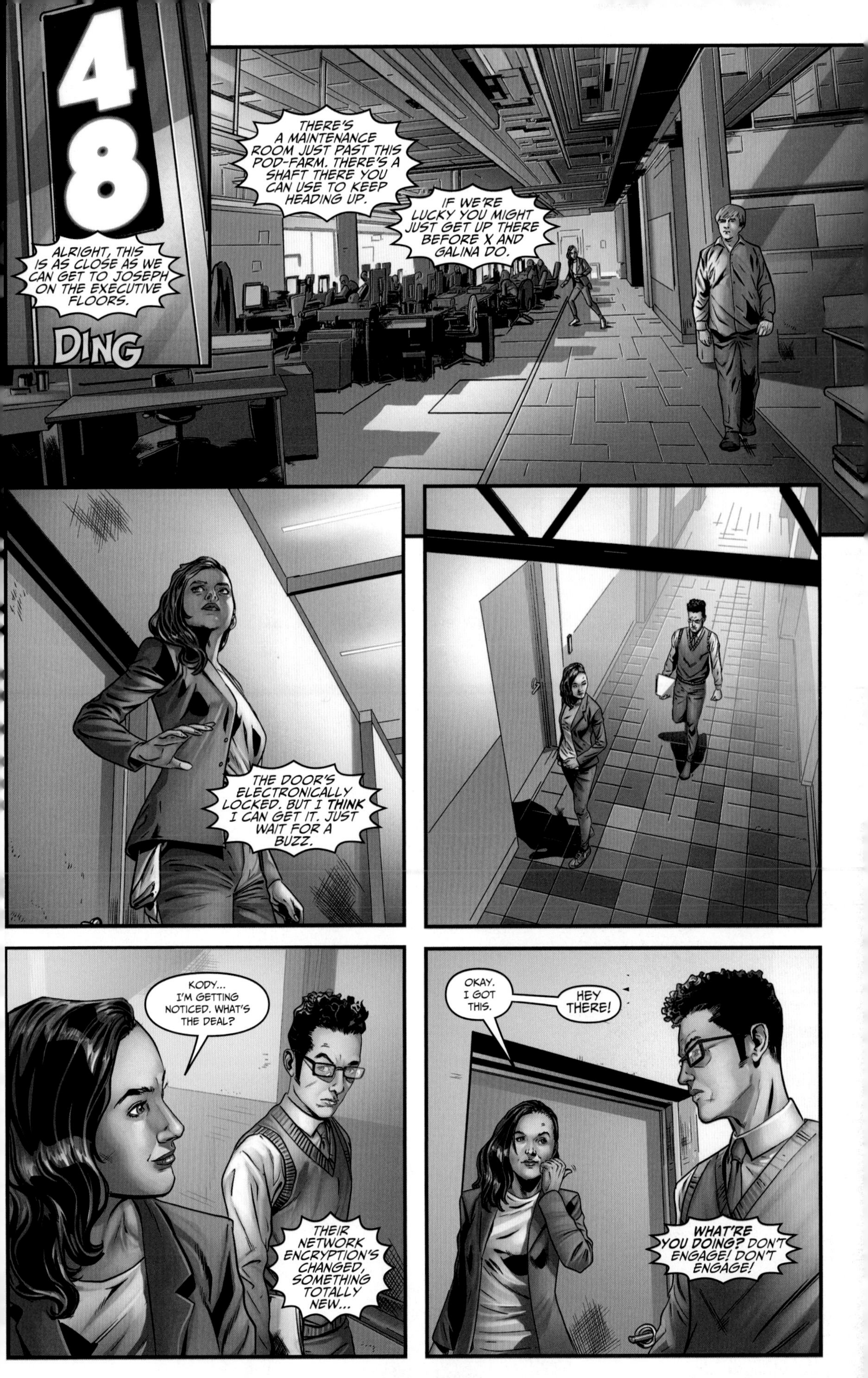
48
ALRIGHT, THIS IS AS CLOSE AS WE CAN GET TO JOSEPH ON THE EXECUTIVE FLOORS.
DING
THERE'S A MAINTENANCE ROOM JUST PAST THIS POD-FARM. THERE'S A SHAFT THERE YOU CAN USE TO KEEP HEADING UP.
IF WE'RE LUCKY YOU MIGHT JUST GET UP THERE BEFORE X AND GALINA DO.
THE DOOR'S ELECTRONICALLY LOCKED. BUT I THINK I CAN GET IT. JUST WAIT FOR A BUZZ.
KODY... I'M GETTING NOTICED. WHAT'S THE DEAL?
THEIR NETWORK ENCRYPTION'S CHANGED, SOMETHING TOTALLY NEW...
OKAY. I GOT THIS.
HEY THERE!
WHAT'RE YOU DOING? DON'T ENGAGE! DON'T ENGAGE!

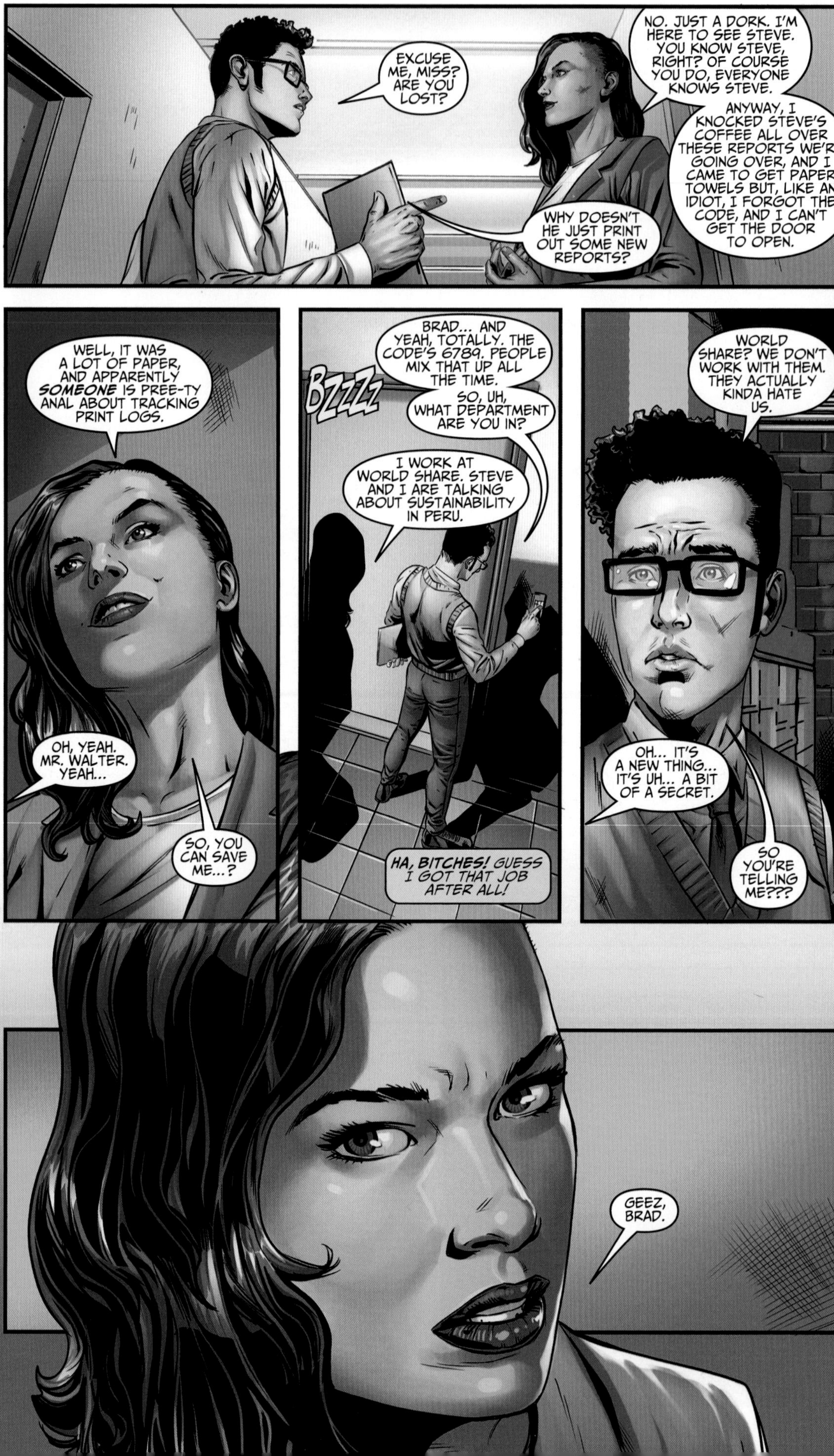
EXCUSE ME, MISS? ARE YOU LOST?
NO. JUST A DORK. I'M HERE TO SEE STEVE. YOU KNOW STEVE, RIGHT? OF COURSE YOU DO, EVERYONE KNOWS STEVE.
ANYWAY, I KNOCKED STEVE'S COFFEE ALL OVER THESE REPORTS WE'RE GOING OVER, AND I CAME TO GET PAPER TOWELS BUT, LIKE AN IDIOT, I FORGOT THE CODE, AND I CAN'T GET THE DOOR TO OPEN.
WHY DOESN'T HE JUST PRINT OUT SOME NEW REPORTS?
WELL, IT WAS A LOT OF PAPER, AND APPARENTLY *SOMEONE* IS PREE-TY ANAL ABOUT TRACKING PRINT LOGS.
OH, YEAH. MR. WALTER. YEAH...
SO, YOU CAN SAVE ME...?
BZZZZ
BRAD... AND YEAH, TOTALLY. THE CODE'S 6789. PEOPLE MIX THAT UP ALL THE TIME.
SO, UH, WHAT DEPARTMENT ARE YOU IN?
I WORK AT WORLD SHARE. STEVE AND I ARE TALKING ABOUT SUSTAINABILITY IN PERU.
HA, BITCHES! GUESS I GOT THAT JOB AFTER ALL!
WORLD SHARE? WE DON'T WORK WITH THEM. THEY ACTUALLY KINDA HATE US.
OH... IT'S A NEW THING... IT'S UH... A BIT OF A SECRET.
SO YOU'RE TELLING ME???
GEEZ, BRAD.

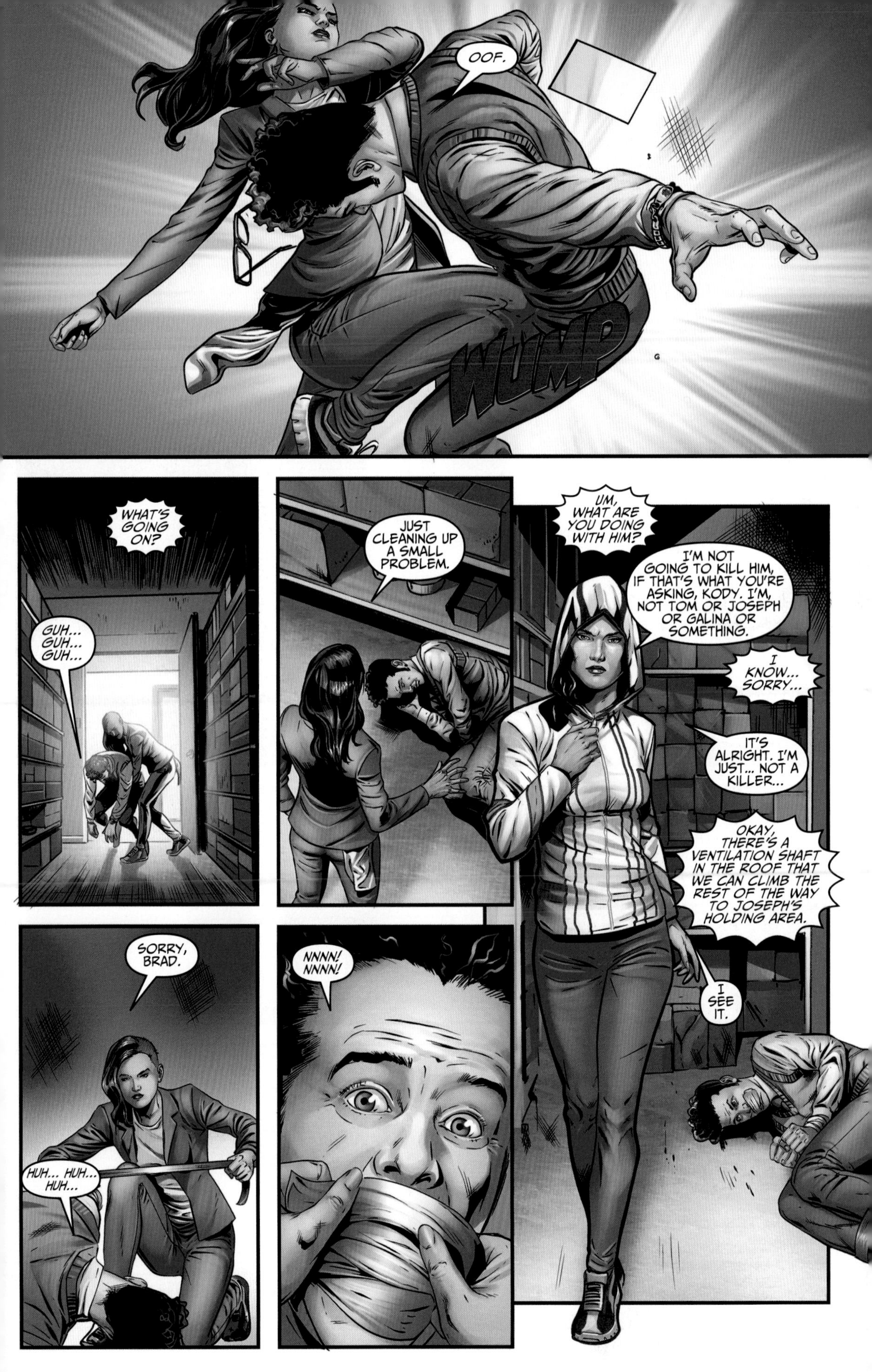
OOF.
WUMP
WHAT'S GOING ON?
GUH... GUH... GUH...
JUST CLEANING UP A SMALL PROBLEM.
UM, WHAT ARE YOU DOING WITH HIM?
I'M NOT GOING TO KILL HIM, IF THAT'S WHAT YOU'RE ASKING, KODY. I'M, NOT TOM OR JOSEPH OR GALINA OR SOMETHING.
I KNOW... SORRY...
IT'S ALRIGHT. I'M JUST... NOT A KILLER...
OKAY, THERE'S A VENTILATION SHAFT IN THE ROOF THAT WE CAN CLIMB THE REST OF THE WAY TO JOSEPH'S HOLDING AREA.
I SEE IT.
SORRY, BRAD.
HUH... HUH... HUH...
NNNN! NNNN!

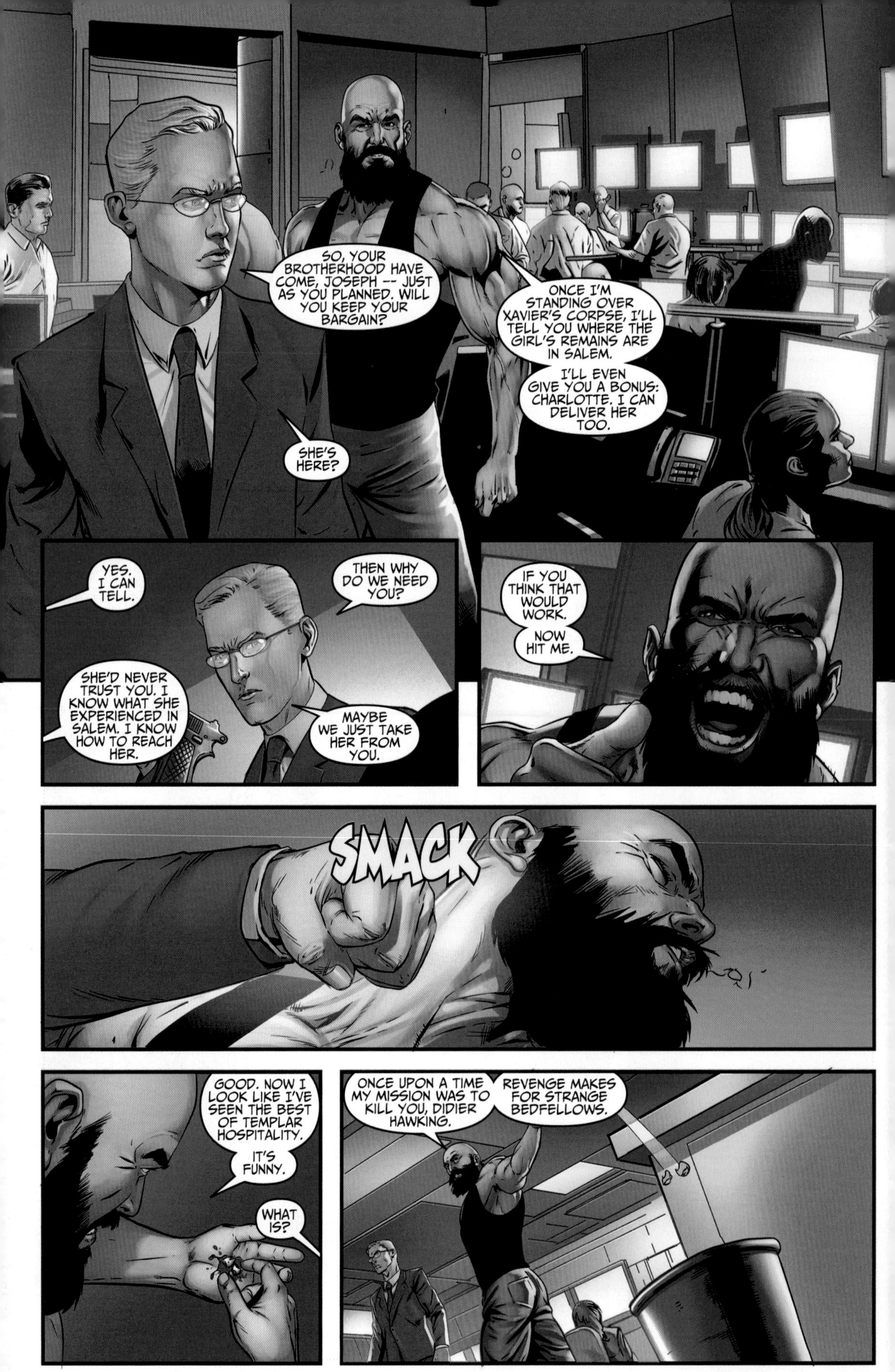
SO, YOUR BROTHERHOOD HAVE COME, JOSEPH -- JUST AS YOU PLANNED. WILL YOU KEEP YOUR BARGAIN?
ONCE I'M STANDING OVER XAVIER'S CORPSE, I'LL TELL YOU WHERE THE GIRL'S REMAINS ARE IN SALEM.
I'LL EVEN GIVE YOU A BONUS: CHARLOTTE. I CAN DELIVER HER TOO.
SHE'S HERE?
YES. I CAN TELL.
THEN WHY DO WE NEED YOU?
SHE'D NEVER TRUST YOU. I KNOW WHAT SHE EXPERIENCED IN SALEM. I KNOW HOW TO REACH HER.
MAYBE WE JUST TAKE HER FROM YOU.
IF YOU THINK THAT WOULD WORK.
NOW HIT ME.
SMACK
GOOD. NOW I LOOK LIKE I'VE SEEN THE BEST OF TEMPLAR HOSPITALITY.
IT'S FUNNY.
WHAT IS?
ONCE UPON A TIME MY MISSION WAS TO KILL YOU, DIDIER HAWKING.
REVENGE MAKES FOR STRANGE BEDFELLOWS.

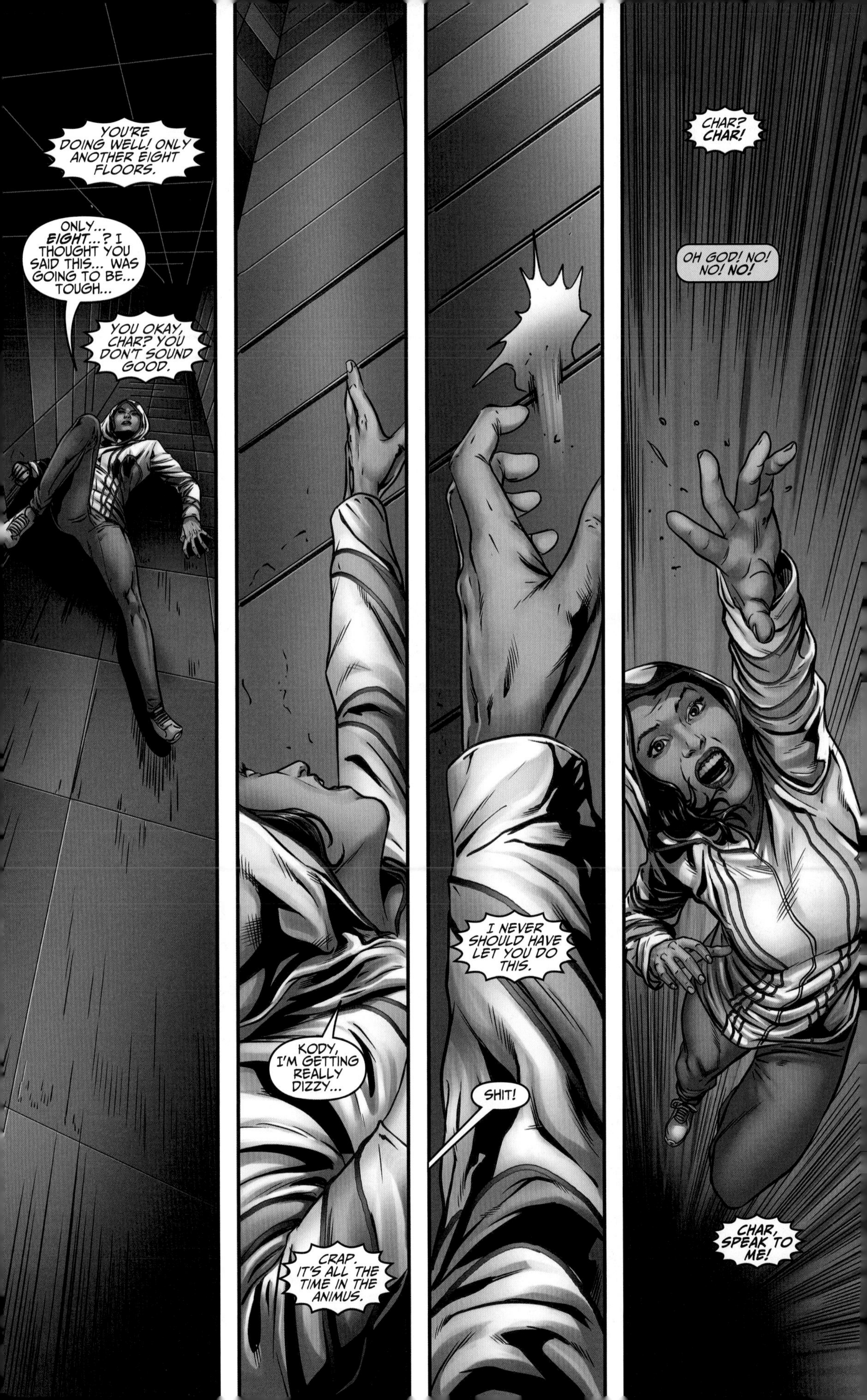
YOU'RE DOING WELL! ONLY ANOTHER EIGHT FLOORS.
ONLY... EIGHT...? I THOUGHT YOU SAID THIS... WAS GOING TO BE... TOUGH...
YOU OKAY, CHAR? YOU DON'T SOUND GOOD.
KODY, I'M GETTING REALLY DIZZY...
CRAP. IT'S ALL THE TIME IN THE ANIMUS.
I NEVER SHOULD HAVE LET YOU DO THIS.
SHIT!
CHAR? CHAR!
OH GOD! NO! NO! NO!
CHAR, SPEAK TO ME!

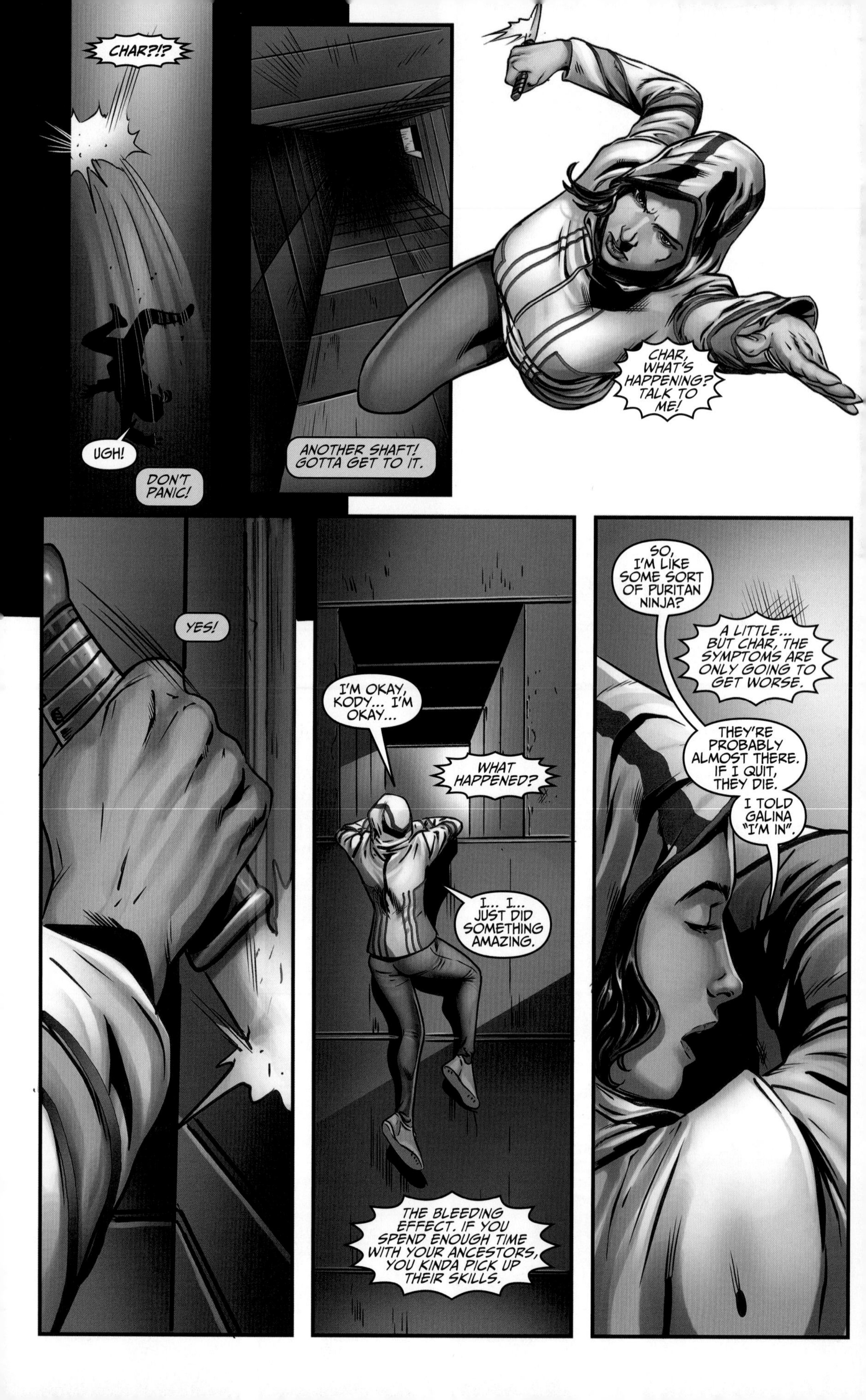

CHAR?!?
UGH!
DON'T PANIC!
ANOTHER SHAFT! GOTTA GET TO IT.
CHAR, WHAT'S HAPPENING? TALK TO ME!
YES!
I'M OKAY, KODY... I'M OKAY...
WHAT HAPPENED?
I... I... JUST DID SOMETHING AMAZING.
THE BLEEDING EFFECT. IF YOU SPEND ENOUGH TIME WITH YOUR ANCESTORS, YOU KINDA PICK UP THEIR SKILLS.
SO, I'M LIKE SOME SORT OF PURITAN NINJA?
A LITTLE... BUT CHAR, THE SYMPTOMS ARE ONLY GOING TO GET WORSE.
THEY'RE PROBABLY ALMOST THERE. IF I QUIT, THEY DIE.
I TOLD GALINA "I'M IN".

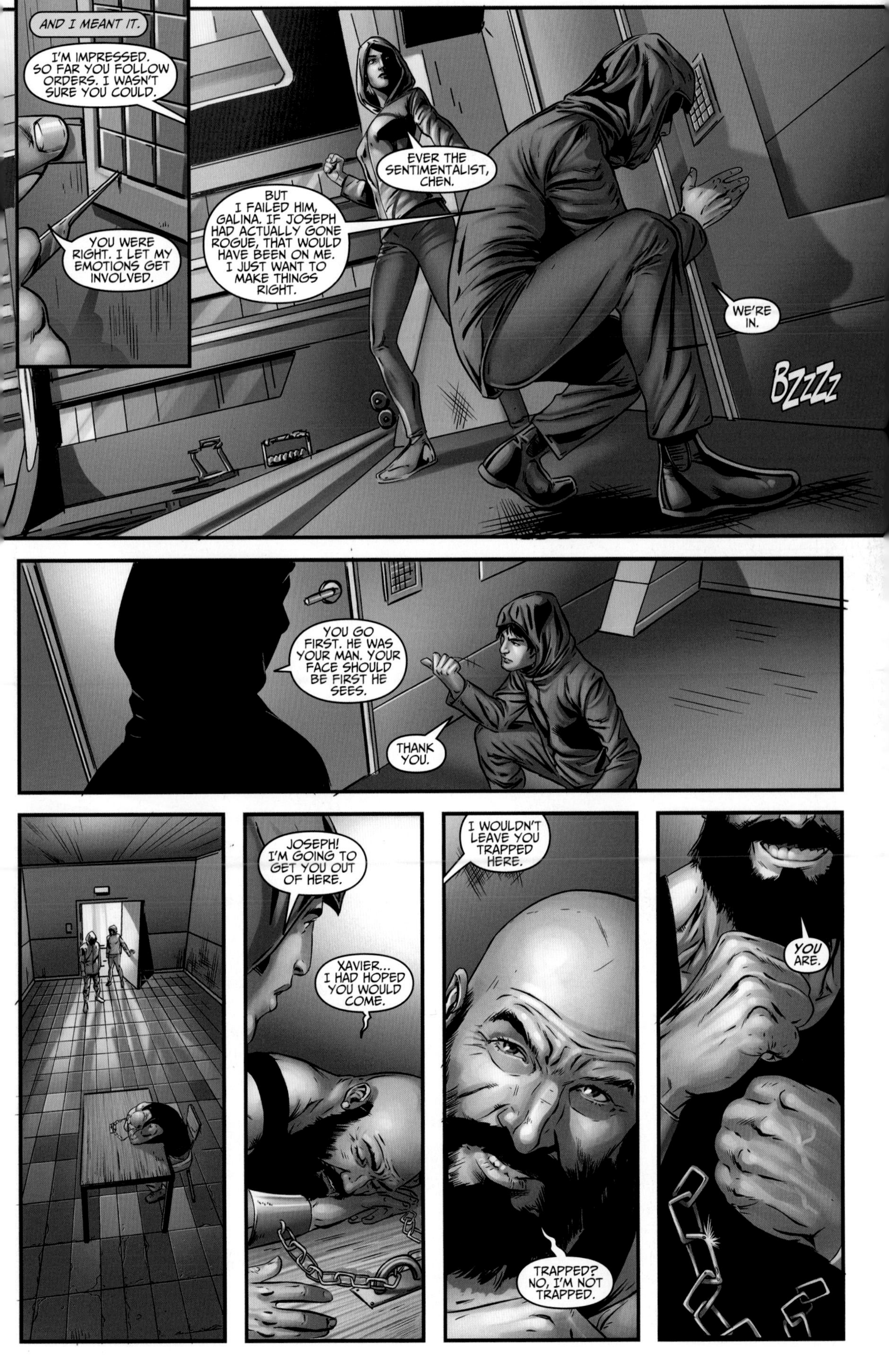
AND I MEANT IT.
I'M IMPRESSED. SO FAR YOU FOLLOW ORDERS. I WASN'T SURE YOU COULD.
YOU WERE RIGHT. I LET MY EMOTIONS GET INVOLVED.
EVER THE SENTIMENTALIST, CHEN.
BUT I FAILED HIM, GALINA. IF JOSEPH HAD ACTUALLY GONE ROGUE, THAT WOULD HAVE BEEN ON ME. I JUST WANT TO MAKE THINGS RIGHT.
WE'RE IN.
BZZZZ
YOU GO FIRST. HE WAS YOUR MAN. YOUR FACE SHOULD BE FIRST HE SEES.
THANK YOU.
JOSEPH! I'M GOING TO GET YOU OUT OF HERE.
XAVIER... I HAD HOPED YOU WOULD COME.
I WOULDN'T LEAVE YOU TRAPPED HERE.
TRAPPED? NO, I'M NOT TRAPPED.
YOU ARE.

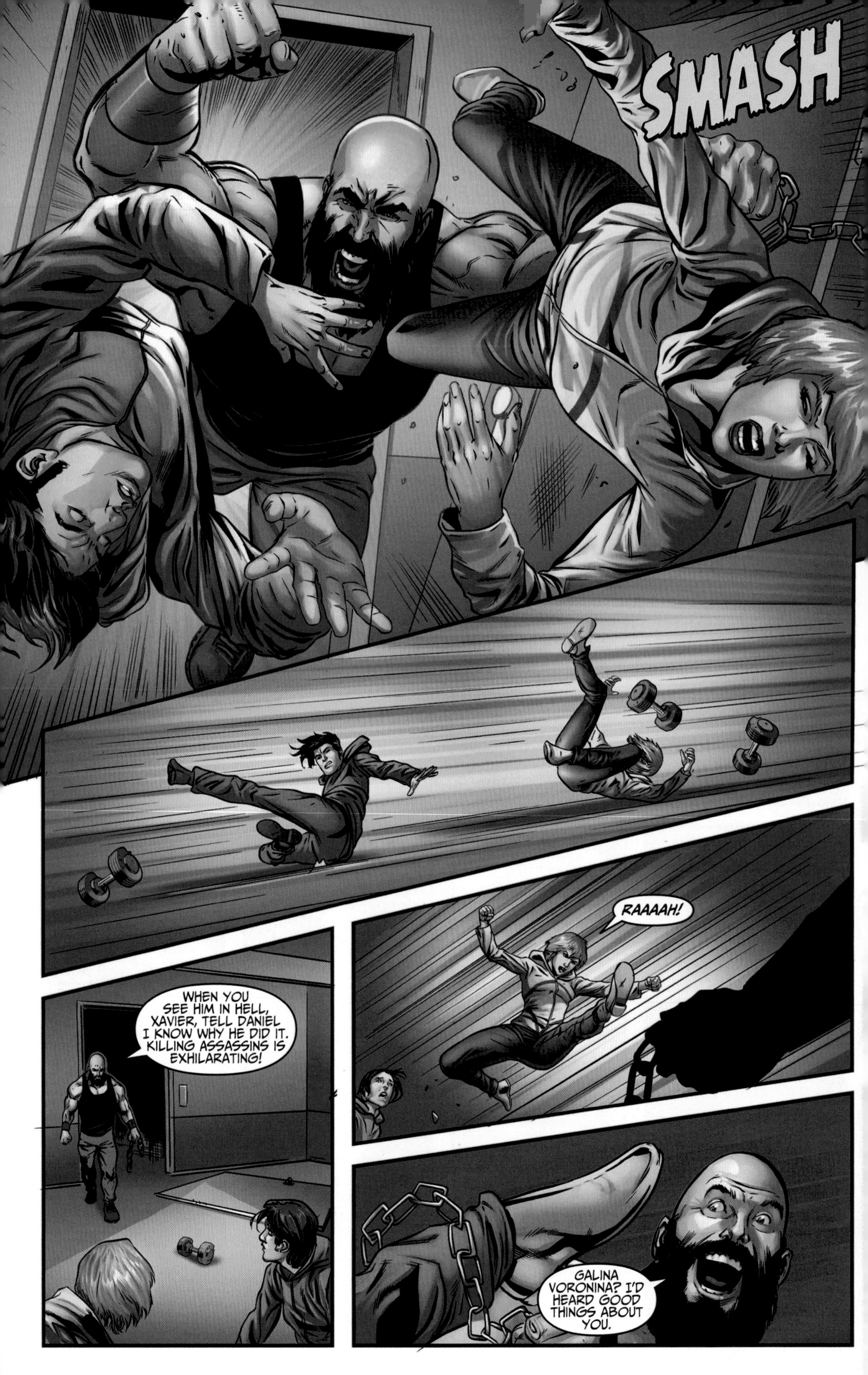
SMASH
RAAAAH!
WHEN YOU SEE HIM IN HELL, XAVIER, TELL DANIEL I KNOW WHY HE DID IT. KILLING ASSASSINS IS EXHILARATING!
GALINA VORONINA? I'D HEARD GOOD THINGS ABOUT YOU.

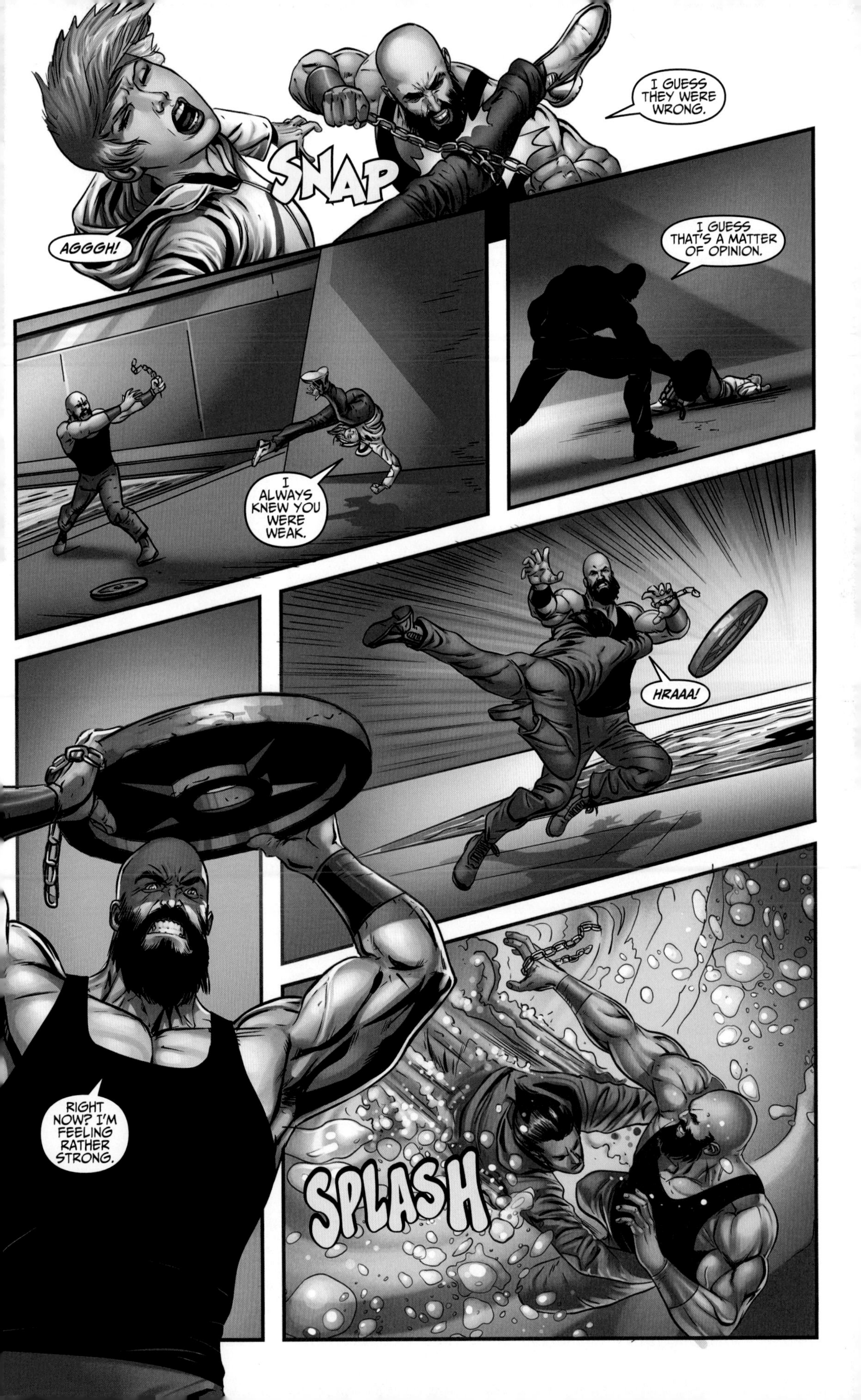
I GUESS THEY WERE WRONG.
SNAP
AGGGH!
I GUESS THAT'S A MATTER OF OPINION.
I ALWAYS KNEW YOU WERE WEAK.
HRAAA!
RIGHT NOW? I'M FEELING RATHER STRONG.
SPLASH

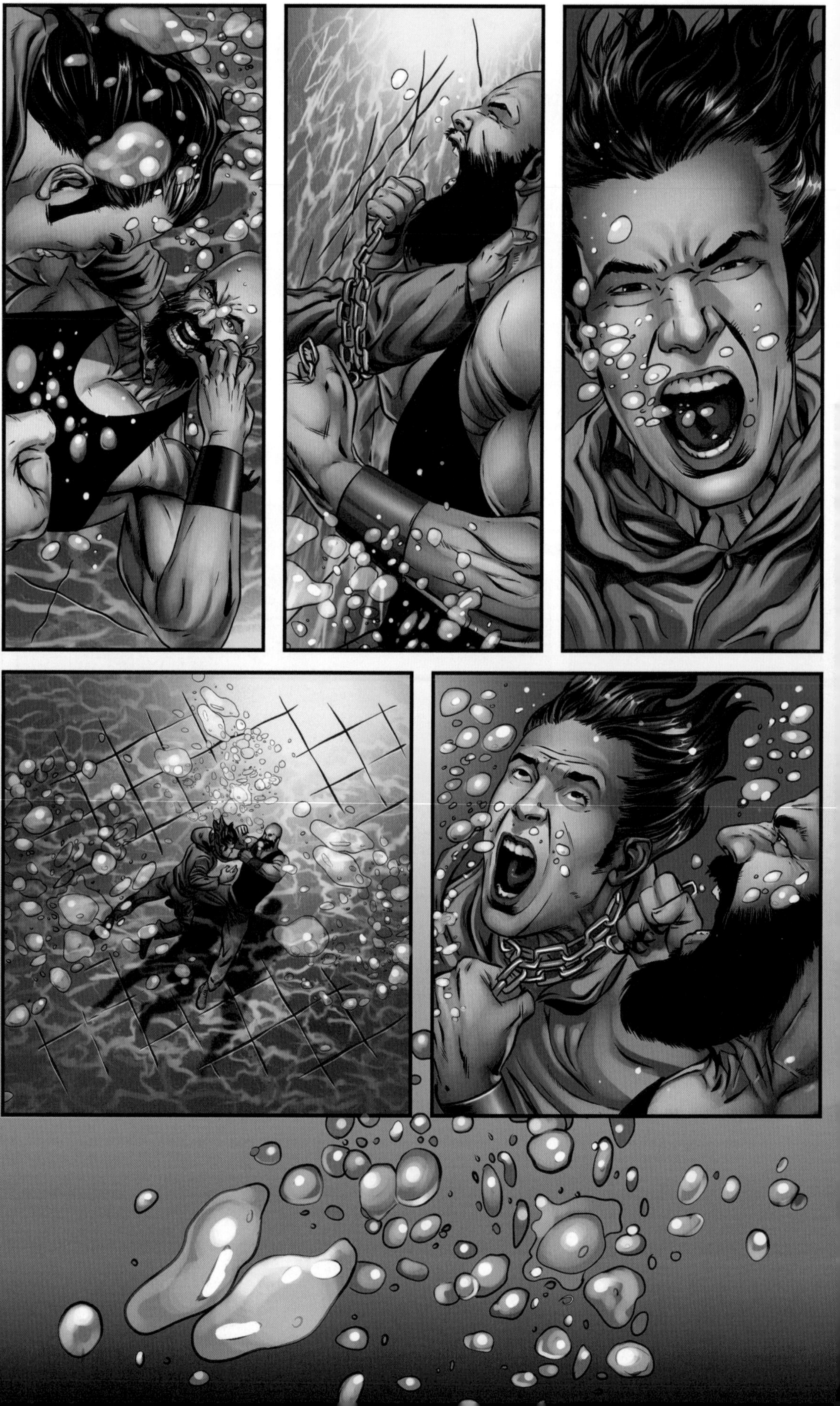

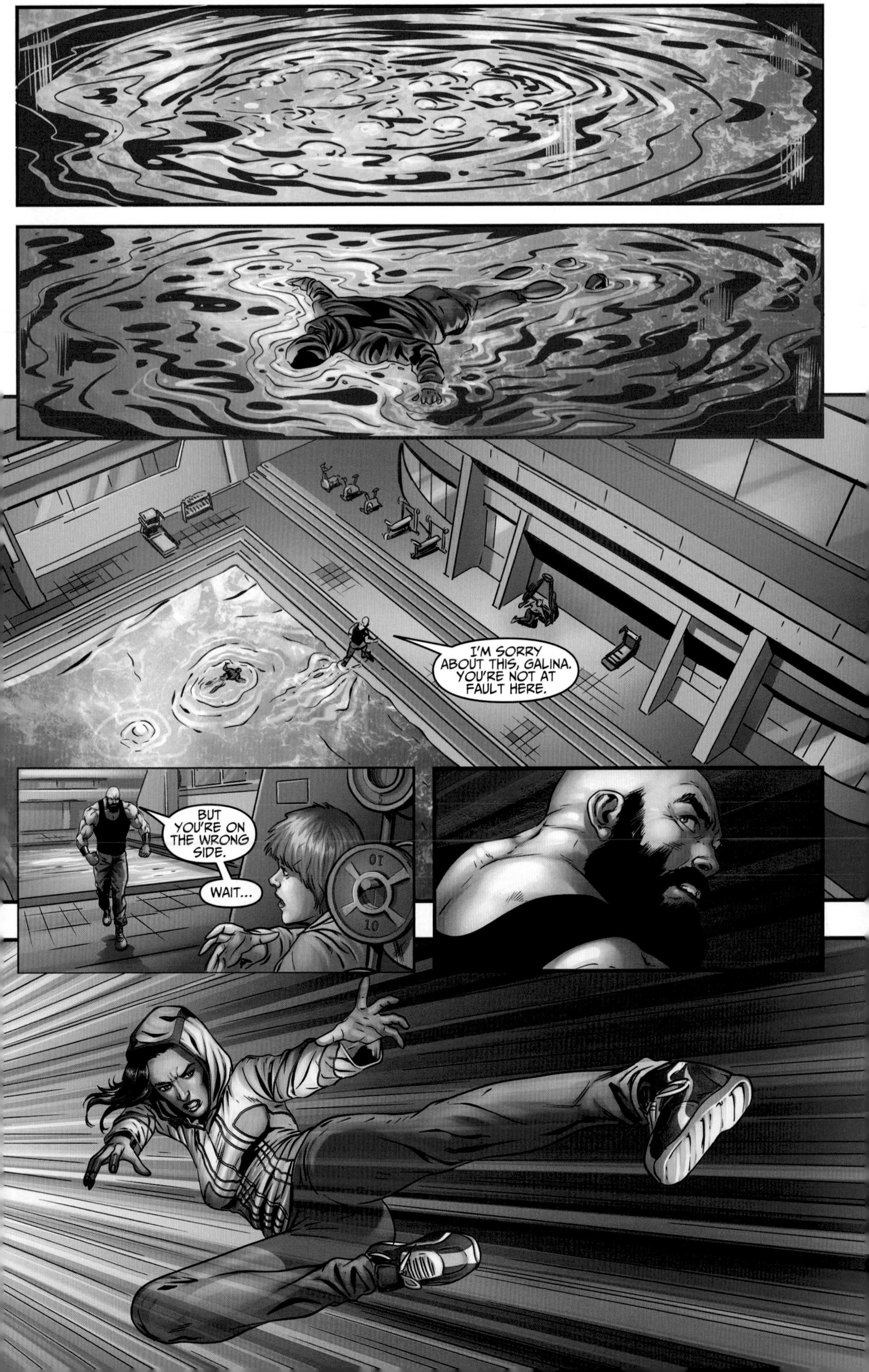
I'M SORRY ABOUT THIS, GALINA. YOU'RE NOT AT FAULT HERE.
BUT YOU'RE ON THE WRONG SIDE.
WAIT...

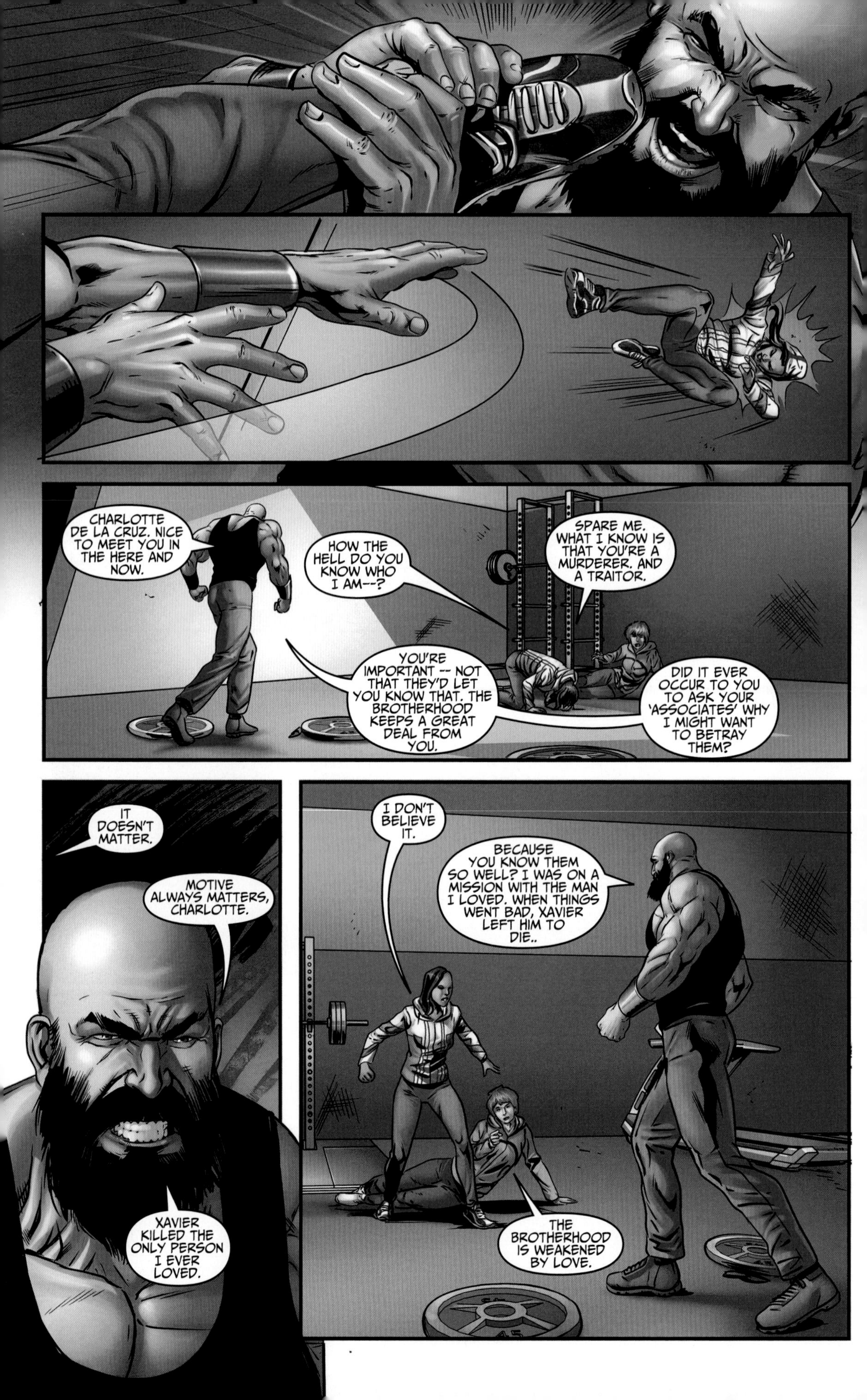
CHARLOTTE DE LA CRUZ. NICE TO MEET YOU IN THE HERE AND NOW.
HOW THE HELL DO YOU KNOW WHO I AM--?
SPARE ME. WHAT I KNOW IS THAT YOU'RE A MURDERER. AND A TRAITOR.
YOU'RE IMPORTANT -- NOT THAT THEY'D LET YOU KNOW THAT. THE BROTHERHOOD KEEPS A GREAT DEAL FROM YOU.
DID IT EVER OCCUR TO YOU TO ASK YOUR 'ASSOCIATES' WHY I MIGHT WANT TO BETRAY THEM?
IT DOESN'T MATTER.
MOTIVE ALWAYS MATTERS, CHARLOTTE.
XAVIER KILLED THE ONLY PERSON I EVER LOVED.
I DON'T BELIEVE IT.
BECAUSE YOU KNOW THEM SO WELL? I WAS ON A MISSION WITH THE MAN I LOVED. WHEN THINGS WENT BAD, XAVIER LEFT HIM TO DIE..
THE BROTHERHOOD IS WEAKENED BY LOVE.

WEAKENED BY LOVE? CAN YOU IMAGINE SUCH A THING, CHARLOTTE?

XAVIER COULD HAVE TOLD ME CHRISTIAN WAS IN DANGER, BUT HE DIDN'T, BECAUSE HE KNEW THAT WOULD PULL ME AWAY FROM OUR PRECIOUS MISSION.

THERE!

JUST LIKE STODDARD IGNORED THOSE WOMEN. LEFT THAT BOY TO DIE. ALL IN THE NAME OF DUTY.

THE BROTHERHOOD IS USING YOU, CHARLOTTE. HAVE THEY TOLD YOU WHY THE REALLY WANTED YOU?

KEEP HIM TALKING, CHAR.

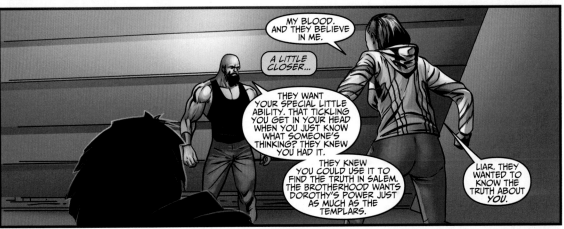

MY BLOOD. AND THEY BELIEVE IN ME.

A LITTLE CLOSER...

THEY WANT YOUR SPECIAL LITTLE ABILITY. THAT TICKLING YOU GET IN YOUR HEAD WHEN YOU JUST KNOW WHAT SOMEONE'S THINKING? THEY KNEW YOU HAD IT.

THEY KNEW YOU COULD USE IT TO FIND THE TRUTH IN SALEM. THE BROTHERHOOD WANTS DOROTHY'S POWER JUST AS MUCH AS THE TEMPLARS.

LIAR. THEY WANTED TO KNOW THE TRUTH ABOUT YOU.

I'M JUST A SIDELINE.

NO! NOT NOW!

THE BROTHERHOOD ALWAYS GET WHAT THEY WANT, REGARDLESS OF THE COST.

LOOK AT YOU, CHARLOTTE, YOU CAN BARELY STAND.

SO WHAT'S THE OTHER OPTION? JOIN THE TEMPLARS LIKE YOU?

NO. YOU MISUNDERSTAND. DESPITE EVERYTHING, I'M A GOOD SOLDIER. I FINISH MY MISSIONS.

THAT TICKLING... I FEEL IT...

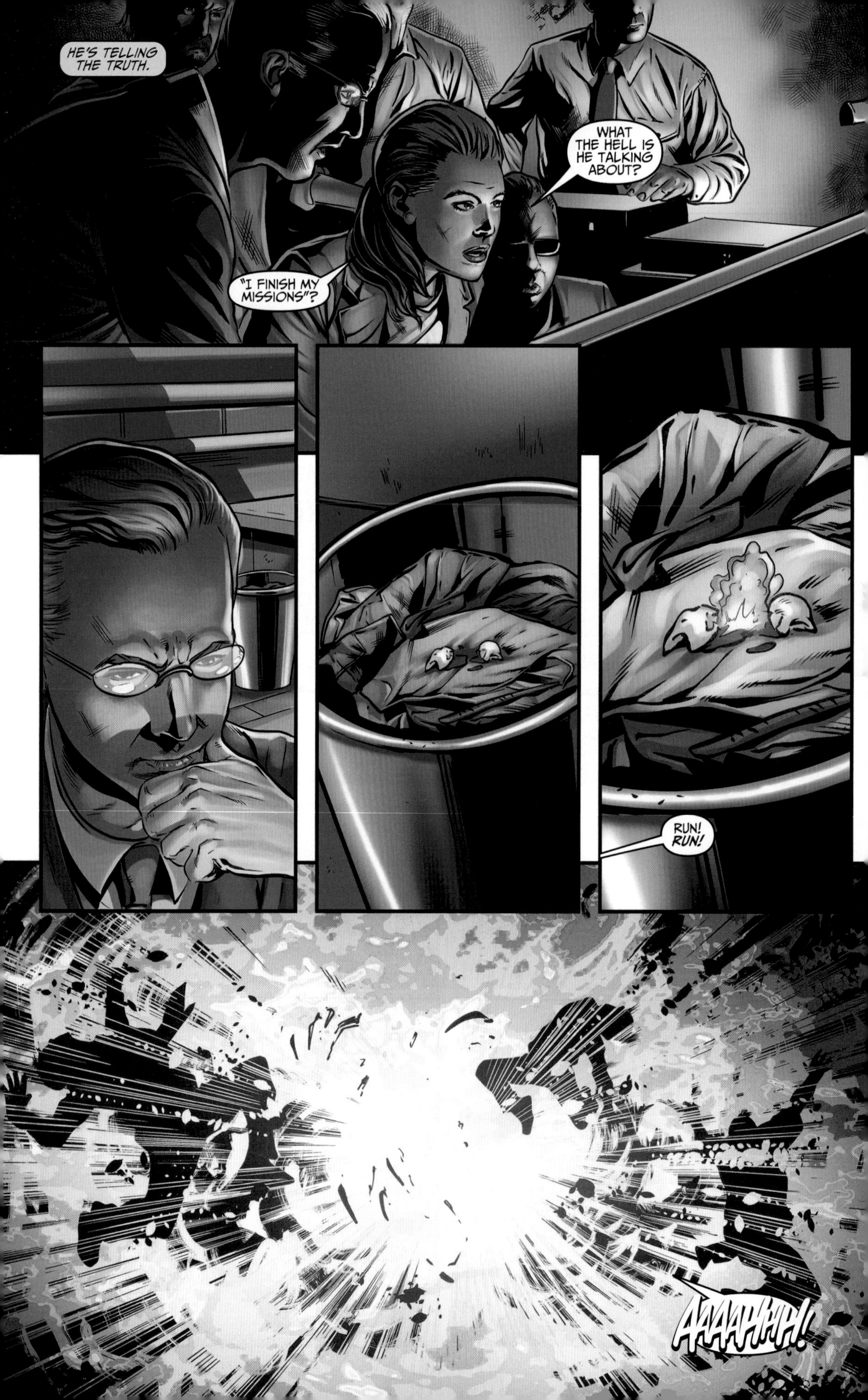
HE'S TELLING THE TRUTH.
WHAT THE HELL IS HE TALKING ABOUT?
"I FINISH MY MISSIONS"?
RUN! RUN!
AAAAHHH!

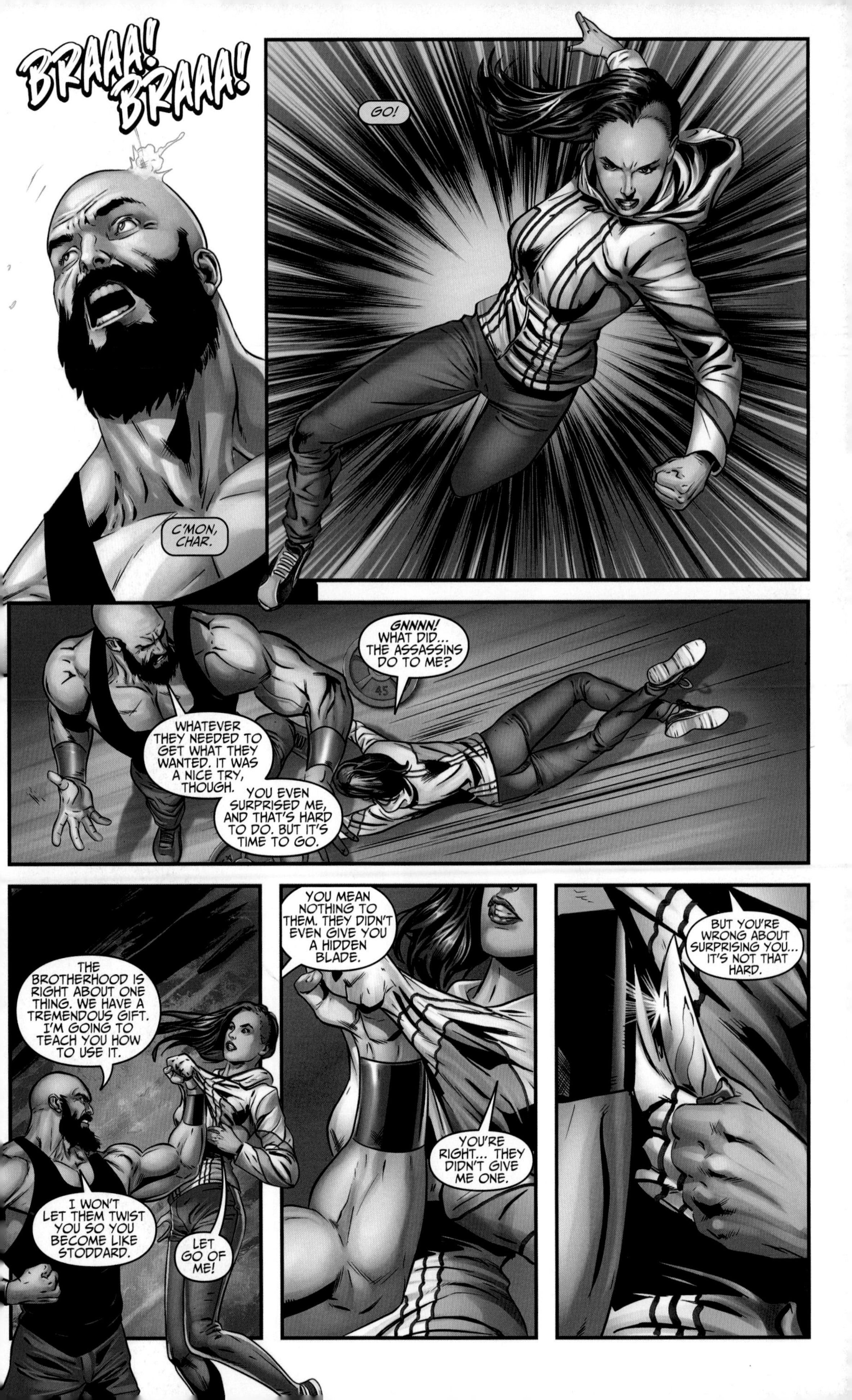
BRAAA! BRAAA!
GO!
C'MON, CHAR.
GNNNN! WHAT DID... THE ASSASSINS DO TO ME?
45
WHATEVER THEY NEEDED TO GET WHAT THEY WANTED. IT WAS A NICE TRY, THOUGH.
YOU EVEN SURPRISED ME, AND THAT'S HARD TO DO. BUT IT'S TIME TO GO.
THE BROTHERHOOD IS RIGHT ABOUT ONE THING. WE HAVE A TREMENDOUS GIFT. I'M GOING TO TEACH YOU HOW TO USE IT.
I WON'T LET THEM TWIST YOU SO YOU BECOME LIKE STODDARD.
LET GO OF ME!
YOU MEAN NOTHING TO THEM. THEY DIDN'T EVEN GIVE YOU A HIDDEN BLADE.
YOU'RE RIGHT... THEY DIDN'T GIVE ME ONE.
BUT YOU'RE WRONG ABOUT SURPRISING YOU... IT'S NOT THAT HARD.

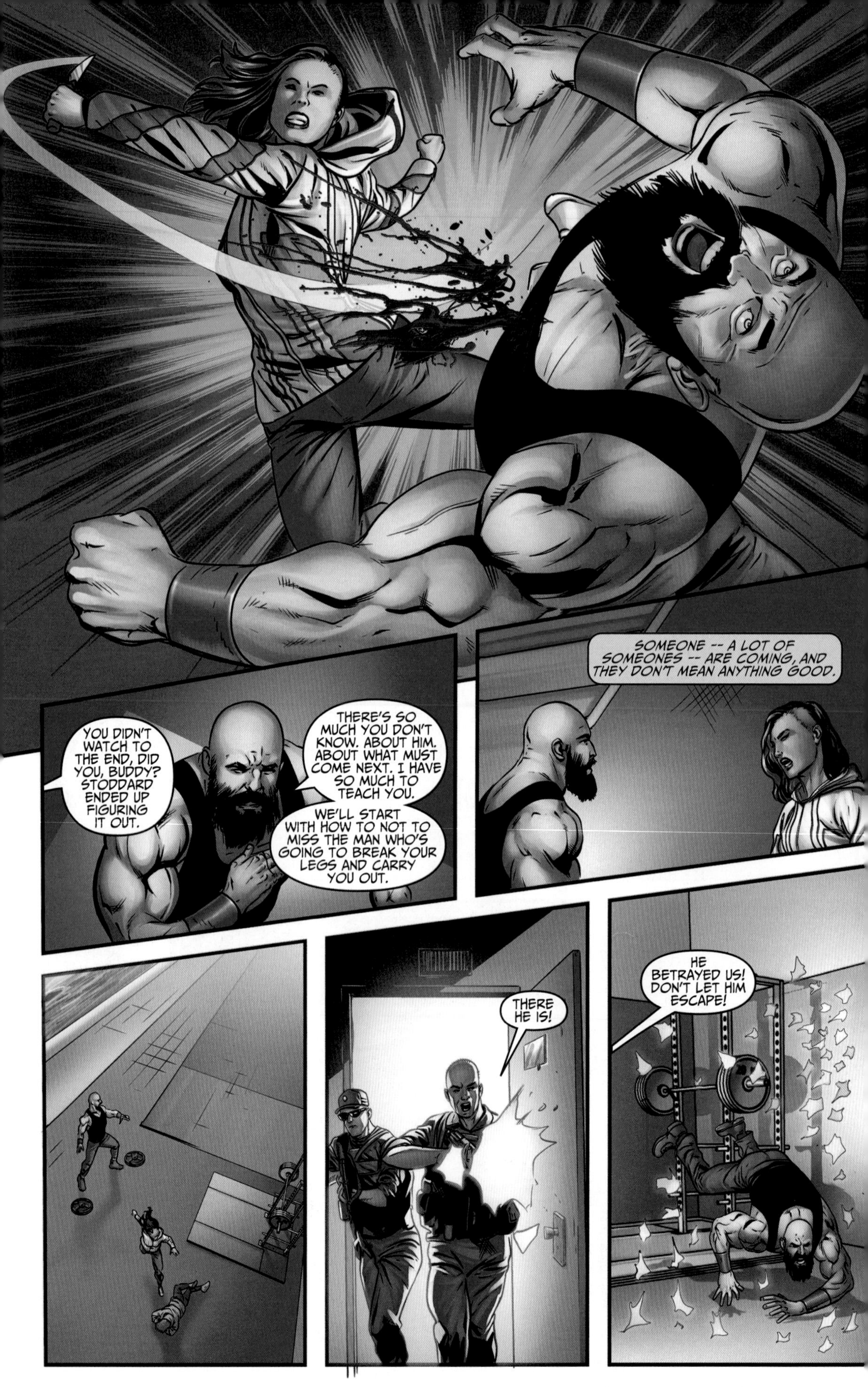
SOMEONE -- A LOT OF SOMEONES -- ARE COMING, AND THEY DON'T MEAN ANYTHING GOOD.
YOU DIDN'T WATCH TO THE END, DID YOU, BUDDY? STODDARD ENDED UP FIGURING IT OUT.
THERE'S SO MUCH YOU DON'T KNOW. ABOUT HIM. ABOUT WHAT MUST COME NEXT. I HAVE SO MUCH TO TEACH YOU.
WE'LL START WITH HOW TO NOT TO MISS THE MAN WHO'S GOING TO BREAK YOUR LEGS AND CARRY YOU OUT.
THERE HE IS!
HE BETRAYED US! DON'T LET HIM ESCAPE!

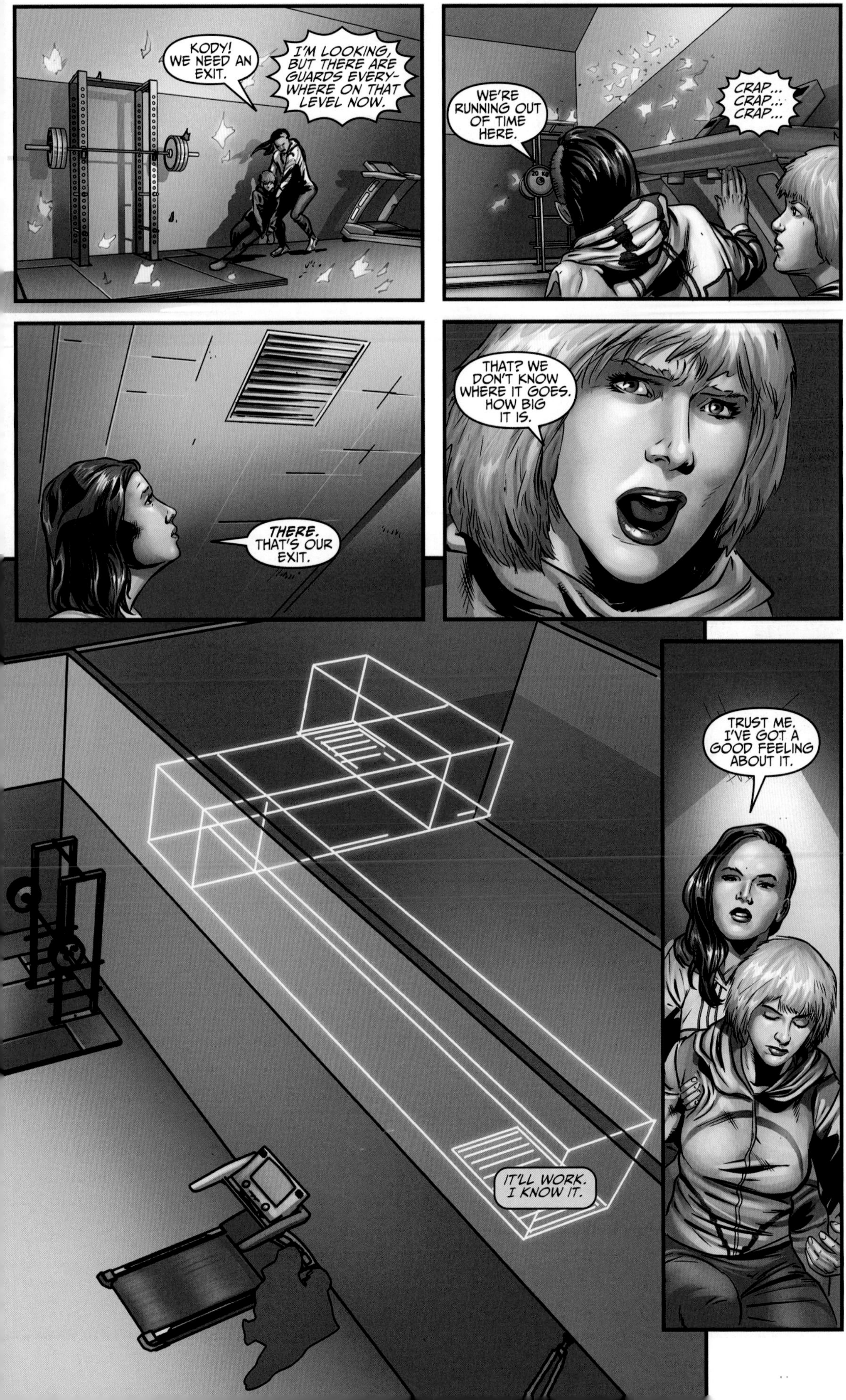
KODY! WE NEED AN EXIT.
I'M LOOKING, BUT THERE ARE GUARDS EVERY-WHERE ON THAT LEVEL NOW.
WE'RE RUNNING OUT OF TIME HERE.
CRAP... CRAP... CRAP...
THERE. THAT'S OUR EXIT.
THAT? WE DON'T KNOW WHERE IT GOES. HOW BIG IT IS.
TRUST ME. I'VE GOT A GOOD FEELING ABOUT IT.
IT'LL WORK. I KNOW IT.

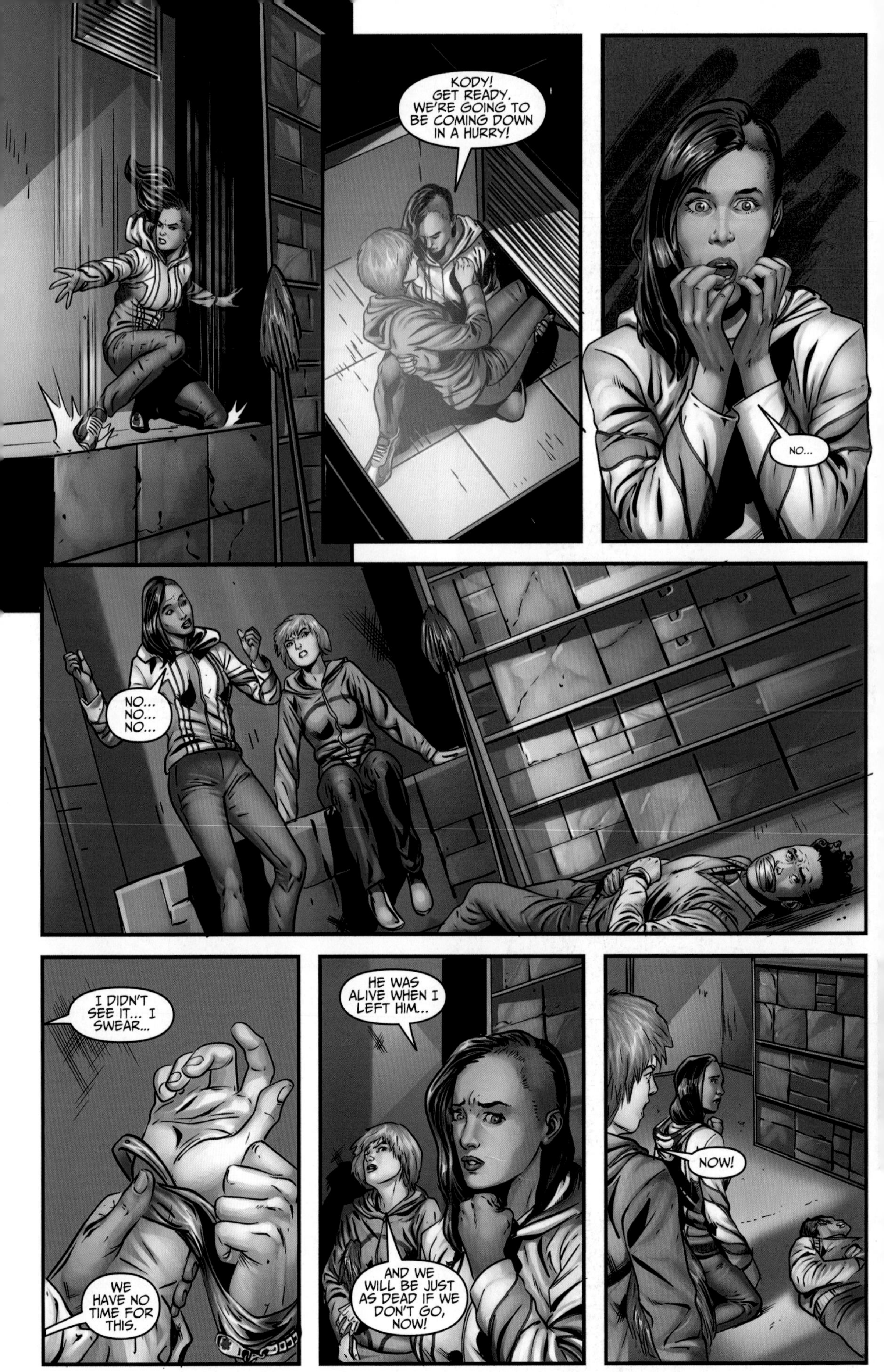
KODY! GET READY. WE'RE GOING TO BE COMING DOWN IN A HURRY!
NO...
NO... NO... NO...
I DIDN'T SEE IT... I SWEAR...
WE HAVE NO TIME FOR THIS.
HE WAS ALIVE WHEN I LEFT HIM...
AND WE WILL BE JUST AS DEAD IF WE DON'T GO, NOW!
NOW!

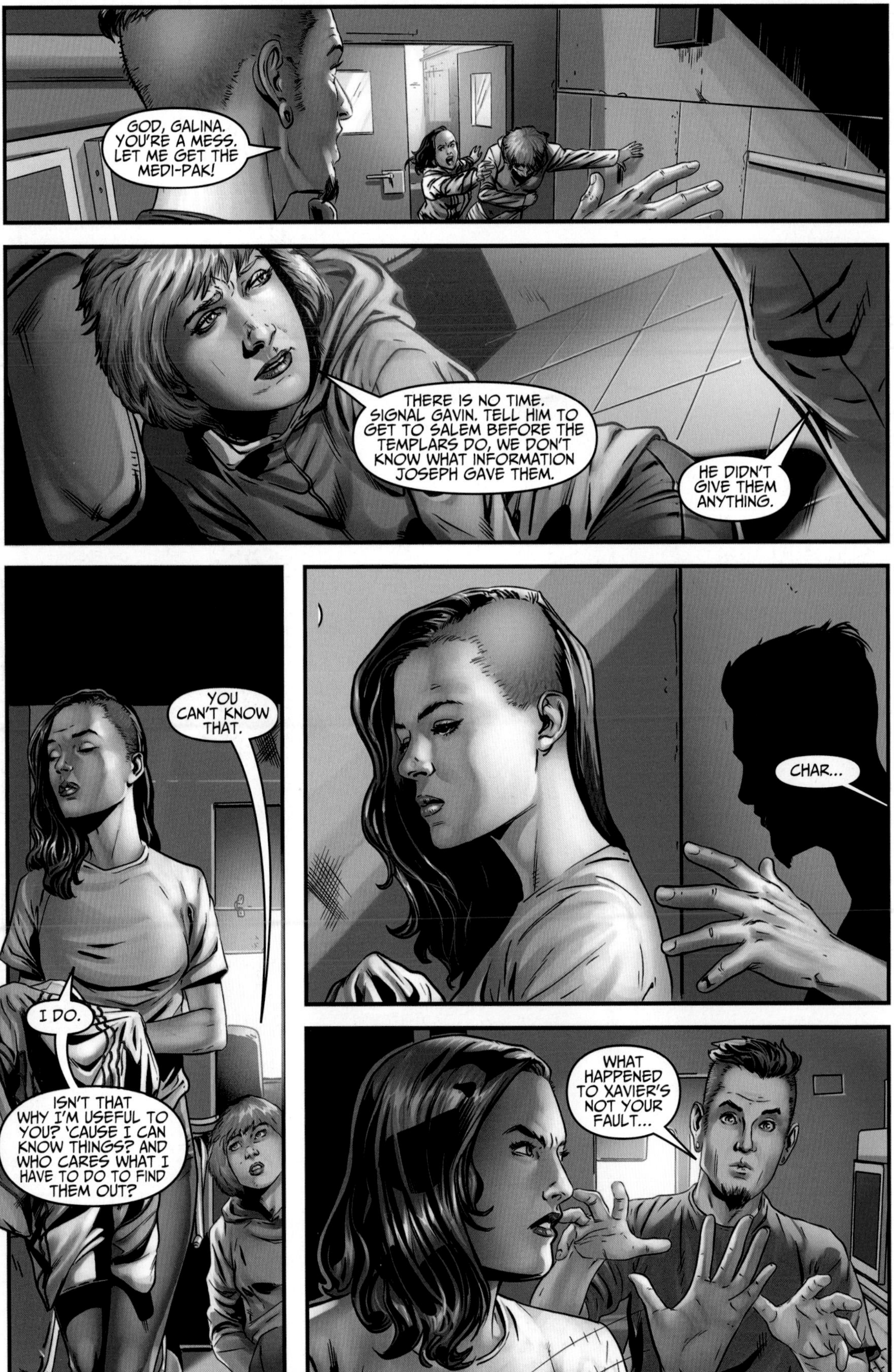
GOD, GALINA. YOU'RE A MESS. LET ME GET THE MEDI-PAK!
THERE IS NO TIME. SIGNAL GAVIN. TELL HIM TO GET TO SALEM BEFORE THE TEMPLARS DO, WE DON'T KNOW WHAT INFORMATION JOSEPH GAVE THEM.
HE DIDN'T GIVE THEM ANYTHING.
YOU CAN'T KNOW THAT.
I DO.
ISN'T THAT WHY I'M USEFUL TO YOU? 'CAUSE I CAN KNOW THINGS? AND WHO CARES WHAT I HAVE TO DO TO FIND THEM OUT?
CHAR...
WHAT HAPPENED TO XAVIER'S NOT YOUR FAULT...

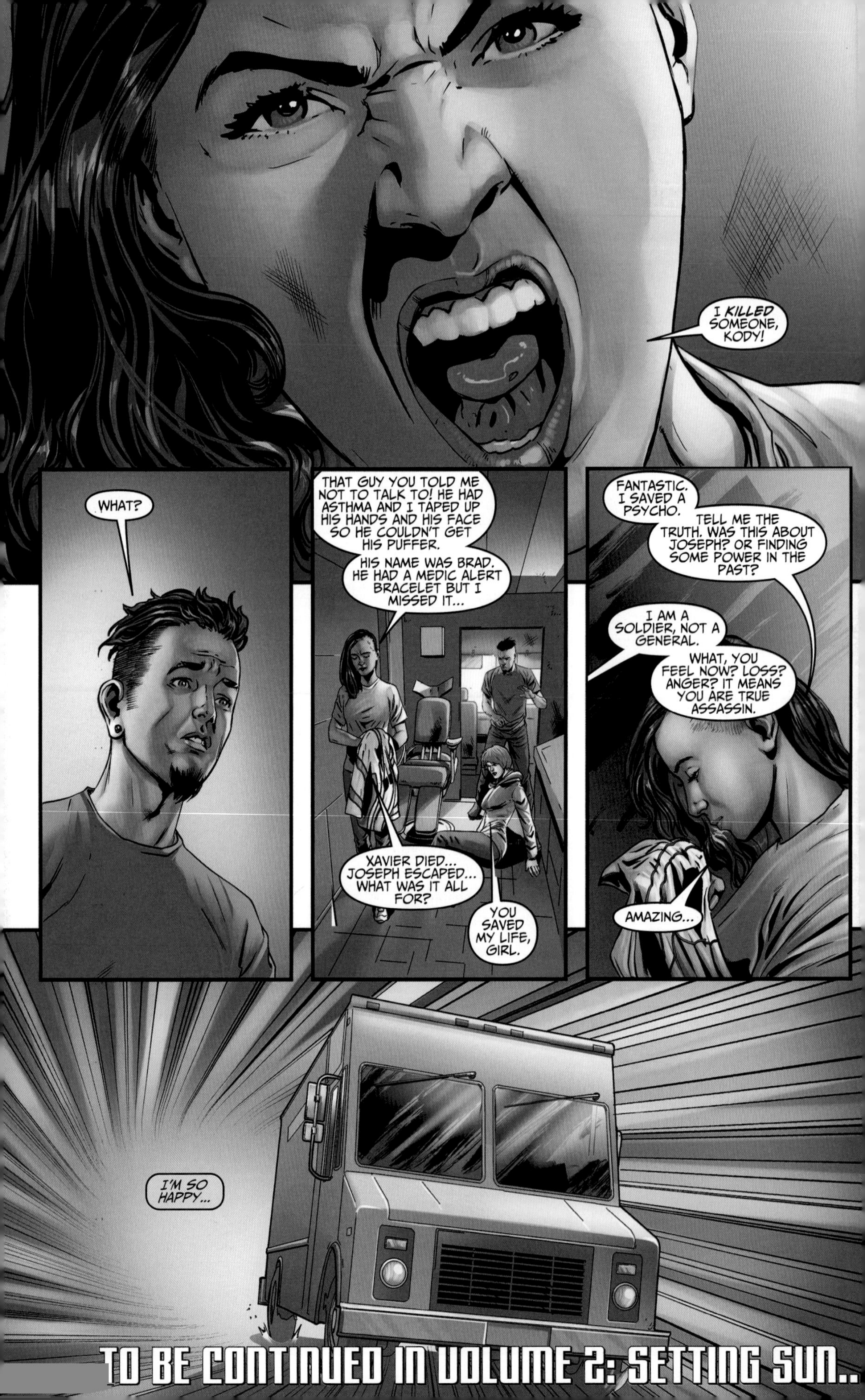
I KILLED SOMEONE, KODY!
WHAT?
THAT GUY YOU TOLD ME NOT TO TALK TO! HE HAD ASTHMA AND I TAPED UP HIS HANDS AND HIS FACE SO HE COULDN'T GET HIS PUFFER.
HIS NAME WAS BRAD. HE HAD A MEDIC ALERT BRACELET BUT I MISSED IT...
XAVIER DIED... JOSEPH ESCAPED... WHAT WAS IT ALL FOR?
YOU SAVED MY LIFE, GIRL.
FANTASTIC. I SAVED A PSYCHO.
TELL ME THE TRUTH. WAS THIS ABOUT JOSEPH? OR FINDING SOME POWER IN THE PAST?
I AM A SOLDIER, NOT A GENERAL.
WHAT, YOU FEEL NOW? LOSS? ANGER? IT MEANS YOU ARE TRUE ASSASSIN.
AMAZING...
I'M SO HAPPY...
TO BE CONTINUED IN VOLUME 2: SETTING SUN...

SALEM

IN 1692, A QUIET PURITAN COLONY WAS THE SETTING FOR DISTURBING EVENTS THAT WOULD ECHO DOWN THE AGES...

In 1626, a small group of Puritans founded the town of Salem on the mouth of the Naumkeag river. They obtained a charter from the British monarchy that gave them the right of free rule so they could practice their Puritan beliefs free from the interference of the Church of England. It was that charter that created the perfect conditions for the horrors to come...

While the name "Salem" is mostly associated with the Witch Trials, it actually refers to both Salem Village (now called Danvers) and Salem Town. The first accusations of witchcraft were made in Salem Village, but the courts, and therefore the trials, were held in nearby Salem Town. However, the accused came from all over Essex County. In fact, the vast majority of the accused were from the nearby villages of Andover, Ipswich, Beverly, Haverhill, Topsfield and Gloucester, among others.

In the years leading up to 1692, Salem Town and the surrounding villages had been in a state of near constant turmoil. Despite being issued a charter in 1629, after the establishment of the colony, that would allow them to practice their Puritan beliefs, the people of Salem were subject to numerous changes in government. These were influenced in large part by the shifting politics and civil war taking place in Britain, which had a significant impact on migration to the colonies.

The increasingly insular members of the Massachusetts colony were well-suited to self-governance, however, and elected their own leaders who supported and reflected their religious beliefs. It was a controlling environment. Puritanism was an extreme form of Protestantism, with origins in Calvinism, that believed wholeheartedly in Original Sin. However, where Calvinists believed they could seek salvation through

good deeds, and therefore absolve themselves of sin, Puritans instead believed they were the chosen people of God, and were therefore required to live by the teachings of the scriptures and set an example for the heathen followers of the Anglican and Catholic churches. Church attendance was absolutely mandatory, and Puritan life revolved around the meetinghouse, with villagers and townspeople required to attend services lasting two to three hours every Wednesday and Sunday. This atmosphere of fear and control was fed by the Puritan belief in the Devil, and in witchcraft. It was an accepted fact of life that the Devil existed, and was constantly trying to tempt the Puritans into blasphemous behavior.

The Massachusetts Bay Colony was also subjected to devastatingly cold winters, and the land was not ideally suited to farming. Crop yields were poor, food was scarce, and the long winters were dangerous, not least due to increasingly frequent attacks by Native Americans on British settlements along the East Coast. With internal fighting, and external threats, life in the colony was fraught with anxiety and paranoia.

However, over time, increased prosperity in Salem Town, a port engaged in trade, shipbuilding and fishing, resulted in a wealthy merchant class, who had little in common with the poorer farmers who lived in Salem Village and other outlying settlements. This led to simmering tensions between the

"Witchcraft at Salem Village" likely by F.O.C. Darley, Granville Perkins or William Ludwell Sheppard, ill. Published in "Pioneers in the Settlement of America: From Florida in 1510 to California in 1849," by William August Crafts, Vol. 1, p. 453, Boston: Samuel Walker and Co. 1876.

town and village, as the villagers believed they were due greater autonomy. However, they were not united in this belief, as around half of the villagers remained loyal to the town and wished to remain affiliated with it. The issue was couched in religious terms; the villagers seeking autonomy felt that the thriving economy of Salem Town made it too "individualistic", which was directly opposed to the communalism that a Puritan belief system called for. Eventually, Salem Village was allowed its own church, and was given the freedom to employ and support their own minister – one Samuel Parris, recently installed in Salem along with his wife Eliabeth, his daughter, Betty, niece, Abigail Williams, and house slave, Tituba.

This compromise was not enough to quell the mutterings of the discontented, though. Factions developed within factions, and tensions rose further still. When some of the villagers refused to finanacially support Parris and his family, bitterness and anger flourished on all sides, and the accusations of witchcraft soon followed, coming first from the mouths of Betty Parris and Abigail Williams.

It was on June 2nd of the year 1692 that the famous trials of Salem began. The Governor of Massachusetts, William Phips, created a Court of Oyer and Terminer to try the cases. These courts, so named for their Anglo-French roots, were commissioned to hear (oyer) and determine (terminer) felonies, treasons, and misdemeanors. The court was comprised of seven members of the community, including William Stoughton. It was these seven men who would condemn 19 people to death, and allow the deaths in prison of five more.

The trials were beset by sensationalism, with spectral evidence admitted in the form of testimonies from the afflicted, with displays of possessions and fits prevalent in the proceedings. 'Spectral evidence' was testimony from the afflicted, girls like Abigail Williams and Betty Parris, that the accused had appeared to them in a dream or vision and perpetrated some harm on them. It was admitted as evidence by William Stoughton.

The first victim of this court was Bridget Bishop. She hadn't been the first accused of witchcraft, but was the first to be tried for the simple reason that it was believed her trial would be the easiest to win. Bishop was a well-known figure in Salem, but for the wrong reasons. Married three times, she was regarded as having loose morals and a poor character. She dressed flamboyantly, for the time at least, and was known to engage in drinking and gambling. It was not the first time she had been accused of witchcraft, with rumors flitting around the countryside a few years before. She was brought up before the court on the June 2nd. On the 10th, she hanged.

Sarah Good met the same fate. Desperately poor and pregnant, she could often be seen begging door to door. Along with Sarah Osbourn and Tituba, she was one of the first women accused of witchcraft by the girls Abigail Williams and Betty Parris. She was hanged on July 19th. Four other women were hanged that day: a poor widow named Susannah Martin, a farmer's wife Elizabeth Howe, Rebecca Nurse, and Sarah Wildes. The executions of the latter two show just how dangerous the community in Salem had become if you refused to conform. Nurse was a pious and popular woman,

but had a longstanding feud with the wealthy Putnam family, and disapproved of the appointment of Samuel Parris as the new minister. It was the Putnams who were her main accusers. She was found to be not guilty in the original verdict, but the "afflicted" girls protested vehemently, and the jury reconsidered and returned a guilty verdict. Nurse hanged alongside Good and Howe. Joining them that day was Sarah Wildes, another victim of the Putnam family. Wildes was the wife of the local judge, and had previous brushes with the law to condemn her. She had been accused of fornicating out of wedlock in 1649 when she was 22, and charged with the heinous crime of wearing a silk scarf in 1663. Her marriage to John Wildes enraged his sister, Mary Gould, who used her friendship with the Putnam family to ensure Sarah Wildes stood trial.

24 people lost their lives between June and September of 1692, the last being Giles Corey. He had refused to enter a plea, and was tortured in a field in Salem Town by being pressed with stones. He died after three days.

THE END, THE AFTERMATH AND THE LEGACY...

In the early months of 1693, the last of the trials in Salem were taking place. The fervor of the first hearings had dwindled, and the court of Oyer and Terminer had been dissolved by Governor Phipps in October of the previous year. As the court slowly worked through the charges laid at the feet of those who remained in prison, public support for the trials diminished, and the townspeople were slowly waking up to the horrors they had perpetrated. By May of 1693, all those still in prison on charges of witchcraft were released and eventually pardoned.

The year of madness had ended. Lives had been lost. Strangely, however, the lives of the "afflicted girls" – the accusers responsible for the majority of the charges - continued much as they would have done had they never decided to portray themselves as victims. While the dissolving of the court brought a certain amount of closure to the events of 1692 and 1693, it is interesting to note that only one of the "afflicted" girls ever apologized for her part in the deaths of innocent people.

Ann Putnam, Jr. had accused sixty-two people of witchcraft, and finally issued a public apology over a decade later, in 1706. Interestingly, her apology was couched in religious terms. She professed herself to be extremely sorry, and believed that, "It was a great delusion of Satan that deceived me in that sad time." The irony would be laughable, if it weren't so awful. While none of the other girls accepted any blame at any point in their lives, twelve members of the jury did concede that their actions were "sadly deluded and mistaken." Samuel Parris did allow that he "may have been mistaken," in 1694, but the damage to his reputation had already been done, and he was replaced as minister for Salem

Village in 1696. His reticence may have been due in part to the fact that his daughter, Betty Parris, was one of the first girls to make any accusations. Betty herself never faced any censure for her part in the trials. She went on to marry and have four children, never being persecuted for her behavior.

William Stoughton had been appointed Lieutenant Governor and Chief Justice of Massachusetts by Governor Phips, and was head judge of the court of Oyer and Terminer until it was dissolved. While many of his decisions were questionable, he was generally held to be a fair man. This was made very clear when Governor Phips attempted to shift his portion of the blame onto Stoughton following the change in public opinion. He did this by chastising Stoughton in a letter to the King of England. This tactic backfired, as Phips was recalled to England, where he died. Stoughton succeeded him as Governor of Massachusetts and served until his own death in 1701.

The greatest indication of the horror the members of the community felt for their actions came in October 1711, when a Reversal of Attainder was signed into law by the Massachusetts legislature. Attainder, in English law, is the metaphorical "stain"

caused by high treason or capital crimes. It essentially stripped the receiver of their rights. The order for reversal nullified all the judgments cast against the majority of those convicted. It was also decreed that reparations were to be paid to the families and heirs. A sum totalling almost £600 was distributed, though only to those families that had specifically asked for it. The Reversal of Attainder applied only to those specifically named, and was not exhaustive. Over time, this oversight would be recified, but when Elizabeth Johnson wrote to the committee asking that her name be included, as she too had been condemned, the committee demurred, on the basis that the business was finished with. It is unknown as to whether Johnson ever managed to clear her name.

In 1957, the Massachusetts Governor signed another bill into law, officially apologizing for the Salem Witch Trials and clearing the names of the remaining accused, though not stating them explicitly. This law was amended in 2001 to correct this error. Included in the correction was the name Bridget Bishop, finally cleared over three hundred years after she was the first person to be hanged in what are the now infamous Salem Witch Trials. +

IN MEMORY OF THOSE INNOCENTS
WHO DIED DURING THE
SALEM VILLAGE WITCHCRAFT HYSTERIA
OF 1692

The Salem Village Witchcraft Victims' Memorial of Danvers (formerly called Salem) was dedicated in 1992 and stands as a reminder that each generation must confront intolerance and "witch hunts" and must always seek the truth, as represented by weighty granite used in the construction of the monument. Commissioned to commemorate the 300th anniversary of the beginning of the hysteria.

COVER GALLERY

ISSUE 01

A COVER AA
MARCO TURINI

B COVER B
DENNIS CALERO

C COVER C
ADAM GORHAM &
JASON LEWIS

D COVER D
NEIL EDWARDS

ISSUE 02

E COVER PRIME
MARCO TURINI

F COVER B
ADAM GORHAM &
JASON LEWIS

G COVER C
JOE CORRONEY

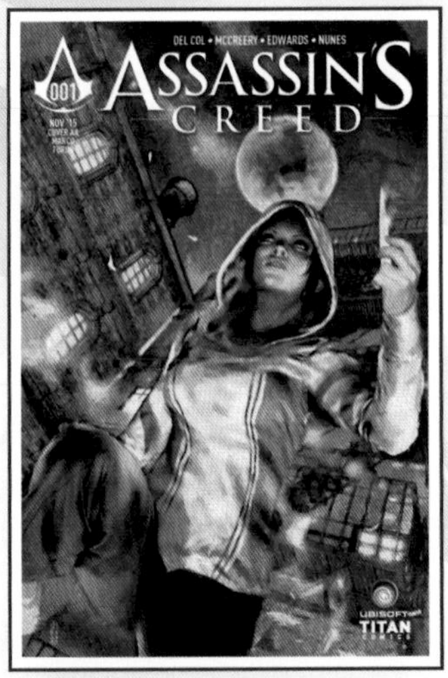
DEL COL • MCCREERY • EDWARDS • NUNES
001
ASSASSIN'S
CREED
NOV '15
UBISOFT
TITAN

A

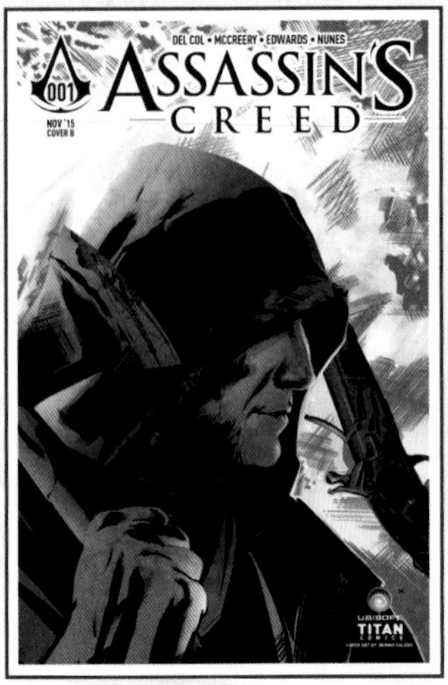
DEL COL • MCCREERY • EDWARDS • NUNES
001
ASSASSIN'S
CREED
NOV '15
COVER B
UBISOFT
TITAN

B

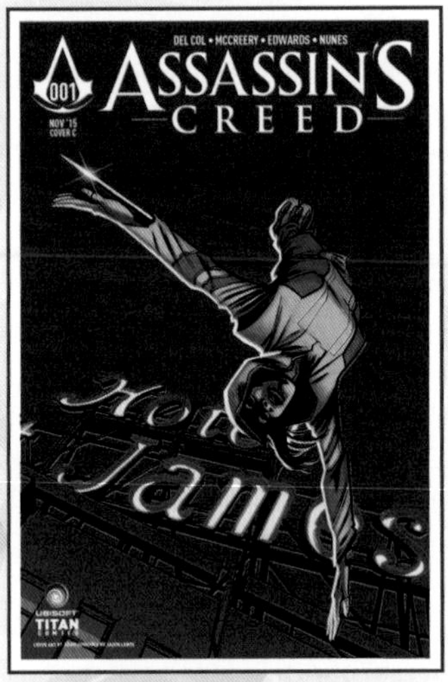
DEL COL • MCCREERY • EDWARDS • NUNES
001
ASSASSIN'S
CREED
NOV '15
COVER C
UBISOFT
TITAN

C

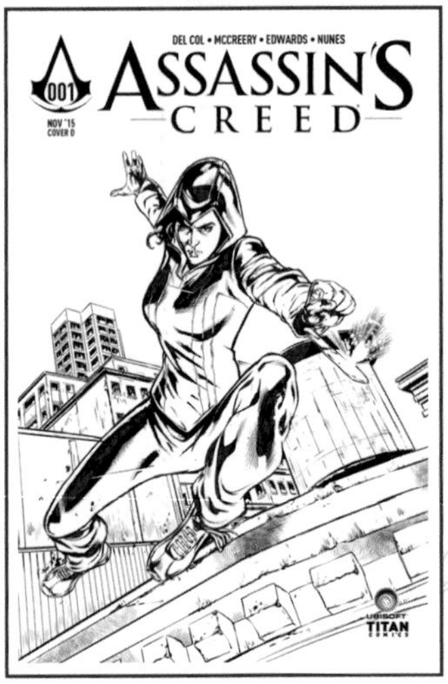
DEL COL • MCCREERY • EDWARDS • NUNES
001
ASSASSIN'S
CREED
NOV '15
COVER D
UBISOFT
TITAN

D

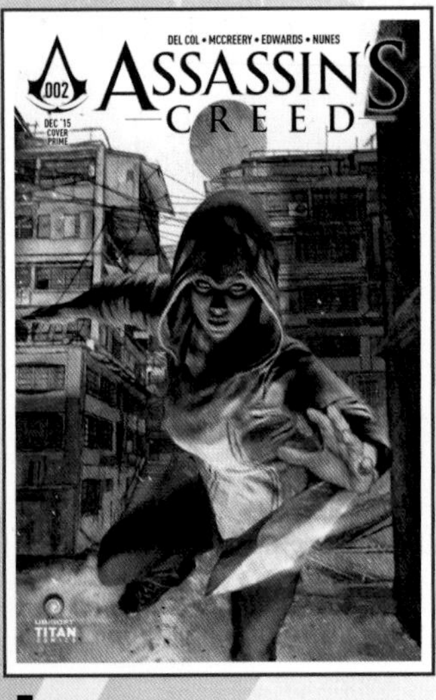
DEL COL • MCCREERY • EDWARDS • NUNES
002
ASSASSIN'S
CREED
DEC '15
COVER
PRIME
UBISOFT
TITAN

E

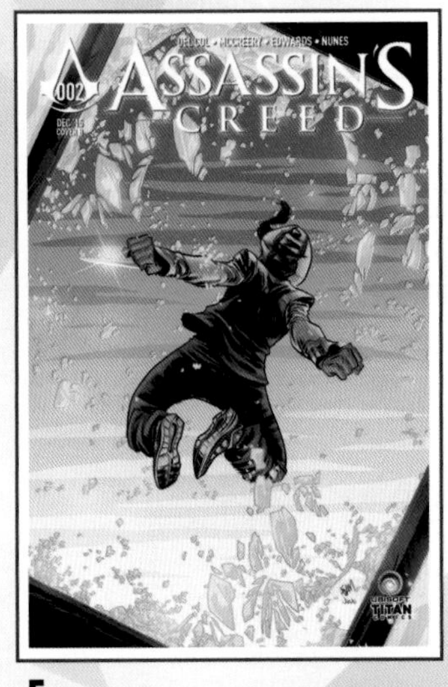
002
ASSASSIN'S
CREED
UBISOFT
TITAN

F

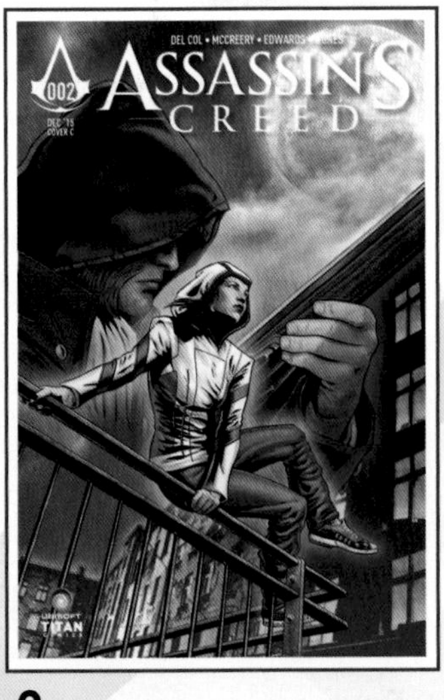
002
ASSASSIN'S
CREED
DEC '15
COVER C
UBISOFT
TITAN

G

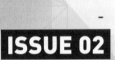

A

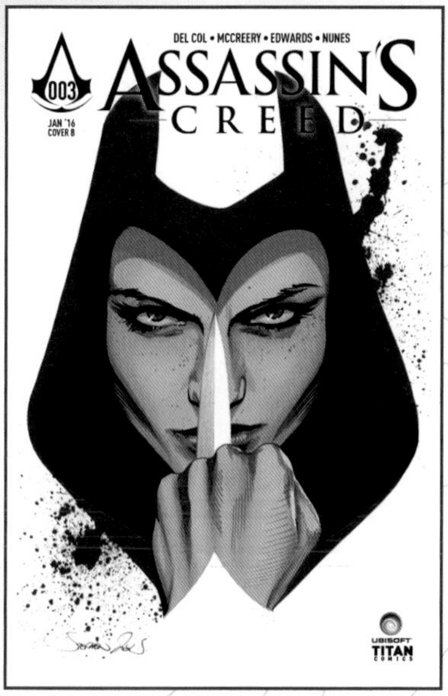
DEL COL • MCCREERY • EDWARDS • NUNES
003
ASSASSIN'S CREED
JAN '16
COVER B
UBISOFT
TITAN COMICS

B

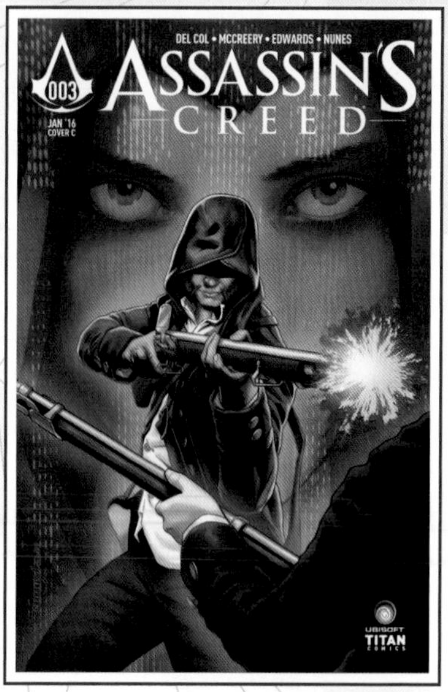
DEL COL • MCCREERY • EDWARDS • NUNES
003
ASSASSIN'S CREED
JAN '16
COVER C
UBISOFT
TITAN COMICS

ISSUE 03

A COVER B
STEPHEN MOONEY

B COVER C
JOE CORRONEY

C

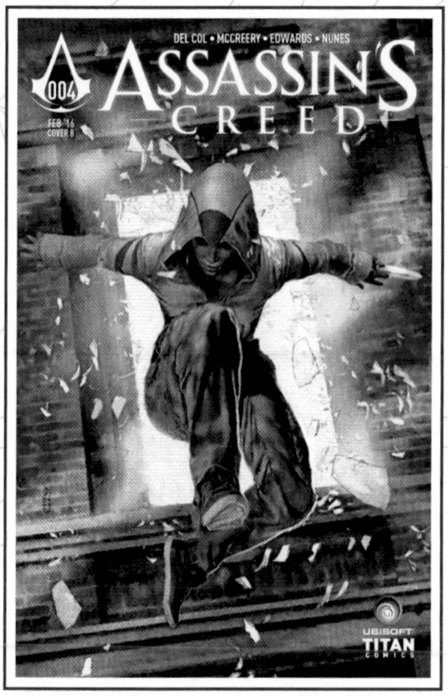
DEL COL • MCCREERY • EDWARDS • NUNES
004
ASSASSIN'S CREED
FEB '16
COVER B
UBISOFT
TITAN COMICS

D

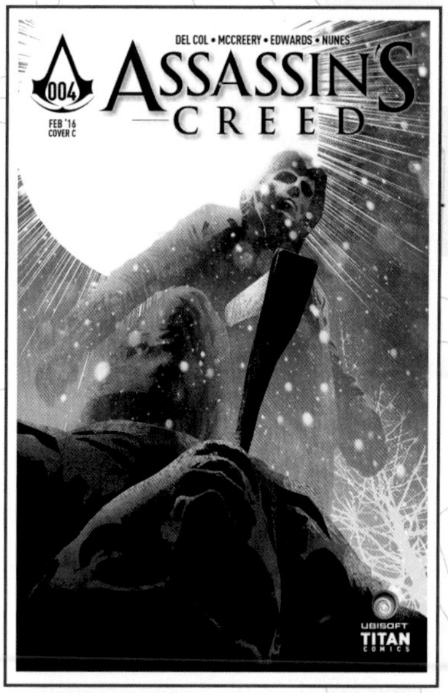
DEL COL • MCCREERY • EDWARDS • NUNES
004
ASSASSIN'S CREED
FEB '16
COVER C
UBISOFT
TITAN COMICS

ISSUE 04

C COVER B
MARCO TURINI

D COVER C
DENNIS CALERO

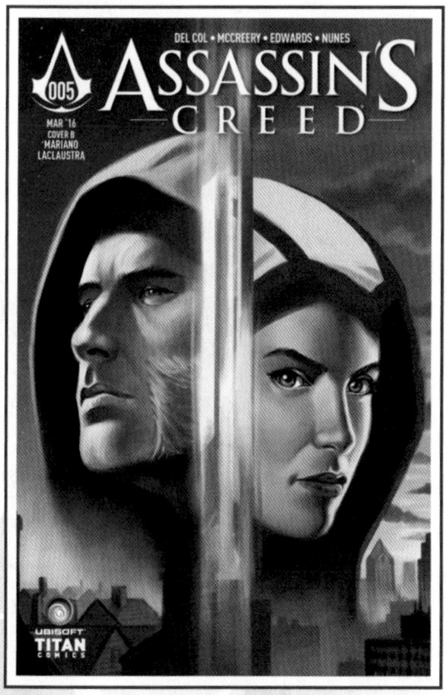
DEL COL • MCCREERY • EDWARDS • NUNES
005
ASSASSIN'S CREED
MAR '16
COVER B
MARIANO
LACLAUSTRA
UBISOFT
TITAN COMICS

E

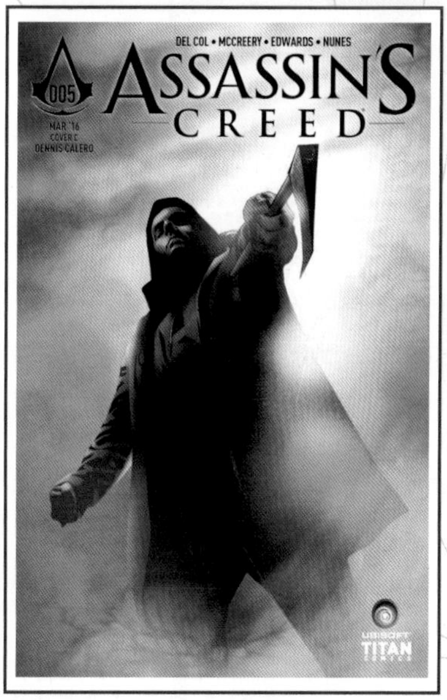
DEL COL • MCCREERY • EDWARDS • NUNES
005
ASSASSIN'S CREED
MAR '16
COVER C
DENNIS CALERO
UBISOFT
TITAN COMICS

F

ISSUE 05

E COVER B
MARIANO
LACLAUSTRA

F COVER C
DENNIS CALERO